# Documentary Filmmaking

## A Contemporary Field Guide

JOHN HEWITT
*San Francisco State University*

GUSTAVO VAZQUEZ
*University of California at Santa Cruz*

SECOND EDITION

New York    Oxford
OXFORD UNIVERSITY PRESS

Oxford University Press is a department of the University of Oxford. It furthers the University's objective of excellence in research, scholarship, and education by publishing worldwide.

Oxford New York
Auckland   Cape Town   Dar es Salaam   Hong Kong   Karachi
Kuala Lumpur   Madrid   Melbourne   Mexico City   Nairobi
New Delhi   Shanghai   Taipei   Toronto

With offices in
Argentina   Austria   Brazil   Chile   Czech Republic   France   Greece
Guatemala   Hungary   Italy   Japan   Poland   Portugal   Singapore
South Korea   Switzerland   Thailand   Turkey   Ukraine   Vietnam

Copyright © 2014 by Oxford University Press

Published by Oxford University Press
198 Madison Avenue, New York, New York 10016
http://www.oup.com

Oxford is a registered trademark of Oxford University Press

**Library of Congress Cataloging-in-Publication Data**
Hewitt, John, 1943-
Documentary filmmaking : a contemporary field guide / John Hewitt, San Francisco State University, Gustavo Vazquez, University of California at Santa Cruz. — Second edition.
pages cm.
Includes index.
ISBN 978-0-19-930086-0
1. Documentary films—Production and direction. I. Vazquez, Gustavo. II. Title.
PN1995.9.D6H49 2013
070.1'8—dc23
2013007159

Printing number: 9 8 7 6 5 4

Printed in the United States of America
on acid-free paper

*To our parents*
*Gerald and Ellen Hewitt and*
*Silvano Vazquez Larios and Rebeca Orozco de Vazquez*
*who gave us wonderful lessons in life*

# BRIEF TABLE OF CONTENTS

# CONTENTS

# PREFACE

The documentary landscape has changed dramatically since we published the first edition of *Documentary Filmmaking: A Contemporary Field Guide*. It's time to update crucial chapters with the exciting advances.

## NEW TO THIS SECOND EDITION

In the second edition, we'll be exploring how short-form documentaries now play a role in a new, social-media-fueled, interactive participatory culture. Emerging ad hoc communities are fueling public discussion by uploading videos under 10 minutes long to YouTube and other sites. Often these short pieces are specifically designed for the mobile screens of smart phones and tablets. We will analyze their design points in several chapters.

Since the first edition, it also is becoming clear that filmmakers must become more Internet savvy when connecting with audiences and the general population. They must be comfortable using sites like Facebook to gather research and beg for archival, YouTube to promote or distribute programs, and file-sharing Internet sites to promote global collaboration. New material in several chapters explores these significant developments.

In the same manner, with the words Kickstarter and Indiegogo solidly part of our lexicon, this second edition celebrates the arrival of crowdsourced funding as an antidote to the always-difficult grant world. These imaginative fundraising sites can bring in thousands of dollars in pledges, and that can be enough to shore up an independent producer's challenging production budget. Chapter 4 explores this encouraging development.

In this new edition, we do our best to keep pace with fast-moving technological change. New cameras with bigger chips and more robust formats arrive almost daily. DSLRs, LED light panels, smart phone video, Bluetooth microphones, and even 3D documentaries are now possibilities. And at last, filmmakers shooting video can control the ever-elusive depth of field. This second edition explores the upsides and downsides of tech changes in our chapters on production.

These technical advances have provided another new development: simplified crew sizes and less expensive production days. Lighter cameras have enhanced the abilities of documentary shooters to go it alone, the so-called "one-man-band." We'll recount producer Ken Kobre's solo odyssey covering photojournalists for *Deadline Every Second* that led him to the tunnels of Gaza, grueling days on the Tour de France, the Parliament in London, skyscrapers in New York, and the forest fires of Santa Barbara, shooting all of it in beautiful high-def with solid audio. We take a look at the implications of the solo practitioner in our revised chapter on preproduction.

In our first edition, we relied on the wisdom of many documentary stalwarts. In this new edition, we have added significant interviews and other commentary from producers and directors of recent works. These include CJ Hunt, Heidi Ewing, and Rachel Grady, Barbara Grandvoinet, Ken Kobre, John Leaños, and Jennifer Maytorena Taylor.

And finally, although the business world remains a tough slog for filmmakers, we'll explore how digital files have now contributed to the ease of making multiple versions of documentaries. We've expanded our section on distribution by separating this information into its own chapter. We've also added new insights from filmmakers who have had telling experiences when turning over rights to commercial sellers.

## DOCUMENTARY FILMMAKING'S BASIC MESSAGE

These fast-moving chaotic changes, however, have not altered the very basics of documentary work. We still believe that carefully planned documentary production is important and that our films need to be visual and involving. As a filmmaker, you must continue to find fascinating characters and strong sequences, lots of time to produce a film, the guts to ignore friends who tell you this is a crazy idea, and a willingness to launch yourselves into a prolonged adventure that transforms your idea into a film.

We are lucky that documentaries are still a hot commodity. Around the world, theater and broadcast audiences have a continued enthusiasm for this challenging factual genre. Festivals touting international documentaries have bubbled up in every crossroads around the world. And each week some Internet website surprises us with a bold new avenue for distribution.

We hope the second edition of *Documentary Filmmaking: A Contemporary Field Guide* will help you pursue, develop, produce, and distribute your ideas. With foresight, it will steer you around the nasty pitfalls that derail even the most professional documentary teams. These pages are full of their suggestions, observations, and fresh alternatives. We encourage you to select what you need for your particular project.

So, whether you are a penniless, street-smart documentary hopeful wanting to distribute on Internet mobile screens, a student expecting to make it to Sundance, or a recognized documentary giant like Ken Burns with an exclusive

PBS contract for the next 16 zillion years, we hope you find this book useful and revealing.

Enjoy it.

## ACKNOWLEDGMENTS

Many associates and friends aided us in forging this book. We especially acknowledge the contributions of our faculty colleagues from the *University of California, Santa Cruz*: Chip Lord, Larry Andrews, Irene Gustafson, and Eli Hollander; from *San Francisco State University*: Ron Compesi, Skye Christensen, Scott Patterson, Hamid Khani, Steve Lahey, Rick Houlberg, Robin McLeod, Grace Provenzano, and Alison Victor; and from *Dominican University*: Melba Beals and John Duvall.

Industry professionals provided us with real-world knowledge and stories. We would like to thank Kelly Briley, Ellen Bruno, Oxana Chumak, Jon Dann, Vicente Franco, Yvonne Ginsberg, Barbara Grandvoinet, Maureen Gosling, Bill Hewitt, Lynn Hershman Leeson, Micah Peled, Russ Johnson, David Kennard, Emiko Omori, Lourdes Portillo, Joan Saffa, and Ralitsa Stoeva.

No textbook can be published without guidance and assistance from many others. We'd like to recognize our editors Mark T. Haynes and Caitlin Kaufman at Oxford University Press; project manager Diane Kohnen at S4Carlisle Publishing Services; and the reviewers who took the time to suggest improvements, including Robert Arnett, *Old Dominion University*; Marta Bautis, *Ramapo College*; Ralph Beliveau, *University of Oklahoma*; Thomas Britt, *George Mason University*; John Craft, *Arizona State University*; Woodrow Hood, *Wake Forest University*; Matthew Irvine, *DePaul University*; Gabor Kalman, *University of Southern California*; Madison Lacy, *University of Kansas*; Kurt Lancaster, *Northern Arizona University*; Ben Levin, *University of North Texas*; John Little, *University of Wisconsin–Stevens Point*; Lisa Mills, *University of Central Florida*; Lisa Molomot, *Yale University*; Daniel Nearing, *Governors State University*; Liam O'Brien, *Quinnipiac University*; Andy Opel, *Florida State University*; Penny Perkins, *Russell Sage College*; Swarnavel Pillai, *Michigan State University*; Mary Jackson Pitts, *Arkansas State University*; Geoffrey Poister, *Boston University*; Sally Rubin, *Chapman University*; Travis Simpson, *San Francisco State University*; Ramon Soto-Crespo, *SUNY Buffalo*; Jan Thompson, *Southern Illinois University*; and Jonah Zeiger, *DePaul University*.

Our families were patient through the long and difficult hours of preparing the manuscript and gathering the photos. We especially want to thank our spouses Annette Blanchard and Cynthia Luna Vazquez.

Again, to all, our most grateful thanks.

## THE AUTHORS

**John Hewitt** is Professor Emeritus in the Broadcast and Electronic Communication Arts department at San Francisco State University. His specialties included documentary production, broadcast journalism, and international broadcast systems.

Over the past 40 years, he has been working as an independent documentary producer, cinematographer, and editor. Most recently, he was co-producer and editor for *Deadline Every Second*, an international look at the dangerous world of the photojournalist. He was Director of Photography on *America's Chemical Angels*, which explored drug therapy for children with Attention Deficit Hyper-activity Disorder; co-producer, shooter, and editor on *Landmines of the Heart*, a probe into political reconciliation in Cambodia; and held various crew positions on *Smokestack Lightnin': The Legendary Howlin' Wolf*, *A Passion for Horses, Staying Lost and Found in Bahia, The Summer of the Amigos,* and *Tremors in Guzman*. His documentaries have appeared on both commercial and public channels and in film festivals throughout the United States and Europe.

**Gustavo Vazquez** is a professor in the Film and Digital Media Department at the University of California, Santa Cruz, where he specializes in video production. His latest documentary, *Jugando con Fuego* (Playing With Fire), explores the world of provincial fireworks makers who live in Celedin, high in the Peruvian Andes. Before that, *Que Viva La Lucha* looked into the arena of Mexican masked wres-tling. It premiered at the Mill Valley Film Festival.

Among his other documentary works are *Corazón de Seda* (Heart of Silk), a biographical documentary on the composer Agustin Lara; *The Great Mojado Inva-sion,* an ethnographic mirror/vortex on historic racist fictions; *Free from Babylon*, a documentary about "Treehouse Joe," a self-made architect and naturalist; and *Comedy of the Underground*, a portrait of George Kuchar, one of San Francisco's best known experimental filmmakers.

His major awards for achievements in film include the Rockefeller Media Fellowship Award and the Eureka Visual Artist Fellowship from the Fleishhacker Foundation.

# Getting Started

# CHAPTER 1

# Begin the Journey by Developing Your Idea, Diving into Research, and Nailing Down Access

Production crew during filming *New Muslim Cool.*
Courtesy of Kauthar Umar

> There are people who believe that if their technology is good enough and they are forging ahead with HD, that's what matters. [But] If the story doesn't have a soul and isn't alive, it doesn't matter what technology you bring to it. It's not going to make a good film.
>
> PRODUCER/CINEMATOGRAPHER ELLEN BRUNO

Documentaries are artful, engaging stories about vital social issues, little-known cultures, curious natural matters, hidden injustices, singular events, or fascinating people. They are impassioned, on-site, fact-filled, entertaining truth-seeking films or videos, explorations that transport and inspire their audiences.

Early British theorist John Grierson wrote that a documentary is "the creative treatment of actuality"—the actuality being the thousands of images and sounds filmmakers capture in the field. We are not, he cautioned, holding up a mirror to nature, but using a creative hammer to mold those filmic images. So whether the inspiration for a documentary begins with a curious idea from a chance meeting or boils up from a producer's lifelong concern, it still must be shaped into a message that makes the most of the film medium.

This chapter is designed to help you go beyond the first inspiration, test the workability of your idea, and set out on what might be a fascinating but consuming adventure.

## GLOSSARY

**B-roll** An industry term for film or video that literally illustrates the spoken story narrative. Usually prominent in issues films.

**Character** An individual who appears in the documentary. Could be the protagonist, an interviewee, a family member, a professional expert or the opponent.

**Dramatic arc** From theater, the rise and fall of story tension throughout your program that leads to a climax that engages and captivates an audience.

**One-offs or standalones** Individual documentary programs, not part of a series.

**Scene** A major structural segment for longer documentaries. In documentaries, scenes are usually composed of sequences.

**Sequence** The basic visual storytelling unit. Centered on a single location, time, event, or process. Made up of wide, medium, close-up, and various other types of shots.

**Talking head** Slang for on-camera segment featuring an interviewee in a fixed medium close-up shot speaking to an off-camera interviewer.

**TRT** Total running time of your program.

**Vérité** A film style in which the camera is observational and generally follows action that happens naturally.

## SOMEONE SHOULD SEE THIS STORY

Creating a visual documentary is a challenge and an art and, if well done, the process is tremendously satisfying. But the clever editing of field video to create a dramatic arc is only half the compensation.

Documentary producers are usually impassioned about a cause, an issue, a historical period, or even an oddity of natural science, and they feel compelled to tell this story in a visual medium.

Producer Micah Peled, whose latest documentary *Bitter Seeds* (2012) is about farmers in India who commit suicide while in conflict with an international seed company, said the documentary must involve the audience: "I wanted American viewers to spend a little time living with the experience of what it's like for other people in other parts of the world to deal with what globalization brought them mostly as a result of what our multinational conglomerates are able to do."

Your story doesn't have to have the high visibility of an international tragedy. Instead, you could focus on a local group that educates high school dropouts, a violin maker who handcrafts instruments, concerned citizens who want to be anonymous organ donors, or a local community fighting wind turbines. In each case, you ache to tell a story because you want people to see it and experience it.

Perhaps now you, the reader of this book, will want to take the next step and become a producer.

## THE ROLE OF THE INDEPENDENT PRODUCER

The producer is the central driving force behind a documentary. If you want to become one, you will develop the idea, dig through the research, find funding for the project, make contacts and gain access to subjects, resolve questions of truth, manage the budget, hire and inspire the crew to artistic excellence, overcome the headaches of location work, carve out the story in postproduction, and then creatively pursue publicity and distribution.

Depending on skill or budgets, independent producers also combine their overview role with a crew position. The most common is producer-director, but producers also have handled cinematography, audio recording, editing, and even on-camera hosting.

Additionally, the producer must be willing to handle business matters. Producers have to improvise when funding disappears or confront the blizzard of problems when budgets allow extra production days, distant travel for weeks at a time, and bewildering negotiations with owners of archival video or music.

**Figure 1.1** Director Lourdes Portillo directs her crew while shooting in the Mexican desert.
Courtesy Lourdes Portillo, photo by Gabriela Cardona

The producer oversees the crew. He or she must determine who will be needed and how they will be hired or otherwise cajoled to work on the film. If the budget is tiny, the crew might be just the producer and one other person. If there is a generous grant or a big Kickstarter fund-raising campaign, the producer might have the option to hire assistant producers, unit managers, researchers, archivists, interns, international aides such as fixers or interpreters, publicists, and producer's reps for distribution, festivals, and film markets.

Finally, the producer must guard his or her authority to have the final say in the documentary's message. If you have directors, editors, or investors, you must make it clear that the final say is on your shoulders—that you have editorial control.

## BEING A CONTRACT PRODUCER IS DIFFERENT

A contract producer is commissioned by the overseeing executive producer of a continuing documentary program such as *Frontline* (David Fanning) or *American Masters* (Susan Lacy). The contract producer takes on the same content responsibilities of research, directing on location, and scripting, but in essence gets a salary and doesn't have to raise the money.

The contract producer's final edit will be subject to oversight from the executive producer, who manages adjacent series projects and has input into the script by setting boundaries for length and direction. In many cases, the commissioning editor sets out the style that is consistent with the series or program's historic approach.

## THE IDEA IS ONLY A CATALYST

The inspiration for your documentary can come from anywhere. Magazine articles, newspaper stories, Internet blogs, a medical crisis, or work-related concerns can stimulate an idea. Multipart programs like director Martin Scorsese's seven-part PBS series *The Blues* or Ken Burns's historical epics often arise from a life-long fascination with a particular topic.

Many others, producers tell us, have started with chance meetings. Gary Weimberg and his producing partner Catherine Ryan began a two-year-long project for *Soldiers of Conscience* after Weimberg had a locker room conversation at a health club with an attorney who counseled conscientious objectors. Director Maureen Gosling embarked on the film *Del Mero Corazon* when she became fascinated with a song left out of another documentary she was editing. Executive producer Yvonne Ginsberg pursued the question of political reconciliation in Cambodia in *Landmines of the Heart* after hearing about the problem during a Buddhist meditation exercise. Co-producers Vicente Franco and Gail Dolgin began their complex *Daughter from Danang* after a conversation at a party.

### Growing Your Idea Beyond Simple Curiosity

Academy Award–winning producer Arnold Shapiro said in one of his ten golden rules about documentary, "The idea is not everything." That original trigger idea might launch the project, Shapiro cautioned, but it is bound to reformulate into a more complex undertaking, changed by internal or outside influences, theoretical questions, production realities, budget shortcomings, or access and rights questions. In the end, that initial inspiration might only be a subtext in the finished documentary.

Projects can also grow in scope. Director Lynn Hershman Leeson found this out with her internationally recognized *Strange Culture* (2007). Hearing that a friend, a noted U.S. artist, had been harassed by the U.S. government, she "just wanted to do a little $100 DVD to let people know about it." That simple effort snowballed into an exhaustive, fully involving, year-long unbudgeted film that ended up as a 75-minute feature playing at Sundance, opening the Berlin Film Festival, appearing on U.S. public television and cable channels, and getting theatrical release in the United States and the UK before finally going to DVD. Not bad for a project that began as a short, informal DVD.

## Do You Have a Passion for the Topic?

Producer CJ Hunt's *In Search of the Perfect Human Diet* took six years to complete. His advice to beginners starting documentaries is clear: "It is going to take a lot longer than you think."

If you are not on a tight deadline from a class or work assignment, any worthwhile long-range documentary project will soak up at least a year's work in idea development, contacting subjects, solving difficult questions in preproduction, fund-raising, production, and postproduction work. We can guarantee that will be followed by another year or two of intensive work gaining exposure and distribution. Therefore a critical concern is this: Are you passionate about the topic?

Before undertaking this journey, assess how deeply this topic touches you. Do you enjoy reading up on the subject, doing research, or getting into long phone conversations about the issue? Are you ready to exchange endless e-mails with other interested aficionados obsessed with the topic? Would you consider yourself somewhat of an expert? Do you talk to people at parties about it? Are you willing to probe its philosophical and ethical foundations? Would you attend gatherings of like-minded experts to talk it up?

Award-winning editor and director Maureen Gosling says this enthusiasm is a must. She reports becoming fascinated with almost every film she edits or produces. Her latest is an exploration of a women's business culture in Africa. "The Mali film was brought to me by a friend. But in terms of the content, it totally clicked with me. It was something I could get behind, and even though she brought the idea to me, it was something I could identify with . . . was interested in . . . and the idea of doing something in Africa was amazing . . . doing something about entrepreneurial women."

For cinematographer Vicente Franco, every film is a revelation. "Documentaries are a lesson in life. It's an endless learning process about every story you tell and the more profound and more in-depth you get into the story the more you learn."

**Figure 1.2** Cinematographer Vicente Franco has a large support crew while shooting a well-funded documentary on Orozco's frescos in Guadalajara, Mexico.

## TESTING THE WATERS

### Will This Idea Turn into a Powerful Documentary?

It all might begin with an informal conversation or an exciting news report. Like the moth circling closer to the flame, the intrigued producer does some initial research, makes a few calls, and along the way identifies characters and visual sequences that might be enough for a documentary. Is it time to jump in and begin a year or two of hard work?

### Gauging the Scope of the Idea

While researching the idea, producers should evaluate the topic's scope. A documentary idea might be too narrow or too local to intrigue a wider audience.

Producers Gary Weimberg and Catherine Ryan faced this issue when they began their film about conscientious objectors. Weimberg said a simple focus on the conscientious objectors to the Iraq War would limit the film's audience. He knew they had to dig deeper: "In terms of discovering what the film was, the thing we found was that it wasn't about conscientious objection, it's about the burden of conscience when one is asked to kill for one's country. Conscientious objection is one half of that discussion by people who take it seriously and the other half is about the people who say 'I'll do it' and now I have to carry that burden for the rest of my life."

There are other concerns. The topic might have a geographic narrowness, only relating to a particular neighborhood, city, or region, or might be directed at persons familiar with certain music, scientific theories, or ecological questions. Producers need to step back and uncover the more universal themes that reach out to greater audiences.

Then again, it's quite possible your idea's scope is too global. Suppose the plan is for an issues documentary on the elimination of malaria as a worldwide disease. The program would show exciting efforts now underway in a number of countries on two continents. An idea of this scale, though, demands an experienced producer with a staff and a substantial budget for research, travel, and production. For an independent, that might be production suicide. Consider narrowing the focus to make it more manageable. Instead of an all-encompassing program, choose a local or regional story that fits within your technical skills and bankbook limitations. Then abstract from that to the larger, more central theme.

### Test the Idea with Informal Pitches
As the idea matures from a simple interest to a long-running obsession, the topic can be tested on colleagues, friends, family, and others. This gambit helps to develop a standardized statement—sometimes called a pitch—that will help you refine your thoughts. Working and reworking this short 25-word statement will give it consistency. A producer needs to deliver the informal pitch with confidence, something that will be obvious to every contact, including prospective crew or possible subjects. Don't confuse this with a more elaborate formal pitch made later to funders and film markets.

Although your idea might be complex, posing it in this short form is effective. The crew should learn it, too, because all of you might repeat this many, many times during the production. It could be something as simple as one of these:

> "I am doing a documentary on zookeepers who try to provide humane settings for animals in our central city zoo."

> "We are following a local dance troupe on a foreign tour to explore the social interactions based on the universality and power of the arts."

> "This documentary is about a small group of artists who are fighting to retain the community feeling of a small Pittsburgh neighborhood."

> "I am exploring the attraction and effects of a unique music-based after-school workshop for students from troubled neighborhoods."

### Don't Re-Invent the Wheel
It has been said that there are no new ideas, only different approaches. In the world of documentary, this usually is the case.

If you are expecting to distribute your documentary beyond a classroom, carefully research whether or not the idea has been produced before and how recently it was done. For instance, with the malaria example from the previous section, there is little chance a national public broadcaster will be interested if they've just run seven 90-minute *NOVA* documentaries on the world's health problems. You'll have similar difficulty if well-publicized programs have been in theatrical distribution or have appeared on competing channels. Maybe HBO or the Sundance channel or even a commercial broadcast network has just wrapped up a highly publicized series done by the BBC.

Check for documentaries in production that are similar to your idea. Review programs in the PBS pipeline by checking their publication *www.current.org* or look in *Hollywood Reporter* or *Variety* for notices of major documentary efforts.

It can be distressing when the documentary trail you are following is crowded. While shooting a program on a Mississippi Delta blues performer, we became aware of a larger crew making the same rounds, talking to the same people, and filming the same performances. At festivals, their nine-person ensemble and abundant budget dwarfed our two-person crew. They had fancy SUVs, advanced format cameras, and production assistants, all fueled by a million-dollar Corporation for Public Broadcasting grant and a noted national billionaire who backed their project. We had an economy rental car and a single prosumer camera. They shelled out thousands of dollars to get stage access, forcing us to shoot around their cinematographer just to get our pictures.

## SHELF LIFE AND THE PROBLEMS OF CURRENT EVENTS DOCS

Shelf life is not just for bakery items. Documentaries based on current events or immediate controversies might not have the longevity needed for distribution. Once a topic has had a short run in the public's consciousness, audiences are likely to move on to newer and juicier items. In the year it takes to produce the documentary, the topic might fade from the world's media radar and unless you can build the film around abstract ideas, you will be left with a very interesting but orphan program.

Day-to-day political shifts can affect the work already done. An interview shot yesterday could be outdated before the end of the week. The corruption angle in local government might disappear when the main antagonist abruptly resigns and flees to live in a remote village.

Shelf life is a particular problem for independent documentary producers trying to make a living. As producer Gary Weimberg explained about his documentary on Iraq War conscientious objectors: "We had a tiger by the tail . . . that was a great story . . . that was a topical story . . . in the news. We are not a network. We are not an institution. We are not deep pockets. So we were in a race with current events and we were totally underhanded and underfunded for that."

For another producer, changing current events snuffed out the film. A documentary colleague began a major project to explore how a proposed hydroelectric dam would destroy a pristine California valley and the culture of local Native American settlements. He secured a generous National Endowment for the Arts grant, moved up to a trailer in the region, and spent hundreds of hours doing preliminary interviews. After three months and halfway through the environmental planning, the government abruptly cancelled the controversial dam. My friend was left with a lot of field video and no story. Things like this happen all the time.

## CONSIDER YOUR DISTRIBUTION POSSIBILITIES

Producers must envision their likely distribution. Your target audience can play a significant role when developing the idea. Funders, research contacts, commissioning editors, and distributors will want to know how your distribution plans might spread the message. Many subjects will ask where you expect the documentary to play when deciding whether to be in your film.

What kind of audiences would you like? Your peers? Local affinity groups? Local art house multiplexes? Film festivals? National or international public broadcast? HBO? Cable channels? Internet streaming? Public access? University classrooms?

### New Distribution Possibilities Are Exciting

We've mentioned the old standby distribution paths: theaters, broadcast, home DVDs, and educational A/V libraries. But these are nontraditional times. New technologies, platforms, social media, and online channels like YouTube have opened up a participatory culture, one that offers exciting opportunities. The Internet has allowed YouTube communities to create networks; share files, sound recordings, images, and music videos; and gather this material to make short documentaries.

In Fife, Scotland, local groups fighting the installation of huge wind generators used crowdsourcing to gather video of the area, of other wind turbines, of public meetings, and of interviews with residents to make short documentaries against the idea. These were distributed to websites, online networks, and community screenings.

The proliferation of cameras also helps make this crowdsourcing possible. During the Occupy Movement in 2012, many videos uploaded to YouTube on the events in major cities showed hundreds of people filming with everything from professional, prosumer, and consumer cameras to smart phones. The dramatic confrontations with police and Occupy protestors then were edited into short documentary form and uploaded to a sizable audience.

In the Arab Spring, the tumultuous events in Tunisia, Libya, and Egypt went up on YouTube, bypassing the rigid government controls and shutdowns of Internet access. Documentary producers pitched on social media for citizen videos and received thousands of scenes, many of which were turned into documentaries that became iconic pictures of the revolution. In the end, the smart phone played a role in bringing down an old political structure.

And this isn't such a new phenomenon. In 2006 in Mexico, film director Luis Mandoki (*When a Man Loves a Woman*) compiled a documentary on the 2006 Mexican electoral process. In a blog post, he invited Mexican citizens to record and contribute their visual evidence in multiple camera formats. He received more than 3,000 hours of video from 300 electoral districts, resulting in a feature-length documentary *Fraude: Mexico 2006*.

Young documentary producers should be poised to develop these new avenues for communication. This multiplicity of artistic expression bypasses the restrictive

**Figure 1.3** The powerful issues documentary *Fraude: Mexico 2006* was taken from crowd-sourced material from hundreds of contributors.

nature of the official and established networks. The communities that had been passive media consumers now have their chance to create and disseminate the documentaries they believe are important without considering the business angle of distribution or possibly your copyright. And ironically, the producers themselves become the audiences.

### Your Distribution Plans Will Determine Your Total Running Time

As a documentary producer in our fast-changing digital age, you have the opportunity to make not just one, but several films from the same material, all with their total running times (TRTs) keyed to particular audiences. This versatility is made possible by nonlinear editing, digital files, and the ease of uploading short docs to online sites.

If you believe your documentary has elements reaching out to the new participatory culture, you might be best served by short videos, under 10 minutes, uploaded to YouTube or another video site. This would mean you could crowd-source material and deal with the frustrations of multiple formats.

If your documentary is produced for a class assignment, a TRT goal might fall between 6 and 12 minutes. This keeps the project within a manageable scope and would allow you to complete preproduction, production, and editing within a four-month time frame. Although the public distribution might be limited to a joint premiere with two or three other docs in front of a friendly audience, you can certainly distribute this work on YouTube or submit it to selected film festivals as a short.

If you have grander ideas and are determined to reach public audiences, then you have to consider TRTs that fit programming needs. The longest docs land in the epic range—anything over two hours. These have limited distribution potential; they can only be shown in multipart presentations either on broadcast or in museum special showings. David Sutherland's fascinating *The Farmer's Wife* was six and a half hours long; Spike Lee's look back at Hurricane Katrina, *When the Levees Broke,* ran four hours; and many of Frederick Wiseman's institutional observations easily surpass two hours (*Central Park* was just shy of three hours). Production on these projects lasts for months or years. For something of this length, there are very few outlets except for premium cable or PBS.

Feature length (usually 72–110 minutes, and averaging 90 minutes) would kick the budget up by many thousands of dollars and demand higher technical standards and a major production schedule. These projects would be headed for theatrical distribution or specialized cable slots. These are often difficult placements for broadcast distribution. One experienced producer warned that planning for a feature-length documentary is a "beginner's mistake."

At the annual MIPDOC market in Cannes, France, most of the world's production companies were pitching docs in the 52- to 57-minute range, essentially hour-long documentaries. If broadcast is the goal, this is a useful working limit. It permits the use of less expensive formats for production. However, there is no guarantee that the hour length will get it on the air. Public service broadcasters and U.S. public television are more receptive to one-hour programs that are part of a series. Producer Ken Kobre, who spends days breaching the PBS system, says offering a one-off hour-long program is extremely difficult.

If the proposed doc ends up with an irregular TRT that is less than 52 minutes, it doesn't fit neatly into the broadcast blocks. Often, broadcasters will slot these into programs under an umbrella-branded title such as "P.O.V." Premium cable channels like IFC, Sundance, HBO, or Showtime will program TRTs that are feature length or irregular. However, they are attracted to edgy or political themes.

Commercial broadcasters or niche cable channels like the History Channel or the Learning Channel vary in what they acquire, but they like to be production partners. Talk with their acquisition people before beginning any film that you want to see end up there. Projects underway might also be found in *Variety* or the *Hollywood Reporter.* These channels also insert commercials, so the program design must take this into account. This is not a simple task.

### Festivals, Screenings, and the Classroom
For festivals or local screenings, irregular running times will not be a problem. Although this type of distribution can be a pleasant experience (there is usually

applause), the audiences might be small and the process can be demanding or expensive in festival entry fees, press kits, and travel.

The educational market is a definite goal. For classroom use, the TRT could be much shorter, often as little as 12 minutes. This allows a postscreening discussion among students. Producer Ellen Bruno, who self-distributes her films, appreciates the support from universities. "If I can sell one DVD to a university I get 100 percent of the money and there are times when I am really broke and I get on the phone to university media buyers and I say: 'Hey, are you interested?' And my friends call it dialing for dollars but it is exciting that young people are seeing these and it helps me make my next film."

Remember, the destination for the documentary will provide a guide for the TRT and technical level of the film.

## NARRATIVE STRUCTURES

Successful documentaries cross a wide range of storytelling scenarios. We have categorized examples around topics and approaches. This is not a definitive list; many others who study documentaries use different modalities.

Screening previous documentaries in each category might be helpful; it will provide inspiration on how other producers have turned ideas into memorable films. Examples of documentaries in each area are available in the appendix.

### DOCUMENTARY THEMES

1) The *journey* (*hidden city*) documentary takes the audience to a place or introduces them to a culture they would never otherwise encounter. This usually demands a looser vérité style, careful cultural and ethnographic sensibilities, and a skilled artistic crew who can endure exhausting location shoots and travel. A producer would need up-front funding for travel and location costs and be adept at improvising with newly discovered characters and visual sequences encountered at the location. Unless the travel costs are low, this type of doc is the realm of experienced producer/directors.

2) The *process* documentary follows a singular project from beginning to end, such as the building of massive bridge or setting up a regional music concert or health care program. It might be less time consuming than the journey, but it still needs extensive location work. An on-camera host would make it more complex.

3) The *biography* documentary explores the life and works of a single contemporary or historical personality or group. It could involve some location sequences, but will rely heavily on testimonial interviews from colleagues or family, archival research, re-creation docudrama, or possibly foreign shoots. A novice producer will receive memorable lessons from demanding managers, fearful family, and archival owners who want to drive difficult bargains for the rights and editorial control.

4) The *current events* or *issue* documentary makes a rhetorical argument or a deductive journalistic investigation into contemporary topics or concerns. This will demand extensive research, an elaborate interview schedule, and an exhausting and sometimes dangerous effort to gather sequence visuals. There will be ethical and social concerns to discuss. Travel and location costs will be expensive and quickly changing current events might suddenly erase months of effort.

5) The *event* documentary is based on the coverage of a significant happening, concert, convention, or gathering that is over within a short time period. This requires complex planning for an intensive multiple-camera/large-crew shoot. It's an all-or-nothing field production exercise.

6) The *historical compilation* looks at past events or issues. The producer creates a story without rich contemporary sequences but must undertake a challenging and expensive effort to collect every significant historical visual scrap in whatever form it exists. Archival research can be grueling and legally baffling. As with the biography and issues docs, it requires ongoing creativity.

7) The *natural history* documentary expands the viewer's knowledge about science or the environment. It requires a significant up-front budget, extensive travel and location costs, prescripting, and a long-term crew commitment during filming. Hosts are often brought in as a storytelling device and to add credibility.

## Storytelling Approaches

Producers often mix and match styles while producing engaging films. These are some traditional methods that help deliver the power.

1) The sequence-driven documentary relies on powerful scenes captured in exciting or action-filled moments. In its purest form, it eschews on-camera sit-down interviews. Often referred to as vérité, sequence-driven docs offer the fly on the wall point of view. These docs are more likely to be what are called open text, allowing the viewers to draw their own conclusions.

2) The character-driven documentary relies on the powerful presence of one individual or several personalities to carry the story. It presents serious ethical questions in depictions of sympathetic characters and is usually a mix of formal interviews and sequences.

3) The narrated documentary relies on an authoritative voice to make connections and explain complexities of the topic. This is particularly effective in the areas of current events and issues, where sequences might not be readily available but interviews and B-roll can be assembled to illustrate the narration.

4) The hosted documentary has an on-camera personality who acts either as an expert or as a surrogate traveler for the viewer. Although a recognizable host such as Michael Moore will lend a certain credibility, the success of this format relies on the engaging qualities of the host. This type of program needs a large crew, a more experienced producer, a prompter on the camera, and a script.

5) The thesis-first or deductive documentary opens with a thesis statement and follows with supporting testimony, sequences, or archival material. It has a rhetorical structure when presenting cause-and-effect reasoning. It is useful in issues, current events, historical, or science and natural history.

6) The inductive documentary structure is exactly the opposite of the thesis-first. It begins with intriguing sequences and unfolds a story without a thesis statement. More often than not, it is sequence driven and the viewers are left to form their own conclusions.

7) The personal reflexive documentary explores the issue or topic by turning the camera back on the filmmaker. As with the hosted documentary, it often lives or dies based on whether the filmmaker has an engaging personality. Producer CJ Hunt found this structure helpful while building the arc for his successful *In Search of the Perfect Human Diet*. His previous on-camera experience was a great help. However, undertaking this requires a comfort level on your part to let yourself, your family, and friends and associates be exposed in exhaustive, sometimes intimate ways.

8) The experimental or hybrid documentary combines almost any documentary approach with many narrative styles, including performance, actors and docudrama, dramatic re-creations, animation, or any combination of categories. Often called essay documentaries, these can be enormously successful and memorable while baffling critics who reject them as outside the genre.

An extreme challenge for a videomaker is to visualize inner thoughts, feelings, abstract ideas, or philosophical concepts. In some cases, the documentarian will be recounting historical events that predated the existence of the first motion picture cameras in the 1890s; in others, they will be detailing events that had no media record.

To get around this, some filmmakers use re-created scenes. Documentarian Errol Morris shot highly stylized re-creations with actors to B-roll the narration, interview, and interrogation of a wrongly convicted felon in his early powerful documentary *The Thin Blue Line*. Critics were mixed on his approach, saying that it wasn't documentary if it was re-created.

In the recently released documentary *Strange Culture*, producer Lynn Hershman Leeson used actors to portray the key characters, primarily because the elements of the case were still in litigation. She contended this was the only way to document the story, but some critics saw this as a dramatic film rather than documentary.

*Tongues Untied*, by the late Marlon Riggs, mixed a variety of techniques—visual poetic reconstructions, retelling of memory through narration, and staged performances with poetry and songs—to combine the personal and the community story of being black and gay in America. This documentary approach stretched the medium as a tool of expression for Riggs's poetic essay.

In *Capitalism: A Love Story*, Michael Moore utilizes "found footage" archival images, including sources from fiction films, to build an argument in a historical yet humorous context of capitalism in his narrated documentary essay.

Legendary film directors are experimenting with the creative potential of 3D filming in documentary. Wim Wenders's *Pina* is a tribute to contemporary dance choreographer Pina Bausch. His stylized camera choreography mirrors the work of the Bausch. Werner Herzog's *Cave of Forgotten Dreams* explores "a perfect time capsule" on an epic expedition into Chauvet Cave in France, a 20,000-year-old gallery of ancient accomplished art created by humans. Herzog had restrictions necessary to preserve the fragility of the cave, so his crew of three was allowed only four hours per day during one week in total filming. By utilizing modern LED lights and 3D he was able to capture shadows getting elongated with the movement of light, thus providing a very strong sense of formation of space, contributing to the drama of the animal life depicted on the cave walls, in the way the original painters must have experienced it.

A new area pushing the boundaries of documentary is animation. *Persepolis,* directed by Marjane Satrapi, was awarded the Jury Prize at the 2007 Cannes Film Festival. This film was Satrapi's autobiographical animation of a young girl growing up during the Iranian Revolution, who eventually became an expatriate at age 24. The success of this film has inspired others to explore the genre.

Producers like John Leaños are excited by the elasticity of animation to illustrate undocumented events and "to show something that doesn't have any footage or to tell a story that doesn't have any as an alternative to reenactment. The freedom that an animator has to represent a certain series of events is attractive to many producers." Leaños said his conceptual strategy with "animation was a political tactic for me because I was looking for a way to represent taboo issues and document

**Figure 1.4** A storyboard for a scene from John Leaños's animated documentary *Frontera!*, a history of insurrection in the 17th-century American Southwest.

historical legacies of colonialism of violence, or racism and the heavy issues that America has had to deal with . . . and to bring these out . . . to bring them to the surface without alienating certain populations or getting people upset and so in an attempt to get at different places for a dialog I turned to animation as a buffer . . . as a way to lighten the heaviness of the subject matter. You can use the form of animation to, in a way, get at the problems of documentary itself, which is trying to find the truth based on multiple perspectives."

Leaños uses research that combines social science with humanities, archives, original material, archeology, literature, and oral history, and looks at it within an art context. "I've read seven books on the Pueblo Revolt and try to get that into a 17-minute piece . . . and that involves building an archive and how to write the story in an entertaining way and which keeps the integrity of the historical events and at the same time and still offers some form of engagement . . . using humor and layers. The audience is hearing one story but they are seeing another, so I think the possibility where I can approach integrity . . . you are leaving so much out. And through animation you can represent that in many ways."

## GAINING ACCESS TO SOURCES

### The Battle to Reach Subjects for the Documentary

Your documentary will not be successful without access. Contacting and convincing intended participants to appear on camera is a daunting task. It seems that 95 percent of documentary preproduction is pleading with someone to be a subject in the documentary.

If the major focus of the documentary is a famous person, especially one in the political or entertainment field, getting access could be a minefield. Managers and handlers will demand preconditions and even money. Attorneys will stymie archival resources. One well-known but frustrated producer said the secret to independent documentaries is "Don't do films on famous persons."

Even without notoriety, documentary subjects are skittish. Everyday people are reluctant to appear on video or to say anything of substance for a variety of reasons. They might fear for their jobs, their relationships, or even their own personal safety. Perhaps they've had bad experiences with authors, journalists, and other filmmakers. It takes repeated phone calls, cajoling, wheedling, or support from allies to convince some to be on camera. Spouses or partners often hold a yes—no veto over their mate's consent, even when the involvement is noncontroversial.

### Visiting with Possible Subjects at the Shooting Locations

Don't ignore the information a producer can uncover during an initial research visit to a possible shooting location. This kind of a trip can establish a familiarity with the culture, the geography, and residents. While there, contact local historical societies, local newspapers, and neighborhood leaders. Librarians usually know the local history buffs, historical societies, or people who hoard treasures of archival photos and materials. Although this trip might not be planned as a production venture, it doesn't hurt to shoot some footage that can be used for trailers and fund-raising.

Location research will be time-consuming. Producer Ai Omaki did a film on chess players who used rented game tables on an impossibly busy and socially messy street corner in San Francisco. She had to spend weeks hanging out at the location, getting to know the street denizens. Her complex work, *The Slab,* was a portrait of a diverse, rough-edged underclass of chess aficionados who were willing to put up with the chaos at the game tables.

Producer Catherine DeSantis needed to find a trove of couples planning marriages. She made the necessary contacts by spending many hours at the county registrar's office where the marriage licenses are filed. She interviewed applicants and agreed to videotape wedding ceremonies if the couples would agree to appear in her documentary. This personal contact provided a long list of potential characters for the film.

## Look for Strong Allies in Unfamiliar Communities

If you are an interloper in a remote community, neighborhood, or social group, then you must find a collaborator or ally to achieve access. It might take weeks or months to discover who can be your entrée to the others. While shooting *Smokestack Lightnin: The Legendary Howlin Wolf* in rural Mississippi, we spent months gaining the trust of a longtime leader in the African American community where the singer had grown up. He then accompanied us to meet everyone else. With his assurance, we gained access to people who would have been polite but would never have appeared on camera.

Producer Micah X. Peled used the collaborator-ally in a different manner in his doc *Bitter Seeds* (2012). To reach farmers in southern India who were in conflict with a multinational seed company, he worked with a young Indian journalist and gave her a camera, using much of that footage in the doc.

While we were shooting in a remote Mexican town on another documentary, our ally accompanied us to every interview. As we asked questions, he would then ask some himself. We found the residents answering him gave straight answers, knowing they couldn't be gracious and pull the wool over his eyes. It was odd but it worked.

Even when you meet subjects, there's still the problem of trust. Producer Barbara Grandvionet, who shot her doc *Children of the Trains* in Thailand, called gaining their confidence her most difficult problem. "We were talking to street kids who were living in the slums, and I had only been there two weeks and didn't speak their language. Why would they trust me?"

## Don't Be Bashful about Connections

Not everyone can be Alexandra Pelosi, the daughter of powerhouse Democratic congressional leader Nancy Pelosi, whose familiarity with political figures gave her an edge in making a campaign trail insider doc with former President George W. Bush called *Journeys With George.* (It is to her credit that the work stands on her own unique style.)

Access might also be granted based on recommendations from the A-list people already on your side. If you can insert a recognizable name into the initial phone call and say that person suggested you call, then you might succeed.

**Figure 1.5** Producer Micah X. Peled behind the camera in a Chinese jeans factory shooting tired workers. His access was unusual and dangerous.

Access might very well depend on a low profile with a suspicious political body. When San Francisco–based producer Micha X. Peled made his award-winning doc *China Blue* about conditions in the denim sweatshops of China, he and his crew spent months gaining access to a factory. Finally one owner, imagining a salutary program, allowed Peled inside.

Peled managed to shoot for months before the owner became suspicious. The police later detained Peled's crew but finally released them. This emphasizes that working on a controversial issue can be risky. Doc teams worldwide have been attacked, arrested, jailed, and had their field materials confiscated.

Producers often succeed or fail based on the erratic way suspicious persons grant or withdraw access. A key subject's abrupt denial of access could imperil the entire doc. A producer documenting the history of a freewheeling communal living group had been warmly received during initial conversations; the group's leaders had repeatedly agreed to participate. Halfway through the project, after extensive interviews with former commune residents, the producer and her crew arrived at the controversial cult home base for their key three-day on-site shoot. It was to be the heart of the program. They were turned away at the gate by residents who said, "No dice—not now, not ever." The key subjects had changed their mind. This flip-flop was crushing, but not fatal; the producer refocused the program on the disappointed members.

### Don't Let Them Down

Investigative producer Jon Dann says you've got to deliver what you promise. "The truth is a powerful thing. You know ... people will go out on limb if they feel that their story will be told. But you have to be very mindful of your responsibility in that situation ... your ability to deliver. It's really important. If they are going to take risks . . . you have to hold up your end of the bargain, which means telling the story."

Filmmaker Lourdes Portillo believes the defining factor in getting access is truthfulness, trust, and your method of acclimating yourself to the locale. "I never go in with cameras. First we meet and we talk. I tell them what I am doing, what kind of things I am planning. I ask: Would they allow me to do this? It will take time. This could take them away from their things. This will be very intrusive. Do they want me to do that? And they say 'Yes' or 'No.' If they say yes, then I say, 'Let's go have dinner first,' because that would develop, that builds up trust."

## Ethics of Access

Ethics is the study of morality and its effect on decisions. Documentary makers live or die on convincing people to go in front of a camera. If a subject is wavering about participating, then there might be a temptation to bend the truth to get that interview. This could involve hiding the extent of the producer's advocacy for a particular thesis in the documentary, lying about what questions might be asked on camera, or not being truthful about the plans to distribute the final program.

Filmmaker Portillo described an encounter she had with another documentary producer during a panel discussion at a conference. "They asked her (the other producer): 'Would you lie to get what she needed?' And she said 'Of course I would lie.' And I thought . . . well, if you would lie, what's to stop them from lying to you?"

It's also increasingly hard to hide your identity. Producer Jon Dann says that's the downside of the way the Internet works. "They can gather information about you. I mean, people have seen what I have done before I go interview them. They've watched it on the Internet. I'm no mystery to them either. Transparency goes both ways."

Other producers say academic discussions of ethics are helpful but sometimes unrealistic. One told us that 9 times out of 10 he would never lie and that this policy has worked. But he cautioned that there are extreme forces out there, well-funded and powerful, who will come after you if you cross them. He said going undercover was a last resort, and if discovered, be ready to clean up the mess.

Theorists who study ethics have evolved many ways to view ethical decisions. Some break the decisions into whether you focus on the end results (*consequential ethics*) or on personal standards (*morality ethics*).

Professor Louis Day, whose work focused on journalists, suggests you prioritize your list of considerations. For instance, you might ask (in descending order) if the information you provide or withhold when gaining access situation violates any of the following factors.

1) Your own moral standards
2) The well-being of the subjects involved
3) The truthful objectives of your documentary
4) The concept of documentary work itself
5) The professional standards of your colleagues

Creating conflict in ethical areas always means you must be ready to explain your moral stance later. The improper information you provide could even get you into legal hot water. Investigative crews have been sued for fraud and trespassing. A federal jury once awarded over $5 million of ABC's money to a supermarket chain as damages because undercover reporters from *Primetime Live* had entered the store's food processing area working as employees and used hidden cameras to photograph questionable food storage.

Disclosure follows these commonly accepted guidelines:

1) The interviewee must be competent to consent.
2) The producer is straightforward about the thesis and advocacy of the documentary.
3) The producer is truthful about the possible distribution of the video (i.e., it will be broadcast).

## Credibility

A primary consideration in gaining access is credibility. If you are starting out, you might not have any credibility history. You are calling someone out of nowhere. Possible documentary subjects always want to know if this film project is backed by someone they can trust. Does the filmmaker have a recognizable reputation like Ken Burns? Is it being made for a known quantity like PBS or HBO? Is the call from the BBC? These names could open doors.

Credibility also might be borrowed from your funder. It helps to be able to say, "I'm working on a National Endowment for the Arts documentary on zoos," or "I'm working with a department at the university for a documentary on gender image."

Beginning producers without a body of work and few connections have the toughest time. For them, gaining trust and access is more complicated. Beyond simple persistence, one method is to find common ground in initial phone conversations. People might open up if they become comfortable with your personal knowledge or outlook. Multiple conversations with sources help break down reluctance.

If contacts still are reticent to appear, perhaps there's a problem with their perceptions of your advocacy for this issue. Review your website, your treatment, and your synopsis. Are they laced with provocative statements about the idea? Toning it down might help; after all, the goal is information and a dialog.

## Standing Behind the Facts in Your Film

Many scholars and theorists have written extensively about the questions of truth (verifiable fact, conformity to reality) and what documentarians do—represent reality with pictures. The discussion is rich enough to fill books and yearlong seminars.

Suffice it to say, the opportunity for outright deception is readily available and getting easier every moment of our digital, manipulative world. These days, we can flip frames, change speeds, Photoshop out embarrassing elements, crop unwanted backgrounds, lose awkward audio, and easily ignore visual images that change our story.

Fakery in filmmaking is as old as the industry itself. Shortly after the French Lumiere brothers projected movie film for an audience in 1894, filmmakers were caught using battlefield films shot in New Jersey as newsreel accounts of the Spanish American war in Cuba. Robert Flaherty's seminal documentary *Nanook of the North,* released in the 1920s, was the crowd-pleasing story of the bitterly hard life in northern Canadian villages. It was extensively staged.

Do audiences look on documentaries as true? We believe so. Do producers have an imperative ethical responsibility to strive for truthfulness and avoid fakery, deceitful staging, or intentional omission of fact? Yes, it would seem so.

Whatever the producer's personal moral standards, fudging facts, slipping in bogus B-roll, leaving out uncomfortable information, and tinkering with the truth will inflame the critics when they discover it. They'll take apart any documentary scene by scene, question everything, and attempt to rip the producer's reputation to shreds. Michael Moore's first foray into theatrical distribution, *Roger and Me,* had some transpositions of events along a chronological timeline. Critics pounced. Moore responded by saying, "It's not a documentary—it's a film."

## THE LONG-TERM PROJECT AND YOU

Now that you've explored a few crucial questions about the topic, we have one last area to examine. It's time to turn to the spotlight on you, the producer. Heed what one producer noted: "It's going to take longer than you think."

### Maintaining Focus

Maintaining focus is easier when the producer is obsessed with the topic. We've mentioned that already. But your own personal work history on long-term projects could be a key. If you have a habit of concentrating on one topic for a short period and then losing interest, do not begin a documentary. It will only come to grief.

### Your Skill Level

A familiarity with the technical side of production or willingness to learn is crucial to your project. You'll be around cameras and sound recording equipment, shooting and interview locations, workflow and format decisions, editing rooms, and the disquieting world of distribution.

A producer who deliberately ignores the technical side makes production difficult for everyone else. Making poor production decisions can fatally damage crew morale and make postproduction incredibly complex.

### Respect Your Life Outside Production

Personal relationships often suffer during documentary production. Long periods of travel, expensive equipment and crew needs, artistic differences, and a single-minded focus on the project can take a toll on family and friends. If you have any

fragile social situations that require a considerable time commitment (old relatives, sick family members, unstable partners, unusual child care arrangements)
you might want to reconsider the demands of a documentary. Bailing out in the
middle of the production creates animosity with collaborators and crew who have
worked extremely hard.

### Money and Financing

Don't lie to yourself; this project is going to cost someone hard dollars. Draining
your own personal resources, such as savings, credit cards, or retirement accounts,
causes grief and takes years to pay off.

The life of the independent filmmaker can be a rocky one. Some documentary
makers set off on a project and find money as they go; others won't make a move
until the grant check is in the bank. Independent filmmakers cannot make mistakes by spending a year on a film that begs for an audience and misses out on
distribution.

Getting financial backing is an onerous enterprise, one that most filmmakers
despise. Check Chapter 4 for possibilities.

## A NOTE ON USING THE TERMS FILM OR VIDEO

In this book, we often refer to a documentary as a *film*. We use this term for historical
continuity and because it's valuable to have an alternative to the word *documentary*.
However, this is not an endorsement of any particular side in the continuing battle
over which medium provides better pictures.

Both authors of this book have made documentaries using film or video. We
believe, for the most part, that techniques for documentaries are more or less the
same in either medium. What you record on in the field depends on experience,
available equipment, and economic forces.

## SUMMARY

This chapter discusses why undertaking a major documentary project should
depend on the quality of the idea, distribution goals, access to subjects, shelf life of
the theme, and an evaluation of your own personal situation and funds. If the answers here encourage you to proceed, then go on to Chapter 2 for a discussion of
what you'll need to make your documentary an engaging, interesting program.

### Shaping Your Skills

1. Using your documentary idea, write out your pitch. Compose a 25-word
   sentence that explains the project.
2. Investigate current and upcoming documentaries on your topic. Use industry and trade resources as well as the PBS website. See if it is an overworked
   topic.

3. Look at the principal characters for your proposed doc. How will you approach the difficult access problems? Could these people be put off by your aggressive stance on the issue? What common ground might you look for? Will there be ethical questions as you approach them?

## Further Reading

Aufderheide, Patricia, *Documentary Film: A Very Short Introduction,* New York: Oxford University Press, 2007.
Nichols, Bill, *Introduction to Documentary,* Bloomington: Indiana University Press, 2001.

# CHAPTER 2

# Critical Needs: Characters and Strong Sequences

The making of sequences is, for me, at the heart of filmmaking.
CINEMATOGRAPHER RICHARD LEACOCK

Every documentary project, regardless of topic, should strive to tell the story through the engaging characters of its on-screen subjects and its powerful visual sequences. The challenge is this: In a character-driven documentary, can you find visual ways to reveal the rich interior of your on-camera subjects' motives, dreams, energy, spirit, morality, or creative exploits? In a sequence-driven documentary, will your field sequences be engaging and revealing? Will they create the essential drama that interests an audience?

This chapter suggests you work diligently to develop strong characters and sequences. Otherwise, your long days and weeks of documentary work could go unrewarded.

## GLOSSARY

**Beauty shots** Landscape and other shots with striking aesthetic qualities. Might be sunrises, sunsets, or moody golden light shots.

**Cover** Generally applied to interview subjects, these are sequences of everyday activity used to introduce the interviewee's personality.

**Fair use** Copyright law provisions allowing unlicensed use of visuals.

**Golden moments** Startling, disproportionately powerful sequences that are fresh, revealing, and memorable.

**Orphan works** Copyrighted film or photos whose owners are difficult to find.

**Public domain** Visual material or audio for which the copyright has expired.

*(Continued)*

## GLOSSARY *(Continued)*

**Reflexivity** Video or audio revealing the production process. Mild reflexivity could be an interviewer's voice asking a question or a portable light stand in the background; strong reflexivity could be an on-camera host or a character directly addressing the producer during sequences. Self-directed reflexivity focuses the story on the documentary maker, who becomes the chief protagonist in the story.

**Treatment** A written narrative of the visual sequences expected in the documentary (see Chapter 4 for an example).

## THE INTERPLAY OF CHARACTERS AND SEQUENCES: THE VITAL NEED FOR BOTH

Memorable documentaries succeed on the visceral nature of unique characters and jewel-like sequences.

For certain storytelling narratives, the needs are obvious. Biographies and hosted programs concentrate on personalities and are decidedly character-driven; the journey, event, or observational documentaries rely more on powerful narrative moments and are sequence-driven; and journalistic or issues docs use a mix of these techniques. It is the interplay of fascinating characters and powerful sequences, told with an intimacy on film, that intrigues and holds the audiences.

The thin boundary that separates fictional storytelling and documentary is easy to cross. That might be why a number of highly acclaimed narrative film directors also are lauded for their documentary work, including Martin Scorsese, Jonathan Demme, Werner Herzog, and Spike Lee.

### Finding Fascinating, Unpredictable, Energetic Characters

A documentary's lead characters should have energetic personalities. If the filmed images can convey this vitality, the program will hold the audience's attention. A lively film depends on the producer's ability to reveal this in an intimate manner.

Early on, a producer must decide if the cinematic presence of each character comes across on the screen. There are plenty of wonderful, socially important, intelligent human beings who are uncomfortable in production situations and who lack energy when the camera is on them. Countless docs have fallen flat as the producers have struggled to tell a story with very normal but lifeless on-screen personalities.

Enduring documentaries result from choosing your subjects carefully. At the beginning of the twentieth century, Robert Flaherty wanted to bring audiences the story of the difficult life in the Canadian provinces. His film, *Nanook of the North*, was a character-driven doc that still intrigues audiences. Flaherty smartly focused on one fascinating protagonist character with a charming smile, Nanook, and filmed him in a controversial series of re-created hunting and fishing sequences. It portrayed the struggle of an individual against the harshness of the cruel, bitter climate. Audiences loved the film.

Several years ago, Producer Jennifer Maytorena Taylor set out to make a film about Muslims in the United States and after a year of research, she knew it had to be a about a character rather than about a general theme:

I really started looking for characters. And Hamza (a hip-hop artist), the one who became the protagonist . . . was one of a group of young Muslim artists whom I had tested. I didn't like him at all. I hated his act . . . I saw him perform it with his brother in a nightclub in Brooklyn where the atmosphere had been very jazzy and all of a sudden these two guys came screaming out on the stage and waving these swords on fire and yelling at me. And I just sort of said "AAAgh, I can't deal with this guy," but then I went out with the group of musicians afterward and I found out that Hamza and his brother were incredibly nice . . . And I decided I would interview him and I found out that they were very funny and wonderful and very Latino and I thought great, these are the people I should follow.

In *Detropia*, released in 2012, producers Heidi Ewing and Rachel Grady found union organizer George McGregor, video blogger Crystal Starr, and nightclub owner Tommy Stephens, all thoughtful, delightful, and very much a part of a gritty Detroit. They used them to depict their feature-length exploration of the demise of a major American city. Each character had a wonderful presence on screen, and all three of them were buoyant as they took the audience on a guided tour through the city's deserted streets and daily challenges.

## The Need to See the Characters in Action

The producer's challenge is to find situations in which the video images reveal a character's motives, social interactions, dreams, nasty habits, or wealth of human kindness. In most cases, the audiences enjoy discovering these elements in active sequences rather than a parade of talking head testimonials.

As the producer, your job is to ensure that a camera crew is at any occasion that shows the character's mindset and interactions. Director Terry Zwigoff had to do this in the six years it took to make *Crumb*, a portrait of counterculture cartoonist Robert Crumb. Zwigoff's camera seemingly dogged Crumb everywhere, ending up with myriad sequences involving Crumb's relationship with his brothers Charles and Maxon, partner Aline, and other family members and associates.

Sometimes, in distant locations, documentary crews have a tougher time. Les Blank's intriguing and masterful portrait of the enigmatic German film director

**Figure 2.1** Strong characters in *Detropia* documentary included a young video blogger, Crystal Starr (left) and the local auto workers' union president George McGregor (right).
Courtesy of *Detropia*, photos by Wolfgang Held and Tony Hardmon

Werner Herzog, *Burden of Dreams,* required immense effort from himself and sound recordist Maureen Gosling to follow Herzog for months while in production on a feature film in the Peruvian Amazon jungle.

The wise and brilliant Herzog himself has built documentaries around highly interesting characters, including *Grizzly Man, Little Dieter Needs to Fly, My Best Friend,* and others. He is a master of storytelling and opening up the contradictions in his characters.

Film director Woody Allen's public image had taken a hit years ago when director Barbara Kopple followed him with his musician buddies on tour of European cities for the doc *Wild Man Blues.* The cameras shadowed him everywhere, recording many personal moments. The result was remarkable sequences letting us peer behind the public persona of a whiny, brilliant filmmaker while he traveled with band members, his wife, and the tour managers. Tender moments emerged when Allen and his wife shared a room service breakfast in their hotel room.

Producer Ken Kobre followed 12 working photojournalists on dangerous and difficult assignments around the world. The power of his documentary *Deadline Every Second* comes from his subjects' enthusiastic comments and personal asides while working in dangerous situations, traveling in cars, editing, or taking food breaks.

When director Jonathan Demme was shooting *A Man from Plains* about former U.S. President Jimmy Carter, he knew he had only two weeks of access. Each day, Demme dispatched multiple crews, sometimes as many as four, to follow Carter's every movement. Carter was amused when they even filmed his early morning laps in a backyard swimming pool. "Each day someone would come out and shoot every stroke," he said. "One morning, I came out and there was a guy with an underwater camera." That's planning.

### Evaluating a Subject's On-Screen Presence

Phone or in-person preinterviews are a good start. Pose provocative questions and listen with great care, and you should begin to sense the subjects' lively, conversational nature. It is then you can start making choices.

Gregarious, friendly people will most likely come across well. Highly talkative characters who fidget and appear uncomfortable might not. Someone who drones endlessly on topics might send up some red flags for the producer.

Director Spike Lee faced this problem in his four-hour documentary on the destruction in New Orleans, *When the Levees Broke: A Requiem in Four Acts.* Any viewer could imagine that it would be filled with interviews featuring devastated residents. However, by emphasizing certain hurricane victims with stronger personalities and repeatedly following them outside the formal interview, the film avoided the stigma of talking heads.

In an ideal world, the next step for producers would be to exclude all the less exciting subjects; however, for many reasons, they often are stuck with nonsparkling speakers. This is particularly the case if the film is an issues, science, or historical production and requires a mosaic of recognized experts and advocates to support the thesis. An audience for these documentaries could endure a repetitive string of on-camera interviews.

Producers must take creative steps to avoid this. Too many talking head interviewees will displace the timeline real estate needed for the energy of natural sound sequences. Even if the talking head experts are kept to a minimum, their on-camera shots have a monotonous appearance—30 seconds of a medium close-up talking to someone off camera. For the audience, that dull string of talking heads can make the documentary seem like one long static shot. These interviews need additional energy to break up this visual tedium.

### Options When the Main Characters Are Not Cinematic

If a key or central character lacks on-camera charisma but still must appear in the film, there are options for the producer.

In these cases, deemphasize the long, formal, sit-down interview and replace it with a series of conversations done while the interviewee is engaged in an activity. Interview locations could be moved outdoors or the interviewee can be allowed to refer to pictures or objects while being interviewed. Sometimes, allowing the interview to walk while talking helps. Also, more sequences can be built around the character's daily professional life, colorful home locations, and candid social situations.

Another possibility is to expand a back story within the film to add interest. When producer Anne Makepeace turned the camera on herself for a self-directed reflexive documentary, *Baby It's You,* about the medical difficulties involved in pregnancy, she also gave a detailed account of her family and her brothers, one of whom talked freely about becoming a polygamist. And although her story was gripping, the shots of her brother standing out in the Utah desert extolling the virtues of attracting and housing multiple wives was so unique that he was unforgettable.

## CHARACTER-DRIVEN DOCS AND DRAMATIC TENSION

In many cases, documentary films will have an appealing protagonist character—the person who is the central focus. Not necessarily the most adventurous, cinematic, or well-known individual, he or she must be a pivotal presence that embodies the traits or actions examined in the film. Protagonist characters will have a point of view and will confront obstacles, usually presented by a single antagonist adversary, groups of antagonists, or associations and businesses.

Defining exactly who fills each role could help the documentary producer plan the program and define the underlying conflicts. Often, these adversarial roles are exaggerated for dramatic impact. In his 1988 documentary *Roger and Me,* director Michael Moore portrays himself as a naive truth-seeking protagonist trying to meet with his antagonist, Roger Smith, the CEO of General Motors. The film's thesis is that the corporation's lack of a benevolent role in the community led to a decline in the economy of Flint, Michigan. To depict this, Moore serves up a series of confrontations with bizarre characters or low-level company security guards and bureaucrats. Their unwillingness to debate him was portrayed as an example of GM's alleged standoffishness. The *Roger and Me* confrontational model is a package that Moore reprised in his later documentaries: *Bowling for Columbine, Fahrenheit 9/11,* and *Sicko.*

**Figure 2.2** The cinematographer provides the director and editor with a variety of close-up, medium, and long shots, reverses, reaction shots, and two-shots that re-create the action at a location.

## CAPTURING VISUAL SEQUENCES

Documentary producers must brainstorm all visual possibilities for their films. They will be looking for significant observational sequences that can be translated to video by the cinematographer. These individual sequences will bring out the personalities of their characters and multiple sequences will allow the editor to choose the most telling ones. The nuts and bolts of these sequences, the multiplicity of shots, are explored in Chapter 9 on production.

## STORYTELLING NEEDS STRONG SEQUENCES

Documentary producers know that images shot on location during an event will be the heart of the film. Skillfully selected and edited into a story arc, the sequence is the pinnacle of documentary. It can be profoundly revealing and along with its natural ambient sound, it can successfully pull the audience into the story without any narration.

An example happened in director Wim Wenders's *Buena Vista Social Club*. The opening sequences begin the documentary because they are intriguing rather than informational. Only later does the film get to the profiles on the unique Cuban musicians.

Sequences have carried documentaries from *Nanook* through the verite movement in the 1960s and 1970s. Good ones always work. In my film *Playing With Fire*, about a family that constructs handmade fireworks in an Andean town, a remarkable scene unfolds when there is a dangerous explosion in the backyard fireworks workshop, something that happened while I was shooting. This sequence then leads to others as the fireworks maker tries to right his life again after the disaster.

### Each Sequence Needs Energy

Producers should consider that a single strong sequence might not carry a story arc in the documentary; it might take a string of sequences to maintain narrative tension.

The string of powerful sequences represents a natural phenomenon. A television weatherman once explained to me his theories about climate and energy. "The storm hitting us today," he said about California, "is really part of a continuum, a lineup of energy bursts that stretches thousands of miles back across the Pacific Ocean, each storm shoving and pushing and banging into the other as they slowly move in the sky across the top of us."

A documentary's lineup of sequences has a kinship with the forecaster's explanation. Each sequence will come before the viewer's eyes as if it were a singular storm, parading by while it engages and involves the audience. The producer must consider, however, that each sequence is affected by the one before it and the one after it, strengthening or weakening in relation to the power and engaging qualities of adjacent sequences.

This serialized presentation structure also has a lot in common with theater, dance, symphonic music, concerts, or dramatic films. The audience is waiting and the producer's job is to perfect each sequence in this series until it maintains the pace and interest in the topic. Two or three clunker sequences in a row and the audience becomes restive.

## Your Topic Needs to Explore Every Possible Sequence

Hundreds of meaningful documentary ideas turn into forgettable films because the producers did not reach beyond mediocre visuals. A feature-length doc planned for theatrical release will need a warehouse full of rich sequences to make it successful. Indeed, and a bit on the excessive side, the producers of *Detropia* shot 500 hours of field video for a 90-minute documentary.

Gathering any significant amount of location sequences might cover extended periods of months and years. Even for a half-hour doc, the rich visual tapestry must be there, considering that a 30-minute film might require at least 20 to 40 sequences. And if your projected TRT is 6 to 12 minutes, you should still plan for at least 8 to 10 discrete sequences.

## Continually Add to Your List of Sequence Possibilities

As preproduction ideas mature and expand, brainstorm with colleagues to compile a list of strong visual sequence ideas that will carry the story. If there are only 10 ideas on that list, the film will be thin.

Be diligent. Continually update the sequence list, writing down even the most outlandish ideas. Current events, investigative, historical compilation, or scientific and health abstract ideas need the most work.

Imagine following principal characters to every interesting location and to every interaction that relates to the topic. If the character meets annually with others in her profession, go to the convention with her. If the character mentions a barbecue for her extended family, there's another opportunity.

Producer CJ Hunt refers to this quest for tantalizing visuals as a treasure hunt. He advises to listen carefully to what the subjects say, even off camera. If a subject casually mentions something during a postshooting conversation, it might lead to great visuals. When Hunt was interviewing a nutritional advocate for his doc *In Search of the Perfect Human Diet*, the person mentioned that his group was doing an anthropological dig in the south of France to investigate what the early residents ate. Sensing an opportunity, Hunt, a student at the time, enticed two of his school colleagues, maxed out his credit cards for airline flights, and ended up with a sequence in the dig that contributed strongly to the rich visual story flow.

Seemingly routine events can result in usable sequences. A producer colleague was talking about her documentary on a native Hawaiian group coming to the mainland United States to retrieve ancestral bones stolen from island graves years before. The producer remarked that she was helping transport the group and was on her way to the airport to pick up the visitors. We suggested instead that she shoot the arrival. She did, and it became an engaging opening sequence.

### Shoot Multiple Sequences at a Single Event

If a crew is documenting a charitable food distribution network, think of separating the different actions at the location into unique individual sequences. One sequence might involve a key character interacting with workers. Another might be the different produce and foodstuffs available. A third might be the loading and unloading of trucks. A fourth might be exterior wide shots. A fifth might be office personnel on the phone with suppliers. All of these might be combined later into one sequence or they might be split up and used at different points. Versatility results from shooting extensively at each location.

### Avoid Building Repetitive Sequences

How many times, for instance, have viewers seen someone working at a keyboard in front of a monitor, students sitting in a classroom, or musicians rehearsing? The sequences on your proposed list could be overused and stale, and if you plan to rely on these to carry the program, you'll need to make an impressive artistic effort to create a fresh look.

This lack of variety might hamstring the editor in post. A filmmaker I worked with was trying to chronicle the story of a club with eight remarkable individuals. The documentary pieced together eight strong profile segments, but all were similar in rhythm and length. By the fifth remarkable individual, some in the audience were sensing they had seen this structure before.

## BEYOND SEQUENCES: B-ROLL

For journalistic or issues docs, in which the on-screen subject is only used as a talking head interview, the producer will need the crew to shoot B-roll. B-roll in documentary is used to illustrate anything a character or personality has mentioned in an interview or voice under segment. So if the interviewee talks about ducks, then the producer assigns the crew to shoot B-roll of ducks. The crew might

not have any opportunity to make a sequence out of the ducks. So, although a sequence would be nice, it is not expected. Well-crafted duck shots might do.

But B-roll can be tedious. Producers like Ellen Bruno are critical of the use of
mundane B-roll. "There's always the tendency to use B-roll material like wallpaper.
People think it is to illustrate and further support a point that's being made. But
often what happens is that you are not taking the viewer anywhere except to where
they already are." Bruno says she will take another tack:

> I think, to me, what can deepen this experience or bring some surprise or bring
> together a juxtaposition of a particular thought and image that creates an equa-
> tion that leads to a different kind of experience that's not a literal experience. And
> so I don't look for something that's matching . . . I look for something that's a bit
> of a stretch in some way or that gives the audience space to have an experience
> that's prompted by what they are hearing in a voice over interview bit.

If the field visuals are not sequences or B-roll, then most likely they are cover,
which refers to mundane everyday shots of your subject, another character, host,
or interviewee. It usually shows the subject walking by the camera or talking on
the phone, something that the crew has asked the person to do. Producer Jon
Dann says these shots usually look inauthentic. He says there are other ways to
get cover. "I would usually find a way to do it . . . to get the pictures we need . . .
without directly telling somebody to do something. And the way I would handle
it would be to say . . . do what you would be doing now, normally, so we can get
pictures of it."

## Archival Is Not a Sure Thing

Dreaming of fleshing out the story with segments of archival or found footage?
Unless a source is hoarding a trove of newly discovered historical footage, the
visual power of commonly used archival could be diminished in the eyes of an
audience. In short, they have seen it before.

For a documentary that referred back to an event three decades earlier, I
searched until I found the original material at a local television station. Its film li-
brarian graciously gave me a free license to a one-minute sequence, but the images
he provided were identical to those already used in another rather well-known
documentary. I had no choice but to use those same shots, and some of my associates assumed I lifted them from the first film.

For the heavy users of archival in issues, historical, or biography documentaries, the price can be shocking. Producers Gary Weimberg and Catherine Ryan
estimated the total cost of archival for their 90-minute feature was $60,000 plus
another $20,000 in search costs. At the start, they struggled along by only buying
selected rights, but later had to make additional payments to secure broadcast
licenses.

When archival is vital but controversial, certain producers take risks. For her
2007 feature-length doc *War Made Easy,* producer Loretta Alper needed more
than an hour of archival, almost 90 percent of the program. Because the doc's topic
was criticism of politics and media, she used 60 percent of the archival without

license, mostly news clips, under "fair use," a provision of the copyright law allow-ing criticism. She acknowledged that her effort could end up in court.

## The Opportunity for "Free" Archival

There's a good deal of free archival available. Go to www.archive.org and you'll find the Prelinger archives, which allow you to use any download for programs in any market. On other sites, "free" archival is often a teaser or a come-on to buy other archival. U.S. government historical film archives are often free to license, but you must pay for screeners, transfer, and media costs.

In *Detropia,* a feature-length reflection on Detroit's fight against desolation, producer Rachel Grady said they had plenty of archival available but just used a little bit. "We just wanted to give a flavor to the history," she said.

## Beyond Sequences: When Few Visuals Are Available

Producer Emiko Omori faced this dilemma in her documentary *To Chris Marker—An Unsent Letter* about reclusive French filmmaker Chris Marker who died in 2012. While his films were in general distribution, there were no recorded inter-views with him and very few still photographs. Instead, she allowed his friends, associates, and colleagues to tell his story, often referring to Omori in the text because she had worked with him. For visuals, she used her own international location footage, because Marker had been a proponent of various cultures around the world.

A similar challenge faces producers recounting events in a precinematic era. They often use reenactments, staged to depict the historical moments. These can be all-out dramas with actors, costumes, and a script, or they can be vague sugges-tions, often blurred images that portray the times in the past.

Although animation is heavily used in science and natural history docs, it is also used to recount history. Producer Ari Folman used it to tell the horrors of the 1982 Israeli war in Lebanon in his *Waltz With Bashir* that had a theatrical release. Producer John Leanos used full animation in his film *Los ABCs* about how the catalog of 26 alphabet letters each represented someone who had died in war, or in slavery, or in Bho Pal in India.

## "Golden" Moments and Beauty Shots

Even though it took a great effort to position the crew at the scene, unforgettable "golden" moment sequences often are surprises. When cosmic luck is on the pro-ducer's side, the crew can return with sequences that reveal human emotions, struggles, strife, joy, anger, or happiness. The more of these that stack up, the more unique is the program. The key to finding these is simple: A producer has to put a capable crew in place.

In Elena Mannes's *Amazing Grace,* the crew followed a group of singers to a rural picnic. At the gathering, a shy 11-year-old girl was encouraged to sing the film's topic song solo and a cappella. All activity ceased and she gave a haunting rendition. The moment was splendid and the photographer and sound recordist did a masterful job. It was unforgettable.

**Figure 2.3** Beauty shots can provide a transition or set the mood for the documentary.

Equally important are those "beauty shots," the stunning sunrises, sunsets, pastoral landscapes, or frantic urban chaos that add texture or chronology. These don't involve cosmic luck; instead, they involve effort and often are hard to shoot. It might require two weeks of climbing out of bed before dawn to get a striking sunrise.

Director Ken Burns is noted for his constant use of these shots. During one interview, his crew joked that it often takes weeks of rising before dawn to get the sublime golden lighting for a stunning sunrise. For his historical style, the beauty shots often fill in for years and times when no film or video was available.

### When the Documentary's Visual List Is Meager
After completing the visual and sequence list, a producer must face reality. If there is very little chance for engaging sequences, then perhaps it is time to find another way to communicate this story. If the subject leans toward the world of abstract concepts, taking it in another direction could bolster possible sequence situations.

Docudrama segments, animation, and clever graphics might help. Another search might turn up the hidden and forgotten archival material. Artists, designers, and creative computer graphics artists could begin B-roll animation. A documentary idea based on borderline visuals demands substantial creative imagination and effort.

## VISUAL STYLE DECISIONS

When contemplating an individual look for the proposed documentary, there are several considerations.

The technical goals, target audiences, or schedules affect the style. The major release market will determine parameters and aesthetic considerations. For instance, for the theater screens or festivals, a director might employ more wide shots and be wary of off-tripod shaky video or minor focus problems. For television screens, the close-up shot is singularly effective. On mobile or tablet screens, the director might emphasize primary colors, larger graphics, less lens motion, and shorter running times to provide a better viewing atmosphere.

Audience makeup is another concern. Will a more mature audience prefer a relaxed pace with longer narrative sequences? For this audience, a classic collection of traditional shots over a music bed of older pop tunes would suffice for the sequences. Then again, an MTV generation audience is used to quick cuts, tilted horizons, multiple camera shots in a single interview, and a heavy music beat throughout. If so, you have to shoot those in addition to the regular required wide, medium, and close-up shots.

The presentation format is also a consideration. Is it a single, standalone program? Multipart? Or could it be cut into chapters for release over a longer stretch of time? For experimental Internet video, producers have experimented with new documentary mini episodes created and transmitted once a week in serial fashion.

## The Director Aims for a Unique Style

Many documentarians are comfortable with classic doc style formats: cinema verite sequences, sit-down interview support for issues, voiceover narration or poetic images. But occasionally directors have unique requests. They want the colors oversaturated. They like the distortion of wide-angle lenses. They demand long-running shots in sequences, shots that allow the action to happen within the frame. They forbid any portable lights and specify all natural lighting. They ignore tripods and advocate all handheld shots.

Sometimes overdoing a style element such as using only handheld video will force a struggle in the editing room. Experienced producer and cinematographer Emiko Omori shot the majority of interviews for her coproduced film *Passion and Power* on a tilted horizon or "Dutch" angle as it is called. Later she had to backtrack. "So the Dutching irritated plenty of people and it still irritates a lot of people. We get a lot of comments . . . why did you do that . . . but the first time we showed it . . . we noticed that people were a little leaned over when they watched it . . . so I did what I called a double Dutch in the edit room . . . and undutched it . . . and the lines were no longer rectangular. I kind of liked that and in the (frame's) black spaces I put other images."

Producers and directors should settle the question of style elements before production. The more agreement reached about a coherent and consistent style, the fewer problems will arise during postproduction. Changing your style in mid-project can be a disaster.

Multiple shooting styles are more trouble if several different cinematographers shoot over the course of multiyear project or multiple cameras record a single event. When I was editing a piece that included a Las Vegas convention segment shot by three different cameramen, a good portion of one shooter's field

**Figure 2.4** Dutch angled interview from the film *Passion and Power*.
Courtesy Emiko Omori

tape was useless because half his medium shots used the tilted Dutch horizon and the other shooters didn't do this. In post, the tilted images wouldn't cut into sequences.

### The Subject Might Suggest a Unique Style

It's critical for the producer/director to consider how closely he or she will mirror the specific visual culture of the subject. Ideally you want to have an interactive relationship between the producer and the documentary subject. For instance, if the subject is a comic book illustrator, there is an opportunity to emulate the inner universe of the creator with specialized lighting and composition, camera angles, and specific color hue to mirror the illustrator's unique sensibility and vision.

Cinematographer Vicente Franco says it is never too early to study this. "I think each story requires a different treatment so that is why it is necessary to have that conversation to decide what the story is all about to decide what the cinematographic style might be. There are an endless amount of styles . . . but to cite an example . . . *The Fight in the Fields* . . . about Cesar Chavez and the farm worker's movement . . . that I shot for Ray Telles and Rick Tejada-Flores. We decided that because of the nature of the subject . . . which was the farm workers, we wanted to interview our subjects outdoors . . . just to represent a little bit about the connection of the subjects to the land so we made it important to do the interviews outdoors."

Consider contemporary hybrid cultures in our urban centers. A documentary might seek to reveal what's happening in a three-generation Vietnamese family living in an inner-city neighborhood. This might mix the parents' older cultural traditions, the kids' American pop culture, and a conglomeration of the neighbors' and relatives' lifestyles with heavy polarized views on assimilation and politics. Issues of language and traditions are in constant collision. Within this complex scenario the producer must agonize over how to mirror the subject. Adaptation to a new culture is the central theme; therefore, the film needs to capture contrasting images and sounds that are evident in that world: an altar with Buddha next to a Bart Simpson figurine; a traditional family dinner with conversation in Vietnamese while younger family members watch a football game; or a comparison of the changing dress codes across generations. Memory and poetic reconstructions of the grandparents' childhood life growing up in Vietnam's countryside could be contrasted with the grandchildren's daily routines in the contemporary culture.

### Outside Video Might Compromise the Style

It is easy to say: We'll use the archival at this point. However, archival material comes in many sizes, shapes, and formats, and blending these produces problems. For instance, although your film will be in a 16 × 9 horizontal format, many archival stills will have a vertical orientation and your historical clips may have a 4 × 3 format. Converting everything to one format and screen size is time-consuming and requires editorial decisions on how to crop irregular-sized images to fit the program's aspect ratio.

The prime archival that the producer imagines might not be available for practical or political reasons. If the archival film or video involves music or art, there will be rights questions, because each song or image could involve the owner of the archival, the publisher of the music, and the artist or estate of the artist. It's a swamp of permissions, cajoling, wheedling, begging, and so on.

In this search, orphan material for which the copyright holder is unknown often appears. It might be music that common wisdom thinks is in public domain, and it might be an old still portrait or even some newly discovered film for which ownership cannot be determined. Using this could be risky; the copyright holder might appear and demand it be pulled from the program. There is very little defense for this unless there is money to pay the owners when they surface.

## ETHICS AND VISUALS

### Visuals Provided by the Subjects

This is a very difficult ethical question. Sometimes there is no choice if the producer intends to show B-roll. There are industries that will not allow independent crews into factories or onto their property for health or safety reasons; instead, they will offer their own video shot by their camera crew.

Using handout footage can open a documentary to charges of conflict of interest, even though the use is minor. The decision will be based on the usefulness of the handout video. Whatever the decision, anyone using the handouts should acknowledge the origin in the documentary itself, as well as in the credits.

### Staging

The documentary filmmaker's desire to get every crucial sequence can lead to an ethical slippery slope. One problem is staging—creating or significantly altering an event or action that never would have happened or re-creating something the camera missed the first time.

This is a discussion that will never end. Indian writer Ved Mehta, accompanying director William Cran on an extended shoot in India, often marveled at the film crew's boldness in redoing events they missed. In his book *The Photographs of Chachaji: The Making of a Documentary Film,* he notes that even the crewmembers were conflicted about the ethics. In one location, they were re-creating the principal character Chachaji's arrival in a rural village and had enlisted the aid of some villagers to play the part of the Chachaji's relatives.

> Eoin (the sound recordist) mutters something about keeping documentaries pure and truthful. "Documentaries should show only events that really happen and show them only as they are happening," he says, harping on his favorite theme. "You can always tell a bad documentary—the camera is in the room before a person enters instead of coming into the room with that person."
>
> "That is just bad staging," Bill [William Cran, the director' says. "In my opinion, whatever looks good, or can be made to look good, is fine in a documentary."
>
> "Ha!" Ivan [the cameraman] snorts. "That's straight out of the shortest book in the world—The journalist's book of ethics."
>
> Bill laughs.

During the filming, Mehta is forever critical of Cran's director's interference. However, after the screening of the first rough cut, his worries ease.

> Once again, Bill has astonished me. During the shooting, I often wondered whether Bill understood what Chachaji was about. During earlier sessions, I wondered about Bill's judgment and taste. But the rough cut has a meditative tone, a certain lyrical calm. It consummately conveys Chachaji's spirit, and most of it is in good taste. It's as though Bill's frenetic pyrotechnics on location and his brashness in initial editing were just a camouflage for his innate poetic sense, for his instinctive understanding of Chachaji and, by analogy, of India.

For Mehta then, the ethical quandary of staging was soothed by the accuracy of the film's final cut.

Almost every director is a target for this criticism. Robert Flaherty was critically roasted for his re-creations in the seminal documentary *Nanook of the North.* Yet no one said this wasn't the way it happened. Director Terry Zwigoff staged a specialized beauty contest in his biographic study of cartoonist Robert Crumb. Yet the film conveyed a stunning account of the controversial artist's approach to life. Director Michael Moore creates a string of confrontations in many of his films, confrontations that never would happen in everyday life.

The tussle over the problem of staging even reached the stolid BBC. In 1998, they released new guidelines about staging. These said (1) producers must inform the audience of a staging or restaging procedure, and (2) producers must always gauge the significance of the intervention to the film itself.

But if you dislike staging, how do you solve the need for cover footage—the common everyday actions to introduce characters? Camera people have always asked someone to walk down a hall, look at a paper, and work at a computer keyboard. One producer told us that he saw nothing wrong there. "Why should I wait around six hours for someone to clean the dishes?"

Documentarians split about staging and where one crosses the line that adds significant meaning. There only appears to be agreement that the director should not contrive an action that reveals strong emotion, character, decision making, or important points.

### Fictional Re-Creations and Docudrama

An extreme challenge for a documentary producer is to visualize inner thoughts, feelings, abstract ideas, or philosophical concepts. In some cases, the documentarian will be recounting historical events that predated the existence of the first motion picture cameras in the 1890s; in others, events that had no recorded media.

To get around this, some filmmakers use re-created scenes. Documentarian Errol Morris shot highly stylized re-creations with actors to B-roll the narration, interview, and interrogation of a wrongly convicted felon in his early powerful documentary *The Thin Blue Line*. Critics were mixed on his approach, saying that it wasn't documentary if it was re-created.

## SUMMARY

The producer must begin a project by reviewing the possibilities for positive and dramatic visual sequences. He or she must also calculate which aesthetic parameters would provide the most useful and comfortable editing situations while still delivering a powerful program in a useful format, whether theatrical release, broadcast for the smaller screen, or delivery to mobile devices.

### Shaping Your Skills

1. List the three most important characters planned for your doc. What makes them interesting? How does each help build the story? How do they interact and is it possible that the interactions would add more? Do you have any evidence they might be charismatic on screen?
2. List five strong sequences that will reveal elements of your topic idea. Discuss if these are repetitive, might be clichés, or might be stale from overuse in other documentaries.

### Further Reading

Mehta, Ved, *The Photographs of Chachaji: The Making of a Documentary Film*, New York: Oxford University Press, 1980.

Rosenthal, Alan, and Corner, John, *New Challenges for the Documentary*, Manchester, UK: Manchester University Press, 2005.

# CHAPTER 3

# Preparing for Collaboration

The more experienced I get, the more deferential I become and really look to use everybody that I work with and love doing that. As they say, failure is an orphan but success has many fathers. If the project is successful . . . it really is a team sport.
PRODUCER JON DANN

Very few people have the resources or skills to shepherd a documentary from idea to distribution without some help. Producers with robust budgets hire professional crews; those with smaller or nonexistent budgets will enlist the aid of collaborators.

This chapter explores the cross-section of collaborators who join up and influence productions. They might do this out of friendship, as interns, as volunteers, as spec workers with an eye toward a back-end deal, as subjects of the doc, as commissioning editors, or, in some cases, as uninvited participants. For the filmmaker, each could be an asset or a nightmare.

Producers should exercise care when teaming up with collaborators. Producers should protect themselves with a contract to avoid personal troubles and disputes over the long haul. The independence of their documentary might be at stake.

## GLOSSARY

**Back-end deals** Payment to a collaborator that depends on money received from distribution deals.

**Contract** A legally binding agreement setting out the details of the collaboration.

**Nonprofit pass-through** A not-for-profit agency willing to sponsor your documentary to allow donors or grant givers a tax break for their support.

**Spec** Informal term for work done that expects a future payoff down the line.

**Work for hire** A clause in a contract establishing that the employee is working at the direction of the producer and is not entitled to any authorship rights of raw or edited material.

## FRIENDLY COLLABORATION

### Colleagues

Bands that are just starting out, newly formed theater groups, and many nascent documentary teams share a common problem: They work on a shoestring and must take on collaborators.

For documentaries, collaborators often become outstanding contributors. They work long hours on important shoots or months in the edit room. In some cases, they can stay with the project for years.

Even though you don't have to pay them, everyone in the business knows collaborations have downsides. Over a period of time, there can be a rusting of friendships, a nasty clash of creative egos, petty battles, family emergencies, personal problems, new love relationships, or deserters who suddenly move on to more exciting (and paying) projects. A disgruntled crewmember's lack of enthusiasm can create ill feelings and lead to a tremendous waste of personal effort, money, and ambition. It can mean the sudden death of what might have been a stimulating work of art.

### Friends, Classmates, and Associates

The most common collaborators are friends, school associates, family members, or industry colleagues. Generally, for no pay, they provide competent production savvy and work on a simple quid pro quo: They help your project expecting that later, you'll help theirs.

But their volunteer efforts can cause roadblocks. One problem with using volunteer collaborators on every shoot is continuity. You might have a different camera person or sound recordist, each of whom does the job in a completely distinct way. Your field material will have dissimilar styles over time and when you reach postproduction, your editor will go mad trying to match up colorations, shot lengths, interview placements, and oddly recorded sound tracks.

With friends, social pressures might force you to continue their involvement long after they have become problem crewmembers. A local unfunded producer told me she was attempting to finish a difficult profile documentary on deadline but had no money to hire a crew. Instead, she relied on a film school classmate behind the camera. On a do-or-die production day, when her subject had a rare availability window, they shot for 10 difficult hours. Later, her volunteer cameraman announced he had lost the field footage. She was crushed. "It was easily one-third of the film. I want to kill him. What can I do now?" she said. Eventually, enough field video turned up to save the day.

On another shoot, a volunteer cameraman became enraged at the producer and his assistant. He gathered up all the original media for field shoots and stole it, hiding it at his sister's house in a distant city. It took police intervention to recover the material.

## Collaboration with Business Partners

Small production companies often make films where the two partners trade off at production skill positions—including directing. In these cases, co-producing or co-directing can lead to creative disputes. Cinematographer Vicente Franco said co-directing a documentary is like any other relationship. "And then there comes the endless discussions about who is right and who is wrong and who is going to win this battle and it's like life in general. You know . . . the creative discussions are always learning sessions that can help you see the story in a different way and sometimes you win a battle and sometimes you lose a battle but it's all for the good of the story. And the good of the documentary."

## Collaboration Over the Internet

The Internet has allowed documentary makers to work with skilled artists and craft persons around the world. Producers can now reach out globally for collaborators.

Producer Ken Kobre did this on his *Deadline Every Second* documentary, which followed the world of international photojournalists. Working from his home in southern France, he collaborated with his editor in San Francisco, his graphics artist in London, his publicity person in Kentucky, and his international distributor in Paris. All the rough cuts, music questions, revisions, and graphic adjustments bounced back and forth across thousands of miles through large file-sharing sites. When an enormous amount of data needed to be moved, it was shipped on portable hard drives. Crewmembers often never personally met the others.

## Ally Collaborators

Often it becomes effective to tap a character in your story to become a protagonist in the film. Producer Micah Peled did just that in his exploration of the controversy over farm seeds in India. He first went to high schools, looking for the children of the cotton farmers involved in the controversy. He met Manjusha Amberwar, an aspiring journalist whose own father had committed suicide, despondent over the seed issue. She became a character that carried the story forward, interviewing and appearing on camera.

**Figure 3.1** Producer/director Micah X. Peled featured journalist Manjusha Amberwar's research and interviews about the controversy in the documentary *Bitter Seeds*.
Courtesy of Micah X. Peled

## CREWMEMBERS WHO HAVE TIES TO THE SUBJECTS

This concerns a potentially troublesome situation where someone is both a craft skills crewmember on the documentary and a social partner or family member to subjects in the doc. Troubles begin when this individual suggests featuring an associate or asks to exclude certain controversial subtopics or approaches because they might create personal problems for the crewmember-participant.

This happened on one film, where the co-producer's wife was on the board of a nonprofit associated with the topic. Although that relationship provided stellar access for production shoots, it also restricted the story topic when it came to sensitive historical issues. And although the spouse co-producer never argued vigorously against pursing certain avenues, he simply didn't make any effort to do it. As a result, the controversial topics were never filmed and never found their way to the editing room.

This brings up sticky questions of ethics: How should you accommodate that enthusiastic but cautious collaborator? Can a producer craft an honest story without spotlighting the collaborator's associate or avoiding sensitive areas? Even if the producer steers clear of special privilege, doesn't this open the documentary to later criticism? The trade-off for access meant doubt about the extent and truth of the documentary.

Once again, the solution involves preproduction discussions. If the key access person is a controlling sort, the producer is very much in danger of losing editorial control of the documentary.

## SUBJECTS OF THE DOC WHO BECOME UNWELCOME COLLABORATORS

There are times when the subjects of the documentary decide they are producers. Consider what happened to a local crew producing a documentary on an outstanding youth urban gardens program. Initially, everyone with the nonprofit gardens organization was delighted with the idea and was unflinchingly cooperative. The confident producer began research, preproduction, and even some shooting. But then there were subtle hints from the organization about the direction they'd like the project to take. They intimated that the film shouldn't mention certain embarrassing events. They suggested that the producer was working for them. They pointed out that the very existence of the project, into which the producer had invested months of work and out-of-pocket money, depended on how the story conformed to their wishes. The atmosphere became hostile and they threatened to pull the plug if the script distressed them. Finally, some delicate negotiations freed up the project, but on a limited basis.

Welcome to a collaboration gone sour. The nonprofit board had become uninvited collaborators. The question of complete editorial control should have been set down in an agreement before production started. There should have been a written contract at the beginning, detailing who has final editorial control, who owns the field material, and what review is available to the participants. Put in as many details as possible regarding screenings and critical reviews. Hopefully, this will preempt a battle, which happens more often than you think.

## OFFICIAL GOVERNMENT COLLABORATORS

When producer Barbara Grandvoinet traveled to Thailand to shoot her documentary *Children of the Trains*, she was warned she had to go to a government office to get official permission to shoot everything. She said they would send a minder out to watch over the project. "Well, we were shooting street kids in the slums and how the kids were sniffing glue and living in the train yards. We knew this was not an image that the Thai government was going to approve." Her solution? She didn't go to the office to get official permission.

When I was shooting in a Mexican city or town, for instance, we would usually first visit the mayor and the chief of police and present letters of introduction. These officials then added a notation with their name or signature to a copy we carried with us. This step helped smooth access to sites and allowed us to shoot throughout the city without unexpected hassles. But in one large central Mexican city we skipped this protocol. Three days into our shoot, the hotel clerk warned us the police were after us and wanted money. He said "You'd better get out of town." And we did.

## FINANCIAL COLLABORATORS

Another set of unexpected collaborators comes on board when the project is teamed with an institutional financial source.

This collaboration is usually formal. It could be a series producer restricting flexibility in choosing a crew, a local nonprofit pass-through demanding restrictions on travel and expenditures, or a distributor that forces the producer to pull out favorite sequences to make the film acceptable to certain markets.

I was producing a grant-funded documentary on a state's death penalty initiative. We had a crucial one-time-only shoot within a state prison and the grant manager demanded I use a distant television station's cinematographer. We spent a 12-hour day shooting inside a maximum-security prison. Out of four hours of footage, I ended up with about five minutes of usable material. The rest was badly framed, badly exposed, out of focus, or filled with pans and zooms that were a terror to edit. This institutional interference is more than annoying: It can be the origin of serious dissension within the original crew.

### Money Can Come with Strings Attached

Any donated production funding provides touchy situations. With the success of crowdfunding sources like Kickstarter and Indiegogo, many more contributors are ponying up support for programs. Wise producers like CJ Hunt, when seeking individual contributions for his *In Search of the Perfect Human Diet,* put the following transparency notification on the website seeking money:

> Transparency notification: All contributors do so for these reasons. In addition, corporate contributors acknowledge they have not been involved in the filming process in any way, *and must agree* that they have no influence whatsoever on the content or editing of the film in order to contribute.

Even if you have an arts agency like the Independent Television Service (ITVS) backing you, you need to read their agreements carefully. While ITVS funding does not impinge on editorial control, it can specify restrictions on exclusivity and distribution.

What's the solution? Read the contracts carefully. Get information up front on possible format or production limitations. Demand the use of production crews who are familiar with your project and who you trust. Firmly establish who has editorial control if the program is shortened.

## COMMISSIONING EDITORS AS COLLABORATORS

Accepting a paid commission to produce a documentary means the producer is beginning a relationship with an executive or series producer who will oversee the project. It could be someone as experienced as *Frontline* Executive Producer David Fanning. He has worked with 200 producers over 20 years to ensure a journalistic quality to the program that has won 32 Emmys, 22 duPont-Columbia University Awards, and 12 Peabodies. In the case of *Frontline,* they have producers above you who might review budgets, rough cut style, and oversee content and scripts. This shouldn't be a surprise, though. Being a commissioned producer is completing a work for hire. As a photographer once told me, "I work hard to provide the best pictures. In the end, the executive editor chooses what he wants. It's his candy store."

## CHOOSING COLLABORATORS

Choosing a crew is like casting actors for a dramatic film; their personalities are often as important as their professional skills.

Some useful concerns include the following:

- Do you know this person well? Is it a friend with whom you've shared experiences or is it someone your partner heard was interested in the topic? Does this person have a passion or appreciation for the topic?
- Do you like them? Will they like you? Be honest! Could you travel on the road and eat dinner for two straight weeks with this person?
- Do you respect them?
- Does this person have any hint of financial problems? Or substance abuse?
- Will this person be troublesome when interacting with subjects of your shoot?

Ask yourself which set of skills the collaborator will bring to your project. Does this strengthen the project? Does this person have extensive production experience on a long-term documentary? Can he or she provide references from others? The slightest hint of unreliability suggests trouble. "Oh yeah, but she is never on time" can be a red flag.

## FIVE DANGEROUS FLASHPOINTS WITH COLLABORATORS

Most collaborators are longtime friends or co-workers who volunteer. But with their skills, some might be headstrong about directorial choices, scheduling attempts, equipment rentals, project directions, or decisions to spend scarce resources. When that happens, they are on a path to becoming ex-friends.

We suggest settling the following sticky areas up front.

### 1. Money

For the multitudes making documentaries on the cheap, the once-idealistic adventure of attacking an intriguing subject often gets messy in two areas: out-of-pocket spending and postdistribution revenues.

In a very mundane sense, independent doc crews consume a lot of fast food and have to buy supplies on the road. If volunteer collaborators discover the costs are not spread around equally, there can be grousing. A useful solution is to have a producer buy everything from a petty cash fund.

What happens when the doc goes to distribution is much more serious. Although nothing might ever have been said about it, some colleagues believe secretly that working on spec means they will share in any revenues when distribution brings in real dollars. They expect to share substantially in royalties. Bitterness results when the producer keeps the money in an attempt to recover his or her own personal funds that were spent. A contract, discussed later in this chapter, is the only answer.

### 2. Scheduling

Where, when, and how often you shoot can become a sore point. A producer must balance the needs of a spec crew against the deadline of getting the job done.

Although the producer might want to stay in one location for an extra interview or sequence, the tired, unpaid crew might be at the end of a long day and looking for some downtime or needing to pick up a child from day care. Maybe a less important interview or sequence can be postponed.

### 3. Equipment

Should you borrow a collaborator's camera, microphones, lights, or editing gear without payment? Who carts it around? Who pays the bills if it gets broken? Suppose another crewmember thoughtlessly bumps it off a ledge onto some cement steps. Bad feelings are usually the result.

Get all equipment responsibilities straightened out ahead of time. Don't innocently borrow it. Write out a contract specifying who will pay for broken, lost, or stolen equipment.

### 4. Credits

On many documentary shoots, the collaborators fail to set out agreements on who gets which credits for the program. Who is the producer? The co-producer? The executive producer? The director of photography?

Everything then must be resolved after the fact. A person who shot half of the documentary but left after a dispute with the producer might have his or her efforts erased from the credits. Who will be listed as the editor if the producer sits down and edits most of the film herself? Sometimes projects are abandoned but

**Figure 3.2** Smaller documentary units mean everyone does multiple jobs and deserves multiple credits. This crew is in Phnom Penh, Cambodia (left to right): John Hewitt (co-producer, cinematographer in the United States, researcher, writer, editor); See Yun Mun (Khmer interpreter, program character, fixer, driver); Yvonne Ginsberg (executive producer, producer, researcher, interviewer, writer); and Paul Justin Rubicek (cinematographer/sound recordist in Cambodia).

restarted later with another cinematographer or editor. What happens if four different people contribute to a script, but that version gets thrown out and the editor scratches a rough cut as he edits? Who gets a writer's credit?

Credits are important. They recognize real and substantial work that later can lead to other jobs. These should be written into a contract before the project gets started.

## 5. Rights

When the documentary is finished, who owns it? Who is in charge of the copyright? Who will be the caretaker and handle distribution? How will the revenues be banked, accounted for, and distributed?

The rights to the program are a difficult maze. If there is no preproduction agreement about work for hire, then each crewmember probably has a legal ownership claim to the documentary and the field material. By the same token, there may be postdistribution legal troubles with material used in the doc. When the authorship and ownership are vague, the legal responsibility for the use of copyrighted or orphan material can be treacherous. These questions can only be settled if spelled out in a preproduction agreement.

## CONTRACTS

Making documentaries creates long-term relationships and you need written agreements. Collaborators should be willing to sign a contract.

We suggest contracts to deal with all the considerations: direction, money, working conditions (if necessary), final say on edits, rights, and credits. The best bet is to have an attorney draw these up. If you cannot afford an attorney, there are several books that carry simple contracts specifically for the entertainment industry. One I have used is *Contracts for the Film and Television Industry* by Mark Litwak.

If a formal contract seems too intimidating, then a comprehensive agreement might be the next best thing. It gives everyone a chance to think about these sticky issues before they become troublesome and it can provide a legal recognition that you have discussed these elements before the production began. The parts of this working agreement might be as follows:

1) Parties involved. Who is agreeing to this contract?
2) Project covered. Specify what documentary project you are talking about. Give it a working title.
3) Time consideration. How much time does this agreement cover?
4) How long will this agreement be in effect: through the production, postproduction, or time of distribution?
5) What will be the role of each person signing this agreement? What credit will the signer be given for his or her work?
6) Financial arrangements. Who will pay for expenses incurred in the production?

7) Salaries? Who might be paid what? How and when will this money appear? Will invoices be necessary?
8) Financial rewards. How will any money, after expenses, be distributed or shared? This includes all sales through distribution. How will the accounting be done? Will there be any payoff on the back end?
9) Is it a work for hire? Who owns the copyright? Who owns the rights to material shot in the field? Can the individual craft practitioners retain any right to show the material as part of their reel?
10) Who can terminate the agreement?
11) Who will arbitrate disagreements?
12) This agreement will constitute the total agreement of the parties.

---

### AGREEMENT FOR EDITING OF A VIDEO PROGRAM

A. PARTIES TO THIS AGREEMENT. This is an agreement between _____, herein known as Editor, and _____, herein known as the Producer.

B. OBLIGATIONS OF THE PARTIES TO THIS AGREEMENT

1. The Editor agrees to log, organize, rough out, and complete the editing of a 60-minute video documentary on the general topic of environmental concerns about the ducks in Crystal Lake. The working title at this time is "The Ducks."
2. The Producer agrees to provide assistance including construction of the initial scripting, final script review, directing the segments, approval of the rough-cut of the program, and approval of the final program.
3. The Producer agrees to arrange for postproduction sound design if needed.
4. The Producer agrees to arrange for all music and graphic licensing rights.
5. The Producer agrees to handle all sales, promotion, and postproduction duplication and distribution of the program outside of this agreement.
6. The Producer retains final editorial control over the program.

C. PRODUCT

1. DELIVERABLES. The Editor agrees to log and organize the completed video, to deliver a rough cut of the program for approval, to make changes deemed necessary by the Producer, and to provide a final production version of the program with a scratch audio track in the appropriate medium for delivery.

2.  DEADLINES. The Editor agrees to provide this final production version of the program to the producer within 150 days of the delivery of the initial hard drive material. Any extension of this deadline must be by mutual consent.

D. COMPENSATION. The Producer will compensate the Editor $5,000 for his work in the following manner:

1.  $1,000 payable on completion of the logging and organization of the material.
2.  $2,000 payable on completion of the first rough assembly of a 60-minute program.
3.  $2,000 on delivery of the final program on the medium appropriate for duplication.
4.  If the Editor must travel to gain approval of the final edit, the Producer will reimburse for transportation.

E. ADDITIONAL COMPENSATION. The Producer agrees that the Editor will be paid an additional $5,000 only if the following occurs:

1.  The program is sold for distribution and revenues ensue.
2.  The Producer recovers his initial costs from these revenues.

F.  CREDITS. The Editor will receive credit as the editor of the documentary and as a co-writer of the script. If the work is given to another editor after the rough cut, the editor will still receive credit as a co-editor.

G. OWNERSHIP. The Producer will be the owner and copyright holder of the program. Upon payment of the compensation, all production material and editing timelines will become the property of the Producer.

H. DEMONSTRATION OF THE PROGRAM. The Producer will be the sole distributor of the program but agrees that the Editor may show or display the program to others as an element of his professional work.

I. NO UNWRITTEN AGREEMENTS. There are no unwritten or unspoken agreements outside of this agreement.

_____
Name                                    Date

_____
Name                                    Date

## SUMMARY

As they progress through the production process, documentary projects often pick up collaborators. Some are welcome and some are uninvited. Producers must anticipate how these persons will be treated in relation to ownership, credits, back-end payments, and crew morale. A good solution is to sign a contract.

### Shaping Your Skills

1. Assume you are a small documentary unit of producer, cinematographer, and editor. The film is two-fifths shot. Now a colleague must be brought aboard to shoot the remainder of the documentary. You want this to be a work for hire and you want the previous cinematographer to be the director of photography. Construct a contract that includes sections clarifying ownership, rights, credits, and back-end deals on distribution.

### Further Reading

Litwak, Mark, *Contracts for the Film and Television Industry* (2nd ed.), Los Angeles: Silman-James Press, 2003.

# CHAPTER 4

# Paying for It: Fundraising

Crowdfunding pitches like this one have helped many producers pay the bills.

> So, I think that it will eventually return enough to cover what
> we spent on it (*Passion and Power*—her latest film) . . . you
> know we had to take home equity loans on our homes.
>
> PRODUCER EMIKO OMORI

Filmmakers setting out to make documentaries are more likely to be enthusiastic, committed artists than experienced fundraisers, but taking time to secure financial help up front will relieve pressure on the long-term project. It also beats going into debt while waiting for a payback from the elusive distribution deal.

This chapter explores preproject funding strategies involving friends and family donors, affinity groups, crowdsourcing through Internet sites, outside investors seeking profits, and grant proposals.

## GLOSSARY

**Above the line**  Salaries for crew or staff in creative or management positions. Usually a single salary figure covers the project.

**Affinity groups**  Local and national organizations that share concerns in step with your documentary topic.

**Budget**  A spending plan for the documentary, often a combination of hope, fiction, and unavoidable reality.

**Crowdsourced funding**  Well-organized pleas for funds through social media or Internet sites such as Kickstarter and Indiegogo.

**Deliverables**  The format and technical standards of copies needed by the distributor, broadcaster, or buyer of your doc.

**Employee**  A crewmember that works at your behest, showing up on the schedule you set and performing jobs you direct.

**Fringe costs**  Government charges, taxes, health plans, and retirement fund payments made to crewmembers classified as employees.

**Hard costs**  Out-of-pocket spending that cannot be avoided to complete the documentary.

**In-kind**  A budget item reflecting money or services donated to the documentary.

**Request for proposal (RFP)**  The guidelines and requirements for grant submissions; usually found on a foundation website.

**Trailer**  Highly stylized short promotional or fundraising video.

**Work-in-progress**  A term for an unfinished documentary or portion of it shown at a private or public screenings.

## PREPARING FOR FUNDRAISING

A yacht is often defined "as a hole in the ocean into which you throw money." The same might be said for documentaries. They launch with great enthusiasm and then founder in rough waters as needed spending and travel expenses balloon to dangerous limits. The financial stability of independent documentary filmmakers is always precarious, often forcing promising projects into a long-term hiatus while the producer gets a job or conjures up new ways to secure funding.

## THE DOCUMENTARY'S SCOPE DEFINES YOUR FUNDRAISING GOALS

Often, a short documentary will use borrowed or school equipment, volunteer crews, and a home laptop for editing. Often there are short-term distribution goals, such as a single premiere showing and some DVD burns. The hard money expenses will include transportation, food, and media for acquisition, all of which can be kept within $500. With careful video work, you can maintain excellent technical quality on a minimal budget. Fundraising can be ignored and expenses paid as you go.

But grander distribution goals and a broader topic drive up the costs exponentially. If the object is to release on broadcast, in theaters, or on multicity museum tours, or to be distributed to educational or DVD audiences, then the baselines for project length and quality go up. There will be better cameras, more travel, higher crew costs, much more expensive postproduction, and costly licensing fees. Hard money expenses can skyrocket into the hundreds of thousands of dollars.

## YOU MIGHT NEED SEVERAL APPROACHES TO RAISE ENOUGH MONEY

There are no easy ways to get funds for a documentary. For most films, outside money to augment your own personal or family funds comes from various sources, including gifts, grants, Internet pleas with crowdsourcing patrons, and anyone else willing to invest in the project.

Filmmakers can choose different options. There are those who don't bother seeking any money. They pay as they go, hoping that credit card companies will be understanding and that the hard money costs won't bankrupt them. This direction gives them absolute control of the process and removes the distractions of fundraising.

There are independents that undertake films and set up companies but still don't make a concerted effort to raise funding. They hope for small grants or Internet backing to augment the personal money lined up for the film.

Finally, there are those with extensive budgets who actively seek family funds, Internet crowdsourcing, large grants, distribution presales, and investors. This multipronged approach is the only way they can raise the huge sums needed for a feature-length production.

A good example is the documentary *Detropia,* a Sundance winner that was theatrically released in 2012 and on public television in 2013. It started with a Ford Foundation Grant, presold television rights to ITVS, got a Sundance grant, attracted investors through Impact Partners, and crowdsourced $70,000 through Kickstarter. That adds up in the hundreds of thousands of dollars, but that's what it takes for a major feature-length effort.

## GETTING READY TO RECEIVE SUPPORT MONEY

A producer hoping to bring in funds or investors needs to go a step further and set up a legal structure to receive this money. It could be a business in the form of a sole proprietorship, general partnership, for-profit corporation, or limited liability company (LLC). These entities will account for all taxable income that must be reported. Because documentary projects spend hard money up front and can be in production over a multiyear period, producers with multiyear production should investigate the tax advantages of carrying over accumulated costs from one year to the next to balance against the revenues that might come in later years.

Another way is the nonprofit route. The documentary project can become a recognized nonprofit corporation. This legal structure has many administrative and financial reporting requirements. It does allow contributors to take advantage of tax laws when donors give money to the project.

Producers who want to avoid this red tape often find a nonprofit pass-through fiscal sponsor organization to satisfy funders who prefer those tax advantages. Look for established nonprofits with concerns sharing your project goals or go to arts organizations, such as the San Francisco Film Society, the Independent Documentary Association in Los Angeles, or Women Make Movies in New York. Searching for this designation should begin early in the doc's development, because it can take months to get the nonprofit's approval.

There is a downside. Your fiscal sponsor will ask for a percentage (5 to 10 percent) off the top for their accounting and administrative costs. It's worth it.

## MAKING THE ABSOLUTELY VITAL FUNDRAISING TRAILER

In the initial stages of the documentary, producers should concentrate on putting together several trailers. One might be for a crowdsourcing site such as Kickstarter or Indiegogo and is usually wrapped around a direct on-camera pitch by the producer, salted throughout with exciting scenes from the first production shoots or from archives. The other would be for e-mail marketing campaigns and general audiences and would be available on Vimeo or YouTube. The running times range between two and three minutes.

This trailer must draw in your prospective contributors. You should concentrate on powerful sequences and one or two key characters to lend credibility. Trailers often use a heavily edited audio track with a rhythmic music bed that supplies an upbeat tempo, but that is a personal choice. The narrative flow is often nonlinear and is punctuated by intertitles that provide information or emphasis. These trailers should begin with the film's title and end with information about how to reach you by phone, e-mail, or website or social media.

If you are in doubt, go to Kickstarter or Indiegogo and watch the trailers for ideas. You'll get the sense of what is necessary.

Are there any dangers in a trailer? Yes. Because it's a highly truncated snippet of the documentary, it often gives viewers a skewed idea of what will be the final rhythm and style of production. Also, if you have an aggressive advocacy theme and post to a website such as YouTube, future interviewees for the doc might be turned off or reluctant to appear if they see it. Be cautious when distributing the trailer on a shotgun basis to the general public.

## SOURCES OF MONEY

### Family and Local Community

Obviously, you can be the prime source of funds. Documentary filmmakers have worked at outside jobs, freelanced production skills, looted their savings accounts,

**Figure 4.1** Trailers, like this one for the documentary *Bitter Seeds*, are a critical part of the initial outreach and fundraising strategy.

or maxed out their credit cards. This path guarantees full control over the production but promises grave anxiety when the costs add up.

Filmmakers should make an e-mail or postal list of family or close friends. Some fundraising specialists recommend that producers use a business-like manner or online marketing site to approach personal contacts, even local merchants, doctors, associates, or even former film school classmates.

Compose a letter, e-mail, or Facebook statement that outlines the plans for the documentary and suggests amounts recipients might give to support this effort. This is one way to get some working capital.

An e-mail or text would start out informally: "Many of you know that I have been making documentaries for some time but don't know that I am now beginning a new project." Make your new production's pitch here and then appeal to their social awareness.

"To continue this effort, I am asking everyone to think about becoming a funder for this project." Explain how grassroots support allows you to spread the message: "You can do this for (a) $200, (b) $100, or (c) $50." Give them options for payment, especially if the project has secured a nonprofit pass-through, so the check they write is a donation to a legal nonprofit organization.

Follow the suggested payments with details about the expected production schedule and interesting elements of the project. Don't leave out the closer: "Thank you for your continued support."

If someone does send a check, be certain to follow up with e-mailed progress reports, website updates, and invitations to screenings in their area.

### Kickstarter, Indiegogo, and the Internet Crowdsourcing Phenomenon

The most popular fundraising gambit is crowdsourcing, putting up a campaign on a site like Kickstarter or Indiegogo. It has been a godsend for many.

In essence, this means publicizing your project through social media, working blogs, and then setting up a Kickstarter or Indiegogo pitch account to bring in monetary pledges. Both novice filmmakers and Oscar-winning production companies use this approach.

To use Kickstarter or other fundraising sites, you must establish a common-sense goal and then devise a strategy offering people differing rewards for preset pledge amounts. With Kickstarter, you don't get the money unless you reach your pledge goal, but that is not the case with Indiegogo. Wise producers set modest amounts, anywhere from $10,000 to $30,000. The Internet site will take a percentage for their sponsorship. For Indiegogo it is 4 percent if you reach your goal and 9 percent if you don't.

Independent producer Barbara Grandvoinet tried for grants but struck out. She then used the online marketing site Constant Contact for some initial funds, before turning to Indiegogo to raise an additional $2,500 for her documentary on Thai street children, *Children of the Trains*. This supplemented a modest amount she had raised from personal friends who gave money as donors.

One crucial decision in using crowdsourcing pledge campaigns is what you offer your supporters for their contribution. The producers of *Bronycon: The Documentary*, which followed fans of a popular television show to a convention, used Kickstarter to secure more than $300,000 in pledges, more than five times their original $60,000 request. They offered pledge categories starting from $30 that would get you a credit in the thank yous, through levels above that offering swag and original works of art, up to $5,000, for which they promised to interview you and put your sound bite in the documentary, and finally up to $10,000, which offered to place you in the credits as a producer. Although the doc's real producer, Michael Brockoff, seemed to have struck gold, the money totals were not outside the costs of a normal documentary.

Producer Ben Henretig, after saying in his Internet campaign that his doc *The Happiest Place: A Journey Across Bhutan* had been financed on credit cards, offered 15 levels of pledging, starting at $1 (for that you received happiness and updates on the film's progress) and going up to $10,000 (for co-executive producer credits on the film and happiness from the whole crew). At the level of $2,500 or more, producer Henretig would film whatever you wanted for a day and then hand over the footage to you—although you have to pay travel and production costs.

Key elements for Kickstarter success are your pitch line (log line) and your trailer. They have to be engaging and memorable. Some even suggest that they be emotional. But in the end, they need to be well produced. It is understandable that prospective donors might judge your ability to make a quality documentary by the quality of your trailer.

Notoriety alone will not necessarily get you gold through Kickstarter or Indiegogo. Oscar-winning documentary director Louis Psihoyos won more than 100 awards for his feature-length theatrically released doc *The Cove* about activists trying to stop dolphin hunting in Japan. To raise funds for the next doc, *The Heist,* about the disappearance of marine species, he appealed on Kickstarter for funds, setting a modest goal of $50,000 and starting the donation levels at $10. The total was reached some three days before the end of pledge time and more than 1,000 people contributed, but it took some time.

## Affinity Groups or Concerned Individuals Through Social Media

This is a fertile area for fundraising. Researching the blogosphere for contacts with similar concerns can provide names of individuals, companies, and organizations that are potential contributors to your film. They can be sources for cash or they can mobilize screenings, lead you to a list of other donors, secure permissions for location shoots or interview access, and work on licensing artworks, archival, or other expensive-to-obtain access.

Producer CJ Hunt took this route when raising money for his self-reflexive feature-length doc on healthy eating, *In Search of the Perfect Human Diet.*

> At first, I did it the traditional way, with a proposal and fiscal sponsor, looking for local grants or concerned organizations. But in two years, there was very little response. So then I went online, before crowdsourcing, and after I got a PayPal account, I wrote to everybody in the Paleo diet world, and to all the bloggers. If they gave over a hundred dollars, they would get a DVD plus some extra content. If they gave under a hundred, they would be thanked in the credits of the film. Over the next two years, I ended up with over 300 personal contributions, plus money from some companies.

The film, shot internationally over a period of four years, cost between $400,000 and $500,000. He said, "If I finished it in L.A., it would have cost more." The film opened in premieres in major U.S. cities in 2012.

## Donors as Gift Givers

Fundraising specialists advise producers to brainstorm a list of contacts who might have substantial amounts available ($5,000 to $10,000), then approach them in a business-like manner to ask for support. Their gift, given though your nonprofit fiscal sponsor, has tax advantages for them and could be designated specifically to provide money for a single phase of the film, such as preproduction.

Fundraisers also propose a strategy involving a matching grant. The donor is more likely to pledge if you are securing a like sum from another donor. This gives the first donor a sense that he or she is not alone on this project and assures them that you are on a businesslike search for more funds.

### Screenings of the Work-in-Progress

Producers can set up fundraising gatherings in homes or community centers to show the trailer or the work-in-progress and ask for contributions. For these events, it is wise to select a comfortable room, provide a minimum of refreshments, and cobble together a solid program that is short and to the point. To ensure an audience, contact local clubs and affinity groups that have similar interests to the film's topic. If the film is about the environment, then any number of environmental groups might be able to talk up the screening or advertise it in their newsletters or on social media.

At the screenings, you must ask for money. Must. Once the trailer or some rough cut segments have been shown, the producer has to stand up, answer questions, and suggest donation categories. In my own experience, a well-planned night might raise up to $1,000; however, I attended one where they asked for $100 donations, had their nonprofit-pass-through representatives present, took credit cards, and raised more than $10,000 in a single night. They had ensured a receptive audience by aggressively contacting local organizations.

If the topic has socially conscious overtones, then make an appeal to a local community service club such as the Lions or Rotary. A colleague showed his documentary on social activists in a less developed country to a regional service club and they raised more than $3,000 to address the topic covered in the doc. Although the filmmaker didn't get the money directly, it helped his influence with the subjects in the film.

### Concerned Investors

Often, filmmakers can interest investors in contributing significant sums ($5,000 to $50,000) to back expensive documentaries. For this the producer needs ready access to the pool of concerned people with available income, a business plan, and a distribution commitment or a presale that is not pie-in-the-sky. Investors should not be guaranteed a return and should be aware that documentary production is expensive and risky. Still, when the budget creeps up over $500,000, this is one of the only ways to go.

There are investors who have formed groups with the goal of investing in documentaries. Impact Partners currently is assisting in the funding of at least 20 documentaries and works with them through production, postproduction, festivals, and distribution. Their funding has helped theatrically released documentaries such as *The Cove, An Inconvenient Truth, The Island President,* and *Detropia.* Applicants must have a treatment, budget, and trailer, and must fill out application forms.

## CO-PRODUCTIONS AND PRESALES: INTERNATIONAL MARKETS

Co-productions, especially with someone who has the solid financial resources, can be a path to producing your idea; however, you do take on a collaborator and must be amenable to that.

**Figure 4.2** Large production companies spend lavishly at international film markets like MIPTV in Cannes. They are approachable for presales opportunities.

To get funding through international presales, producers need to find a rep or agent familiar with pitch sessions and film markets. Experts recommend that if Europe is your target, then hiring a rep, agent, or distributor is the only way to go. They say it takes three years of working the European circuit for a newly arrived producer to gain credibility and get results.

European funding works on a different model. Europe has commissioning editors from major state broadcasters with budgets who work with international channels such as ARTE to co-fund and co-produce documentaries. They usually fund before production and then encumber distribution, similar to what the ITVS does in the United States. ITVS doesn't give grants; instead, it pays filmmakers for licensing agreements.

An independent producer from the United States would have to attend a series of pitch sessions to interest the co-funders and producers in backing the project. The major pitch meeting in Europe is FORUM, which is part of the International Documentary Festival, Amsterdam (IDFA). All major European commissioning editors attend, as well as American backers such as Sundance, PBS, and ITVS. Producers seeking substantial backing must be ready to prove that their film project is relevant to European and worldwide audiences and has a competent and professional crew on board.

Anyone serious about this approach should research European distributors by checking with other producers or checking out the *Hollywood Reporter's* annual listing of agents and reps. (Their website has this information but you'll pay for the listings.) Be aware that these agreements don't happen overnight, but result from long-term negotiations, and the presales of some rights can provide substantial working funds.

A contracted rep will also attend the international film market gatherings or the international television market at Cannes (MIPCOM in the spring), Toronto, Amsterdam, or Berlin and hawk your idea. Commissions for a rep can be 30 to 35 percent.

## GRANTS

Foundation or endowment money is not a ripe plum awaiting the filmmaker's request. Grants are a well-traveled road and are extremely difficult to obtain.

There are many different grants, from national endowments to local arts organizations. Some provide a lump sum to cover all costs; others mete out the funds in stages as the project progresses. There are development grants that fund research, production grants for shooting, postproduction funds, and distribution money. Some provide in-kind services and equipment. Few, if any, however, compensate the filmmaker for money already spent.

Read the request for proposals (RFP) thoroughly. Your grant application must be in sync with the particular topics and themes of that particular foundation or arts agency; otherwise, you are simply blowing in the wind.

Do not look to foundations as an immediate money source. Yours is not the only application out there. Occasionally, the initial decision letters from grant agencies will report that 2,460 (or some other outrageous figure) applications were received and their committees have narrowed the pool down to 10 finalists. Hopefully, you will be in that group. And even if you are selected, the funds might not come until six months or a year after the approval. Don't count on a future grant as the source for next week's shoot.

Filmmakers interviewed for this book, even those with critically acclaimed documentaries and international reputations as artists, universally cautioned against dreaming of the day the grant money flows into your checking account.

I have worked on six films where grant funds provided some or all of the backing. In almost every case, there were severe restrictions on what could be spent.

Producer Gary Weimberg, whose film *Soldiers of Conscience* (co-produced with Catherine Ryan) received a Sundance grant and support from investors, said the grant world is a tough slog. "On the whole, it is a frustrating way to go. For me, as a professional film editor, I found that if I put the same amount of effort into earning a living and donated that money to myself that I put into researching and writing grants, in the end I found that I was better off earning the money and funding myself than waiting around for grants."

### Hiring a Grant Specialist
It doesn't hurt. If you really intend to base your funding on grants, then someone who has a track record and has contacts and experience in the foundation world has an advantage over a stressed filmmaker trying to do field production at the same time. The grant specialist will plot strategies, hone proposals, and make sure that only the right foundations are approached. He or she will generally work on a salaried rate or for a percentage of the funding he or she gets.

**Available Grant Sources**

There are many Internet lists of foundations and endowments that support documentary projects. Look for agencies that have funded documentary projects in the past. In the United States, the major sources include such as well-known groups as the Ford Foundation, the MacArthur Foundation, the National Endowment for the Arts or Humanities, the Corporation for Public Broadcasting, and so on. Check out their websites for RFPs. These groups usually offer grants or distribution schemes that provide enough money to support professional-level costs of documentary filmmaking.

While probing the major national grantors, also look for local grants that are seldom advertised but that are available. Don't ignore grant agencies in major nearby regional cities.

Smaller grants are offered through municipal arts groups or a local gadfly foundation that has $5,000 grants for topics important to the region. In my hometown, a search turned up grants for specialized topics (environment), starter grants from the county arts agency that supported video projects every other year, and grants from a local private arts group. There was nothing very big, but a small grant of a few thousand dollars can be stretched to help with hard costs. It can even be used to get a matching gift from a donor.

Another source of grants might be employers or groups associated with the industry in which you work. Many companies have funds for community projects that advance their corporate image. For one documentary, I amassed enough money from small research grants to shoot for two weeks in a foreign country.

Do not make the foray into the grant world a one-time adventure. Organize and manage a campaign that includes calling grant offices and chatting with managers to find out if your project fits into their guidelines.

Deadlines come in all months and each grantor requests different material. Most will want parts of the projects proposal package that is described in the next section. Some have rather imposing applications (the National Endowment for the Humanities form is 54 pages long). Different foundations have different timetables. Some are pretty quick in making the first cut, but others won't respond for months.

There is other help available. Producers who need a continuing source for grant possibilities can usually find it with a local or national arts association or strong university media program. There are also technical websites that offer particular help for artists seeking funding. Often, local community colleges or arts organizations offer seminars on foundation fundraising.

## THE PROPOSAL

Besides talking up and pitching the idea, putting it into proposal form will help the focus. Although this document might change in substantive ways when submitted to different funding sources or private entities, having a tight proposal with a core set of elements ready and poised will speed up the process of responding to RFPs.

The standard proposal (averaging 8 to 10 pages) usually contains some or all of these elements:

- A hypothesis/summary of your idea.
- Topic research backing this up.
- A review of previous docs on this topic.
- A bullet point list of strengths.
- The conflicts and characters in your film.
- A treatment describing the visual story flow.
- A distribution plan.
- A funding strategy.
- A discussion of special and intended audiences.
- A discussion of unusual technical elements.
- Crew bios.
- A budget or budget outline.

## The Hypothesis

This is the introductory paragraph setting the tone for the proposal. It contains an overall statement about the theme of the documentary, a more specific statement of how the producer plans to visualize the story, and a short optimistic assessment of the effect this documentary might have on the audience. It could use a working title for identification.

Here's an example.

> Animal rights activists have become increasingly vocal in the last decade about the unhealthy lifestyles of caged animals in traditional zoo settings. But the McWilliams Zoo in downtown Barth Falls is trying to change that. Led by a visionary zookeeper DeShiba Walsh, the zoo has banned all small cages and has started a program that houses animals in large fields allowing them to interact. This documentary *Future Zoos* (working title) will tell this story so that the audience will discover that it is possible to have more humane zoos.

## Research

The next section details what the research has uncovered. Usually several pages long, it will background the issue, personalities, or events and try to add historical perspective to the story.

In the zoo example, construct a section on the history of zoos and current criticisms. This will lead to more background on how the new zookeeper DeShiba Walsh has developed her vision for a groundbreaking kind of urban zoo, one that is pleasant for both the visitors and the animals. Two or three pages would background this section.

## Previous Documentaries

There needs to be a thorough search for previous documentaries that have touched on the same topic. It's a good guess that if you find the topic interesting, someone else has, too. In certain docs (entertainment or controversial current events), there might have been well financed and extensively distributed documentaries. Any documentary revisiting a well-worn topic, such as homelessness or a popular cultural event like Burning Man, must make a compelling argument that this film will be different. Funders are not receptive to reinventing the wheel.

There is no magic source for this research. It's a combination of search engines, websites, trips to a specialized media library, phone calls, archival snooping in audiovisual libraries, and guessing to find out what's been done and when it was done.

A sample paragraph might go like this:

> My proposal to do *Future Zoos* follows in a long tradition of documentaries on issues in animal care. In 2007, PBS ran a two-part, four-hour series on animal care world-wide, *Our Fellow Creatures*. Niche entertainment cable channels such as Animal Planet produce programs on wildlife regularly. However, *Future Zoos* has a unique focus. No documentary yet has followed the paradigm set by this innovative com-munity zoo.

## Bullet Points: Touting Big Names and Exclusive Ideas

Every documentary project worth doing has its strong features. For the bullet points, highlight the most remarkable elements that will make it unique. This might be a special access you have because you have an inside connection to a principal subject or it could be recently discovered archival film that reveals candid portraits of the central personality.

At this point, you can set out what you expect to happen when the zookeeper shows the newest plans and so on. These can be displayed as bullet points in the paragraph.

> ==>We have approval from the International Fund for Animals to interview Brian McAffey, the world expert on changing zoo conditions.
>
> ==>We have assurances from the International Zoo Commission to film their annual tour of the McWilliams Zoo.

## Conflict and Challenge

Long-form documentary storytelling has roots in the theatrical drama, where conflict and challenge are the lifeblood and where protagonists and antagonists square off with uncertain ends. Unless this proposal identifies the conflict within this documentary, the producer will have a difficult time convincing backers and funders that this project will be worthwhile.

If you say, "I am doing a documentary on a local zoo and how it brings to-gether the local community" you'd better also include a concise background on the tensions that currently exist and why the disparate parts of a fractionalized community are making this effort to gather and speak.

## Characters

Documentaries are stories about people. Who will be depicted in the documentary and why they are important is the core of this section. Explain why these characters are endearing or good motivational models for the audience. If it is an issue documentary, suggest that the film's experts are leaders in the particular field and are admired around the world. Highlighting three or four characters is enough.

A sample might look like this:

> This documentary will explore the motivations and actions of three very important players in the reinvigoration of the McWilliams Zoo. Zookeeper DeShiba Walsh is a 41-year-old Kenyan who studied animal care at the world famous Mombasa Large Animal Institute. Her exciting energy and her new theories on urban zoos were the reason that the zoo's governing board hired her two years ago. Since then her revolutionary policies at the zoo have led to recognition by groups such as PETA.

## Treatment

Writing a treatment is difficult but is an attempt to describe the visual story the audience will experience. It is written to transport the reader to locations and sights in the documentary.

Creating it forces the filmmaker to think visually and to explain the documentary's plan in terms of possible sequences. Funders always want a short treatment. There is a one-page sample of a longer treatment at the end of this chapter.

## The Distribution Plan

Before writing the distribution section, the producer needs to identify authentic possibilities for theatrical, festival, broadcast or cable distribution, local screenings, or education. The plans crafted for this proposal must be pragmatic. "I'm hoping this will go on the BBC" is unrealistic.

Any contacts with or promises provided by programmers or distributors should be discussed. Ask these people to write a letter of interest or send an e-mail. These communications from anyone with decision-making power at national channels or distributors should be paraphrased in this section and a copy should be appended to the back of the proposal.

Remember, the evaluation committees reading these proposals usually know when the outlined distribution plans are last-minute thoughts or pure fantasy.

## A Funding Plan

Often, the funder will ask for a paragraph or two detailing where the producer hopes to get whatever funds are needed to complete the budget. For federal grants, the RFP might ask the amount already spent, what is now on hand in the bank, how much is currently pledged from confirmed sources, how much has or will come from other grants, how much might come from presales on distribution, and how much will be given in-kind, which is the price of goods or services donated by interested parties or by the filmmaker.

The RFP might also seek these amounts in relation to its own proportion of expenses. This means that the filmmaker might have to show committed funds equal to the amount sought from the funder. Quite often the filmmaker's deferral of his or her own salary is enough to offset this.

## Intended and Special Audiences

For many funders, especially those with a social mission, this is a crucial section. The producer must demonstrate a well-considered effort to reach those who will have a unique interest in the topic. Some agencies, like ITVS and PBS, hope the proposal will identify underserved audiences. The argument satisfying their curiosity must be in this section.

To explain your outreach to audiences, the proposal needs to address both general and special groups. "We are doing this for a nationwide general PBS audience" is vague but makes the case that you believe the program has wide appeal. In the case of special audiences for a doc on zoo reform, the producer might cite and enumerate animal welfare associations and their members, pet owners throughout the United States, and persons who care significantly for the health of caged animals. These groups might not be underserved, but are populous and would show a wide appeal based on topic.

## Style and Format

Will this documentary be shot in a particular manner that will stylize the elements? Is the director a proponent of handheld verite films? Is there a plan for a host or narrator? Will a celebrity director apply his or her distinctive storytelling talents to the idea? Will experimental technology like 3D intensify the images from the production? If there is a gimmick, now is the time to pitch it.

For example, a well-regarded documentary on the use of hip-hop culture in inner-city education adopted a fast-paced, slightly frenetic style that matched the rhythms of its music. Award-winning cinematographer Emiko Mori said she deliberately used slow pans and long zooms in her *Rabbit in the Moon* to stimulate concentration on the topic. The languid films of Ken Burns also move slowly in a clearly identifiable style, possibly to reflect the careful pace historians wish to maintain.

In *War Photographer,* producer Christian Frei used miniature video cameras to follow the eye movement of combat photojournalist James Nachtwey. Although these moments were only a small portion of the story, the technique was so unique that it was memorable.

The format section is more technical. Will the production shoot in a particular HD format with wide-screen image and 5.1 Surround Sound recording? Will there be a need for larger crews for extensive dolly work, special lighting, or other additional equipment? Will special low-light cameras be employed for unique situations?

**Crew Bios**

This is a critical selling point for the proposal and should be carefully written. One or two paragraphs should extol the skills and experience of three or four crewmembers, including past experience, credits, notable awards, and other recognition. If special filming must be done (underwater, in tropical areas, in war zones) previous successes should be highlighted. Include the filmography of each as an attachment.

This is the fantasy part of this section. Often, producers without crews under contract get permission from well-respected cinematographers and editors to use their names in the grant proposal, even if a realistic budget would never allow hiring them. They often sign a letter of interest or send an e-mail describing their interest in the project. The producer should attach these to the back of the proposal. Be certain these individuals have agreed.

# BUDGET

The budget is the project's spending estimate for all activities through the end of distribution. These financial projections are critical for the proposal. Most funders want to see a budget or budget outline.

At the beginning of the campaign for the documentary, the producer should frame up a simple budget on a spreadsheet program. It should include elements we'll discuss later. During production and post, there should be continual revisions to reflect the realities encountered on the project.

Budgets are a bit of a joke among producers—you don't have one budget, you have seven budgets. And that's true. The version of the budget submitted usually corresponds to the size or objective of the funding agency or support group. If it is a local foundation that gives awards of several thousand dollars, then the proposal should contain a low-ball budget version with no salaries and little else but the hard money costs. If it is a major national funding agency, like a public television service, or a national support foundation like the NEA in the United States, then there must be a realistic budget with professional, market-rate salaries, administrative expenses, and normal business travel and equipment rental costs.

What's realistic? A major feature-length documentary with market-rate salaries, shot in HD, and heavily postproduced can cost between $500,000 and $1,000,000. A producer under contract to *Frontline* for an hour in a PBS format has a budget around $350,000. Complex independent docs without salaries run between $50,000 and $100,000 in hard costs. Of course, you can throw a 10-year-old video camera in a rucksack and set out into a forgotten part of the world, then edit on a home-based editing system, and you might get away with spending only about $10,000 before it is deliverable. Archival and music rights licenses could add another $50,000 to $100,000 to the budget.

Before beginning any kind of budget work, get a good grasp of the extent of the project and the technical deliverables needed for distribution. Once this point is reached, break the projections into each major step: preproduction, production, postproduction, and distribution.

### Preproduction Portion of the Budget
The producer will need to estimate costs for communication (phones, web hookups, faxes, shipping, etc.), crew sizes (researchers, archival researchers, website assistance), and any production you might do to make a trailer for fundraising.

### Production Portion of the Budget
Total up the size and expense of your crew, the costs of media, equipment rentals, the length of the production schedule down to the day, travel, lodging, per diem for meals, local transportation, and insurance.

### Postproduction Portion of the Budget
Estimate the length of time editing will take, add an extra six months, and then total the cost allowed for personnel, equipment rental, specialized transfers, dubbing and transcribing, arrangements for reviews and screenings, quality control checks, color correction and audio sweetening, closed captioning, and transfer to deliverables. For editing, half-hour docs usually take two to three months, hour docs take four to five months, and feature-length docs might be done in seven to nine months.

### Exhibition and Distribution Portions of the Budget
Estimate the costs for publicity, festival entry fees, posters, screener DVDs, graphics for boxes and box covers, shipping, postage, and Errors and Omissions insurance. Rights for distribution are a big part of this. A producer's rep for festivals or international film markets is also a worthwhile line item.

Additionally, there are payments to anyone who is working on spec or expecting compensation for donated time and equipment, amounts that could be critical in major fundraising agencies.

### Sample Budget
There are many different formats. For complex, feature-length documentaries, the budget might cover two or five pages. For an independent producer still in preproduction, this example budget includes contains enough travel and music rights.

As you view the budget, notice certain salaries are paid in total, because the person might be considered a subcontractor. Others are employees and need to have payroll deductions and other state and federal payments. For this, there's a fringe percentage set aside.

In the production section, a shooting day is considered one unit. Therefore, the cost of day rates for salaried workers and equipment rental are lumped into one sum, which is then multiplied by the number of days shooting.

On each line item, you express the unit cost, then multiply it by $x$ for the number of crew involved and the number of days. If this is uncertain, estimate the total and use the word "allow." The budgets that follow should be formatted onto a spreadsheet grid design.

## Budget Outline (for a Short Documentary) in U.S. Dollars

I. Salaries (all deferred)

II. Development & Preproduction

| | | |
|---|---|---:|
| A. | Travel for location scouting | $1,600 |
| B. | Telephone, DSL, communications | $500 |
| C. | Postage/supplies | $100 |
| | | --------------------- |
| | **Subtotal Preproduction:** | $2,200 |

III. Production

| | | |
|---|---|---:|
| A. | 5 Shooting days (Equipment rentals, field media, travel costs, food) @ $100/day | $500 |
| B. | Duplication/rights of archival @ allow | $200 |
| C. | Insurance required for location shoots | $300 |
| D. | Phones/supplies allow | $300 |
| | | --------------------- |
| | **Subtotal Preproduction:** | $1,300 |

IV. Postproduction & Rights

| | | |
|---|---|---:|
| A. | Fine cut edit system rental 3 days at $1,500/wk | $600 |
| B. | Hard drives for postproduction allow | $1,200 |
| C. | Rights acquisition music allow | $300 |
| D. | Telephone/postage/shipping allow | $500 |
| E. | Audio sweetening @ remix allow | $1,000 |
| F. | Color and format correction @ $600/day | $600 |
| G. | Travel and food for screenings | $150 |
| H. | DVD screeners | $200 |
| | | --------------------- |
| | **Subtotal Post** | $4,550 |
| | | --------------------- |
| | **Total Budget** | $8,050 |

---

## Sample Budget for a Major Documentary Project in U.S. Dollars

I. Contract Personnel (above the line)

| | | |
|---|---|---:|
| A. | Producer/researcher | |
| | Preproduction 3 mos @ $4,000 | $12,000 |

|  |  |  |
|---|---|---|
|  | Production 5 mos @ $4,000 | $20,000 |
|  | Postproduction 4 mos @ $4,000 | $16,000 |
| B. | Producer/director |  |
|  | Preproduction 3 mos @ $4,000 | $12,000 |
|  | Production 4 mos @ $6,000 | $24,000 |
|  | Postproduction 3 mos @ $4,000 | $12,000 |
| C. | Postproduction Editor @ $5,000/mo × 2 | $10,000 |
| D. | Postproduction Asst. Editor @ $3,000/mo × 2 | $6,000 |
|  |  | ------------------- |
|  | **Subtotal Contract Salaries** | $104,000 |

II. Salaried Employees

|  |  |  |
|---|---|---|
| A. | Assistant Producer @ $2,500/mo × 10 | $25,000 |
| B. | Fringe @ .18 | $4,500 |
|  |  | ------------------- |
|  | **Subtotal Salaried Personnel** | $29,500 |

III. Development & Preproduction

|  |  |  |
|---|---|---|
| A. | Airfare to research locations | $1,600 |
| B. | Per diem on location | $2,400 |
| C. | Car rental on location | $500 |
| D. | Field media $30 × 20 | $600 |
| E. | Equipment rental | $600 |
| F. | Telephone, communications, office rental | $2,000 |
| G. | Postage/supplies | $100 |
|  |  | ------------------- |
|  | **Subtotal Preproduction:** | $7,340 |

IV. Production

|  |  |  |
|---|---|---|
| A. | Shooting days on location Chicago Crew & Equipment $2,500/day × 10 days | $25,000 |
| B. | Travel 6 to two locations | $3,900 |
| C. | Per diem crew on location | $7,160 |
| D. | Car rental × 3 weeks × 2 | $2,500 |
| E. | Shooting days Europe 5 days | $12,500 |
| F. | Travel Europe round trip airfare × 7 | $10,300 |
| G. | Per diem Europe | $5,625 |
| H. | Car rental Europe × 1 week × 2 | $2,400 |

| | | |
|---|---|---|
| I. | Local travel | $7,300 |
| J. | Still photography | $1,000 |
| K. | Duplication/rights of personal archival @ allow | $10,000 |
| L. | Insurance | $4,000 |
| M. | Media supplies 90 ($30 × 90) | $2,700 |
| N. | Phones/supplies allow | $2,000 |

|  |  |
|---|---|
| **Subtotal Production:** | **$94,485** |

V. Postproduction & Rights

| | | |
|---|---|---|
| A. | Dubbing, TC, transcripts @ $60/hr × 100 hrs | $6,000 |
| B. | Rough cut edit system rental $1,000/mo × 4 | $4,000 |
| C. | Fine cut edit system rental 1 mo at $1,500/wk | $6,000 |
| D. | Online suite/w operator 5 days at $2,000 | $10,000 |
| E. | Tape/computer supplies for postproduction allow | $10,000 |
| F. | Rights acquisition music allow | see note 1 $70,000 |
| G. | Rights acquisition archival film/video allow | $30,000 |
| H. | Honorariums for interviews allow | $10,000 |
| I. | Telephone/fax/postage allow | $3,000 |
| J. | Audio sweetening @ remix allow | $15,000 |
| K. | Computer graphics/art for 16 × 9 | $10,000 |
| L. | Color correction and format | $10,000 |
| M. | Travel for justification/screening 8 rt × $400 | $3,200 |
| N. | Dubbing for predistribution/screening | $5,000 |
| O. | E & O Insurance | $10,000 |

| | |
|---|---|
| **Subtotal Postproduction:** | **$202,200** |
| **Subtotal all:** | **$437,525** |
| Contingency on production 10% | $43,752 |

| | |
|---|---|
| **Total Budget** | **$481,277** |

## Budget Notes

1. Budget includes a total of $110,000 for rights to music, performance, archival film and video, and archival personal still works. This figure could vary depending on preexisting ASCAP/BMI agreements and in-kind courtesies.

## SUMMARY

Raising money to pay the hefty cost of a major documentary is a difficult task. Grants, sponsorship, underwriting, and presales are all avenues to secure funds, but they are difficult paths. Beware of beginning production without any pledged funds; this can send the documentary maker to his or her own credit cards, bank accounts, or kids' college funds.

Now that a funding search is underway, it's time to begin the next chapter—preproduction.

### Shaping Your Skills

1. Write a hypothesis statement for your idea.
2. Research previous docs on your subject and write a paragraph or two explaining why yours should continue.
3. Write the first page of a four-page treatment for your idea.
4. Write engaging crew bios for your documentary team.
5. Devise a short budget for what you project to spend on a 13-minute doc shot locally with borrowed equipment. Don't include salaries.
6. Do a search for local grants in your area. Include arts groups, cultural groups, and foundations.

### Further Reading

Koster, Robert, *The Budget Book for Film and Television* (2nd ed.), Boston: Focal Press, 2004.
Warshawski, Morrie, *Shaking the Money Tree, 2nd Edition: How to Get Grants and Donations for Film and Video,* Studio City, CA: Michael Wiese Productions, 2003.

## SAMPLE TREATMENT

This is a portion of a treatment for *Goodbye Soldiers,* a proposal for a documentary exploring the closing of military bases in a region.

**GOODBYE SAILORS**

A treatment for a documentary

A tight formation of Navy fighter jets screams low over the water. Ponderous gray, military ships appear out of the fog and glide silently under the Golden Gate Bridge and into San Francisco Bay. Sailors in dress white uniforms ring the deck, standing at attention. Chattering helicopters circle overhead. Spectators crowd the shoreline, sitting in folding chairs, hats decorated with American flags, cameras ready, picnics spread out at their feet.

In the Bay Area, this is Fleet Week, the annual October event when the Navy parades its big iron to remind San Francisco that it once was a Navy town.

"We need this. Since the military closed the bases, this is our way of attracting people to our volunteer military." *Navy Commander Jack Hanslick*

"The military used to be a common sight here. You lived near them. You talked to officers and enlisted personnel on a daily basis . . . about daily events. Now, that's all gone." *Retired Army Colonel Jack Stone*

A retired military officer takes us on a quick tour of the military bases closed in the Bay Area: The Presidio, Treasure Island, Hunters Point Naval Shipyards, Alameda Naval Air Station, Mare Island, Ft. Ord. All are former bases that employed thousands of civilian and military personnel. Now the signs say "Closed." Our on-camera guide relates the size of the former civilian workforce at these places. He notes that the Bay Area was one of the hardest hit areas, with almost 90 percent of its bases shuttered.

Shots of a stack of reports . . . and Narrator: Since the federal government began closing bases 20 years ago, it has issued a roomful of reports detailing the economic benefits and cost savings of this shuttering process. (Continues . . .)

# PART II

# Preproduction

# CHAPTER 5

# Preparing for the Long Haul

> You know, a lot of the time, filmmaking is not about equipment, and cameras, and sound; it is about trust and making connections and establishing relationships and you need to be flexible, respectful, trusting and open-minded.
>
> CINEMATOGRAPHER-DIRECTOR VICENTE FRANCO

As your documentary idea becomes robust and viable, preproduction must begin. This chapter discusses how to assemble a crew; intensify your research; and deal with travel, logistics, equipment, schedules, formats, legal matters, release forms, and rights. It is foolhardy to start shooting without spending several weeks or months of intense preproduction.

## GLOSSARY

**Carnet** An "equipment passport" for international travel that authenticates ownership of all cameras, microphones, and other equipment.

**Fixer** On international shoots, a fixer is a local resident hired to provide connections to the industry, officials, and culture.

**Minder** In international work, an official from the host government who shadows the crew for the entire shoot.

**Production book** A file or pocket folder with all hard copy documents, legal material, and e-mails from the production.

**Release** A signed legal contract that assigns video and audio rights to the producer. Used for music, performers, locations, or archival.

(Continued)

## GLOSSARY *(Continued)*

**Upconvert** A transfer process that upgrades a program to a higher quality format.
**Workflow** The set-up of postproduction that considers how the field shooting formats will interface with the editing software.

## A GREEN LIGHT AND THE REAL WORK BEGINS

Up until now, you've been in the world of ideas: "I see this as a journey film. I think my audience will be . . . . I think we finally got so and so to go on camera."

Finally, things are falling into place and you make the commitment to do a documentary. The next step is preproduction. This detailed planning continues until the first day of shooting. It involves diligent research, crew evaluation, equipment gathering, detailed location planning, and attention to a myriad of legal matters.

## DOING THE RESEARCH: DILIGENCE PAYS OFF

Research will continue throughout preproduction and production, but the initial digging should start immediately. This can test the program scope while alerting the producer to events that might need filming.

Internet surfing is a good beginning, working every combination of keywords that represents your topic. Award-winning investigative documentary producer Jon Dann says the Internet has radically changed research:

> Right now it's almost spooky how transparent our society has become. What happens when everybody knows everything? I mean, you can Google anything. Which does not mean that certain elements of our investigations are not going to involve human sources or shoe leather, gaining people's trust, talking to whistle blowers, and everything that goes with that but Google has become a lubricant in that process that is really phenomenal.

As Dann warns, Internet data mining and blogs will need to be augmented by old-fashioned exploration. Start with the following:

1) Major books and research articles on the topics.
2) Explore newspaper archives for articles around major issues in the field.
3) Look in trade journals and popular periodicals.
4) Investigate other films or documentaries about the topic.

Start a file with copies of comprehensive articles. Read the best sellers and specialized scholarly research and make a list of the most quoted and respected authorities whose names are salted throughout these publications. While they might not become on-screen personalities for the doc, the list will provide leads to contacts and locations.

### People as Sources

Once a list of prominent names is assembled, get on the phone. The telephone might be ancient technology but it is the backbone of documentary research.

Talk to as many sources as possible. Find a common ground in your interests when becoming acquainted. The old adage to "stay on the line until you know everything there is to know" still works. You are going to have to get them to trust you.

Again, producer Jon Dann:

> There is no computer-assisted way you can get another human being on the other side of the phone or face-to-face who is going to trust you enough to say "Look, I am going to take a risk either for myself or for people I believe in and hold some trust in me." That only comes with the down time and the getting to know you time during which you have to reveal some of your humanity and to let people know why you should be trusted and to be as transparent as possible. You know, in 30 years, I feel more greatly that kind of responsibility when people put that kind of faith in you. You can wind up having people's livelihoods and lives affected by what you do . . . that means taking things too far or not protecting their identity or whatever.

Record or take extensive notes of phone or in-person interviews with prominent sources. These transcripts can provide crucial ideas and feedback.

Dann also suggests that you go back to these sources again and again. You might not get enough information the first time and they might reveal more in subsequent talks.

## Sympathetic Organizations and Whistle Blowers

Often, organizations in the proposed topic area have done extensive research. These could be political groups, religious, health, nongovernmental organizations, or institutes affiliated with universities. Find those organizations.

When Jon Dann was looking into the problems of labor practices in overseas outsourced products, "through enough phone calls I finally met a guy on the ground here in the United States who was an expert on refugees who worked for a big church group who explained to me that he was in touch with networks of workers in Southeast Asia and would be willing to take me to these people who might be willing to talk to me despite the fact that this is a totalitarian society wherein people were at some risk if I would agree to protect their identities."

## Breakthroughs

Look for a Rosetta stone in the research, something that makes a quantum leap in your efforts. For one documentary, I had been searching in a slow, painstaking way to locate people who had worked on a community project 30 years earlier. The names were dribbling out one by one with old or disconnected numbers. Then one source, while discussing the topic, offhandedly remarked that she had a current phone list of nearly 80 persons involved in the project. This was nothing short of a miracle.

In another instance, producer Gary Weimberg was digging through the CNN database looking for significant archival Iraq war footage. The search was going slowly until he realized that three words were being repeated over and over, and that this phrase would lead to the footage he wanted. "You look at the keywords in the database section . . . and I discovered this keyword 'Unfit for Air.' And suddenly a goldmine of material appeared. Now, to give credit to CNN, I think they were right. This was not political censorship. And a lot of that stuff was unfit for my film as well. But my film can go to places that regular television cannot."

## THE PRODUCTION STAFF

During preproduction, underfunded documentary units suffer. Independent producers operating on a shoestring must do the same amount of work as filmmakers with money in the bank and an office staff. Travel must be booked, equipment rented, crews scheduled, research completed, access to facilities set up, and archival searches completed. If you've got the money or staff, this is the time to look for an archivist, visit a lawyer, and select a unit manager.

### The Unit Manager
A long-term documentary project can always use an organized unit manager. Without one, you'll do all this yourself and it's a difficult slog. The unit manager takes care of administrative details that can sidetrack the producer's quest for the best characters and visuals.

A unit manager should do the following:

- Maintain an organized office.
- Control the production book, which includes the paper trail of all e-mails, memos, meeting minutes, legal releases, travel documents, and account books.
- Handle scheduling for local shoots, setting the crew call, and arranging for all equipment to arrive when needed.
- Book out-of-town travel, including air connections, rental cars, hotels, and arranging for per diem.
- Hire out-of-town crewmembers.
- Maintain a communications central, e-mail or website.
- Do all of this in a pleasant, capable manner.

## PRODUCTION BOOK AND CONTACTS

There should be a production book or file that contains hard copies of all release and consent forms, contracts, agreements, insurance certificates, memoranda, or any communication with distributors, commissioning editors, or postproduction workers. It is important to keep printed copies of all e-mail messages (to avoid later misunderstandings) and copies of logs and transcripts as a permanent reference.

Every long-term documentary project benefits from having its own phone number, e-mail group, and website for the project. The website address and contact information should be printed onto a project letterhead, business cards, and other material that can be handed or sent out.

## THE DELIVERABLES

Preproduction is the time to consider the technical standards for your deliverables and the format that a future distributor might require. Revisit the questions from Chapter 1: Is it theatrical? Is it for broadcast? Is it for international distribution? Is it for local screenings and festivals? Is it for Internet and mobile screens? Each has special technical parameters that will have to be met.

These standards must be considered before a crew goes into the field. A production team that shoots the documentary in a less than acceptable format will be spending a lot of money later to upconvert or correct it.

At this moment, it's time to learn about video formats and standards. If you will need extensive color correction later, then the color space of your format is critical. If your audio tracks have to be stereo, then you should be shooting that during production.

Producers who would avoid this technical part should hire someone who is knowledgeable.

## ACCESS TO PEOPLE, LOCATIONS, AND MEMORABILIA

As research continues, it might mean the producer or assistant producers should make scouting trips to possible locations. During these research trips, be on the lookout for archival materials, such as old photos, home films or videotapes, old posters, or other materials. Contacts or family members might have a stash (or know of a friend with a box in the attic) full of previously unseen memorabilia that that would help the visual side of the doc, especially if this is as yet unseen material.

Also, these research trips can be cultural awakenings. Before shooting in the rural South, we learned on one research trip from our local ally that it was expected out-of-towners would first pay a social call on possible interviewees previously contacted by phone. After some refreshments and gossip about local history, the visitors were expected to leave without mentioning the documentary. Next, a follow-up phone call would again explain our purpose—a documentary— and our request for an interview. After that, there would be more phone calls to discuss the ground rules. Finally, after these preliminaries were settled, we were approved to show up with our equipment for actual production.

### Scouting Locations

An obvious criterion for a location is that it has the essentials: access, electricity, power, manageable noise, light, and crowd control. Be sure to scout the area at the same time of day the crew will probably be shooting.

Director David Kennard, who has worked in many countries over the past 30 years, suggests that you look for locations that are emblematic of the topic or personality. If your interviewee is a reclusive artist, then shooting for a day in his or her hideaway studio would be perfect. If you are exploring the work of a musician who grew up in a chaotic neighborhood, then you've got to go there, despite the drawbacks of noise, congestion, and scheduling. While shooting an on-camera hosted segment for their *Keeping Score* series on composer Aaron Copland, Kennard and company found a location in congested Brooklyn (where Copland grew up) that looked across the East River to the more stylish Manhattan. They arrived ready to conquer the noise and traffic, but ended up in a dispute with a wedding party who claimed to have booked the same spot. This shortened their production time and forced them to shoot everything within a single hour, which they did, despite planning a more leisurely shoot.

It doesn't hurt to scout locations with a small video camera or audio recorder to capture the ambient sounds. If indoors, try to imagine large windows admitting strong light on a sunny day. Listen for traffic or bus or train noise, elevator machinery racket, air conditioning, or other such sounds. A cafe we had scouted for a doc was perfect until the actual production day when the wind shifted and the heavy jetliners from a nearby airport climbed out directly over our location. The noise was deafening.

Often, an anxious owner will deny access to a location. The crew for *Keeping Score* was locked out of a famous palace when shooting in Russia. But later, while making an impromptu tourist visit to the palace, the custodian let slip that authorities often rented the place out for banquets. The quick-thinking crew "rented" the hall for a "banquet" and shot the on-camera hosted pieces and B-roll at their so-called banquet.

Other access problems might require legal contracts or insurance matters. Producers should always carry location releases for signature. See the section Legal Issues later in this chapter.

## SHOOTING ABROAD

International travel is much more difficult for crews who plan on shooting video. There are close to 200 countries and that means there are 200 different interpretations of the rules on how to do this. Any crew planning to travel outside their home country for interviews or sequences will need to research customs regulations, types of visas, work permits, labor laws, and possibly, as producer and director Joan Saffa suggests, hire a fixer. This is a person who takes care of local details, official regulations, location permits, rental cars, local cell phones, and so on. Sometimes, she notes, you have to spend a good deal of time and effort to find a fixer who won't flake on you.

Director David Kennard suggests that there are two types of countries: those that don't care what you say and those that care very much what you say. As the latter group looks at it, there are two types of documentaries: ones that will make them look bad (child slavery, corruption, political instability), and you won't get to do those; and the other topics where you can convince the host country that they will greatly benefit from having your crew there to examine the rural home of some famous person or whatever.

In the countries that are suspicious, you might get a minder, someone from the Ministry of Information whose job is to watch what you do. Kennard suggests you can win this person over by having him or her help in the production, doing crowd control, running errands, or whatever. Now, although you still can't trust the minder, he or she will be able to make it a pleasant experience.

Kennard also advises that you hire at least part of your crew locally. This could be a sound person, assistant cameraman, or gaffer. Locals will be familiar with culture and laws. Even in highly industrialized countries, it could be against the law in certain instances to bring out a camera on public streets; in others, you might be arrested for doing this. In still others, you might fear for your personal safety.

Director Joan Saffa advocates securing a carnet, a certified list of all equipment, with make and serial numbers that prove ownership. Having the camera equipment seized in customs or and held for weeks will put a crimp in the production schedule.

Immigration rules can be tricky. Crewmembers traveling on tourist visas will be suspect if they are bringing large amounts of professional gear into a country. Many have circumvented this by only carrying the lighter DV sized camcorders or DSLRs, many of which appear to be tourist amateur equipment.

Another help would be a sheaf of official-looking letters of reference from universities and officials. Bring many copies of these on letterhead signed by anyone with a title. In many countries, these might help when taking the first and often mandatory step to contact the local authorities and present your credentials.

## SCRIPTING IN ADVANCE

There are genres of documentary that require detailed scripts before production begins. These usually involve on-camera celebrity hosts, historical or biographical themes, or difficult science topics.

When a producer creates a script before any shooting starts, he or she must let the imagination spin freely to envision all possibilities. Quotes can be fabricated and ideal sequences conceptualized as a starting point. Then, once production begins, the script can be revised as some parts fall away and others are successful.

There are times when careful scripting causes trouble. If the director is locked into a script but discovers far more interesting angles while in production (this happens all the time), there must be leeway to make changes.

Lynn Novick, who co-produced *The War* documentary series with historian Ken Burns, told an audience that they started off with a definite framework but as they carried out research and did interviews during the seven years it took to bring the doc to PBS, they changed their direction in very significant ways. In the end, they bundled the entire 15-hour World War II program around the lives of soldiers from four American cities. Then, after postproduction but before the premiere, they listened to criticism from groups and made even more changes to their storyline.

Another example happened on my own international shoot to document the recovery of a town partially destroyed by an earthquake. During production, my crew and I discovered that the townspeople were less concerned about repairing the quake damage than with revealing the corruption of town officials who administered the recovery funds. We shifted from a recovery story to a political story.

For another documentary, we had planned a nonconventional approach to a scene involving the culture of daily commuters who take an old rambling train. The producer did extensive preinterviews with many commuters and was confident we'd get intriguing stories. We wouldn't use a thesis statement but would open inductively, letting the stories draw in the audience. When production began, however, the key shoot on the train turned into a disaster. The railroad's minder confined the video crew to one car and forced the producer to travel through the train to beg busy riders to leave their seats and come back to where the crew was "imprisoned." Most balked and at the end of the trip, we had only four interesting tales, all shot in the same location and with little visual variety. Needless to say, this setback changed the plans for the documentary.

### Finding Visual Metaphors for Abstract, Nonvisual Ideas

Because prescripting works well in the area of abstract ideas, you might have to anticipate visual metaphors to explain these nonvisual concepts. In the science documentary *What the Bleep Do We Know?* the producers made an effort to depict how quantum physics engages our lives. To do this, they hired an actress and built a complex back story about a woman coming to a new consciousness. Some critics took them to task for this, calling it a mishmash; others said it was weirdly entertaining.

In a PBS Nova production on science of string theory, the documentary opened with a long segment of Argentine tango dancers, whose dance steps became the visual metaphor for the theories in physics. As fascinating as it was to watch, tango is a distance from the science.

### Needed Prep on Prescripted Hosted Documentaries

Plans to use an on-camera host in the documentary will require that the producer scout quiet locations where the crew can work for hours without distractions. The director should rehearse the host for the longer segments. Less experienced on-camera hosts can cause traumatically long production days.

If the host is an expert and good on camera, then begin any scripting process by interviewing him or her before writing the first treatment. For the host who is comfortable on camera but unfamiliar with the details of the topic, you'll need to fully script those portions and give the host his or her lines in advance.

When directing the hosted segments:

- Always arrange for a portable teleprompter unit for the main camera.
- Do as many takes as possible within the allotted time.
- Don't make the host do something on camera that makes him or her look awkward. Some brilliant souls cannot walk and talk at the same time. Others have no problem.
- Assess the host's successes and failures by watching dailies.

## LEGAL ISSUES

### Consent and Release Forms

Securing the rights to use either interviews, locations, performances, or archival means that contracts called releases must be signed and dated. (Some suggestions for one can be found at the end of this chapter.) Paying an attorney to draw up a model is a very good idea. This prevents interviewees from changing their mind, threatening you, and demanding that they be removed from the program. This happens more often than you want to believe.

At every shoot, someone must be in charge of bringing a sheaf of releases. That same person should be responsible for getting the right signatures and dates. The signed originals should be kept in a safe place. The copies should go into the production book.

### On-Camera Releases

Sometimes when you are working in the field, getting releases seems like an intrusion on the rapport you have with the characters. Suddenly you thrust this very legal-sounding paper at them and ask them to sign over to you the right to use what you recorded.

Take the time to do it. Companies that write the Errors and Omissions insurance want to see these signed releases for the principals in the doc. Getting signed permissions after the editing has been done is enormously complicated and often impossible.

I've also made it a habit of getting verbal releases from interviewees as the first step during the session. When the recording has started I ask interviewees to say and spell their name and to give the title they'd like used in the documentary (if that applies). Then I say, "And although you have signed a release, I want you to reconfirm that you understand this interview is for a documentary that may appear on television and that you agree to participate in it." So far, I've never been turned down.

### The Release

There are important elements of a release for appearance in the documentary, location, or use of memorabilia or music. Here's our disclaimer, though: This is not legal advice. If you want legal advice, see an attorney. We are only calling attention to something that needs your attention. You need to get a signed release for the use of locations, interview subjects, music performance, memorabilia, photos, artwork, and commercial trademarks. So, for a release, this is a rough model.

1) Put a title at the top that boldly says what it is: "RELEASE FOR APPEARANCE IN A DOCUMENTARY" or "RELEASE FOR USE OF A LOCATION IN A DOCUMENTARY."

2) A paragraph should state "I hereby irrevocably agree and consent that you (put your name and or production company) may use all or part of your videotaped interview of me for your documentary program about (subject of doc)."

3) This next paragraph is more specific: "I give you the right to use my picture, silhouette, image, voice, and other reproductions of my likeness (or location, or whatever) in any motion picture, television program, or Internet program in which this documentary may be a part of or in any publicity materials promoting it."

4) A paragraph saying there are no conditions: "I do this for no fee and give you title and interest and all results and proceeds from such use."

5) A paragraph that says you have control over the material: "I agree that you may edit my interview as you see fit and are under no obligation to use all or any of it."

6) This paragraph expresses duration: "These rights are perpetual, worldwide and include the use of this interview in any medium now in existence or which may yet be invented."

7) Finally, include an affirmation of the release: "I have read and understand the meaning of this release."

Follow this with lines for the printed name, the signature, date, and possibly phone number.

## Location Legal Questions

Producers thinking it would add a little spice to an interview by shooting it at a local Starbucks or shopping center might be in for a surprise. In the United States, documentary crews on public property can shoot anything visible without extraordinary means. But when the crew sets foot in a commercial store or on private property, they must get permission. Technically, a crew can enter areas open to the public during business hours to shoot, but must stop if asked. The company personnel or security guards cannot seize your cameras or footage but can escort you off the property.

What the crew cannot do is trespass into areas closed to the public. For this access, they will need prior express consent from the local manager and possibly from corporate headquarters. If it is a large corporation, you'll have more red tape and will be less likely to get permission to shoot. Private property extends out to the public street. A shopping center can stop you from shooting in the parking lot. The crew will have to leave.

What if you are shooting in a public location and you photograph someone in the background. Do you need to get their release? Probably not. Documentaries are considered journalism; as such, unless a person is put into a false light by implication that these people are doing something illegal, it is possible to use the pictures. If, however, the very ordinary picture of a person coming out a doorway is covered by narration that says "The house at 121 Elm has been a crack house for five years," then the film is implying a crime and putting the on-screen subject in false light. That person can sue for invasion of privacy.

Can a camera person use powerful telephoto lenses or hidden microphones and cameras? Usually this leads to a violation of invasion of privacy statutes. The law varies from state to state and internationally, so it's worth checking the rules of your local state or country.

## HIRING AN ARCHIVIST

Chasing down archival material in old news reports, libraries, personal holdings, broadcast banks, or commercial file film companies is a grueling chore for someone intent on making a documentary.

Spend some money and hire an experienced freelance archivist to conduct the basic research. That person's familiarity with procedures will allow them to scour both the major and obscure sources in the time it would take you to get started. When faced with an international search, producer Gary Weimberg, who claims he enjoys research, still hired a European archive assistant to look through databases on the continent.

## GRAPHICS, ANIMATION, STILLS, AND MUSIC

Yes, modern editing software programs such as Avid, Final Cut Pro, Adobe Premiere and Photoshop have enough power to do simple text, motion, and graphics and music programs such as Garageband allow you to piece together background tracks; but this doesn't mean you necessarily have the training or background skills to qualify you as an artist or a composer. If you've got any money or connections at all, now is the time to find a person with those talents.

### Music Rights

Understand that any use of popular music will cost buckets of money. There is no way around it. Getting these rights is far more complicated and expensive than a novice producer would like to think. Check out Chapter 11 for more information.

Preproduction, however, is the time to find a composer, a band, performers to build an original score, or performers to cover public domain tracks.

## USING AN ATTORNEY

It is a good idea to have some access to legal advice for a long-term documentary. Legal services, at least introductory consultations, are often available to artists either free or at reduced rates through local arts collectives in major metropolitan cities. These consultations often are limited to one visit, but this can be helpful to clear up some questions regarding the rights to certain material that is already shot or needs to be acquired.

It's true lawyers are expensive and overly cautious in questions of use, but their advice can provide peace of mind.

## CREWS AND EQUIPMENT

Although most documentary producers or directors say they only work with crews they know, there comes a time when colleagues are not available and a crew is vital. Suddenly the producer is faced with the expensive day rate of a camera person plus the dollars for the equipment.

**Figure 5.1** Documentary crew working on CJ Hunt's *In Search of the Perfect Human Diet* preparing to shoot an on-camera segment.
Courtesy CJ Hunt

When hiring crews, we suggest you bite the bullet and pay the asking price for an experienced cinematographer or sound recordist. It's money well spent. Make sure they have been shooting or recording documentaries and not theatrical dramas. Definitely check references to see if a candidate has both skills and a personality that will withstand the tensions of production. Ask if this person has used the equipment format used by the production.

The care and feeding of crews on the road is always a touchy subject. Some professionals told us that a two-week shoot on the road is the preferred length before people began to get at each other. There also have to be provisions for serviceable hotel rooms, decent food, and roomy, secure rental cars (get vehicles with big trunks so equipment is not visible). Also, crews flying to other cities should be paid one-half day rate for travel.

Anyone hiring out-of-town crews should consult with other local professionals. Hire experienced cinematographers who have their own equipment that is compatible with the documentary's format. If there is enough lead time, a producer could request that prospective cinematographers or recordists send a link to their reel and references.

## How to Approach Equipment and Technical Needs?

Technical standards for the planned distribution cannot be ignored. Use the highest quality cameras, lenses, and microphones within the scope of the budget.

As this is written, there are multiple working HD formats (AVCHD, XDCAMHD, DVCPROHD, HDCAM), plus numerous forms of older standard definition formats. Because the distribution world will demand it, we strongly suggest shooting in some format of HD.

Try to stick with one format throughout. During the years it takes to shoot a documentary, you might see new formats arrive as the old drop away. This happened to producer CJ Hunt when he shot the first part of his *In Search of the Perfect Human Diet*. He was broke and had to use an old HDV format camera. Three years later, as he secured more funding, his new crews were shooting all the final stand-ups on DSLRs. Luckily, his editor managed to blend the two formats. Still, a single format makes the workflow easier in post.

When traveling internationally, crews should pay attention to format. Other countries use different recording formats (PAL, SECAM) that are not compatible with U.S. standards. Often, the only cameras available are in the local format and finding an NTSC camera in parts of Southeast Asia is very difficult. Do not count on borrowing local equipment or being able to buy any compatible tape or other recording material in foreign cities or countries. Bring it all in with the crew.

### Advantages of Camera Size and Quality

There are many instances where a particular camera is preferred by a crucial crew-member. Cinematographers like Emiko Mori favor the heavier cameras that rest on the shoulder and have high-quality interchangeable lenses and advanced video signal processing.

The little cameras, she says, are

> very hard to hold steady just with your hands. . . . I'm a bit crooked most of the time. Not being able to change your exposures easily . . . there's a lot of things about the controls that are inconvenient. And I have to rely heavily on autofocus because I can't see focus in those little viewfinders. (If you use smaller cameras) You just have to learn how to do things with it that you cannot do with the bigger cameras . . . for instance . . . different angles like getting under something or over something . . . and . . . learn to do the things it can do well.

Others, like producer and cinematographer Ken Kobre, advocate for lightweight cameras. "I was going to be in the field alone for many hours. I tried to find the lightest professional format camera so I didn't have to carry a huge amount of weight."

The smaller cameras have other advantages. They are easily carried in compact equipment bags and can pass for tourist gear in politically dangerous areas. Also, they are less noticeable. The powerful documentary *Baghdad Hospital: Inside the Red Zone* used a tiny camcorder with a single crewmember. This provided a nearly invisible situation in a chaotic location where apprehensive injured people did not want to be on camera. At times, the video is clearly being shot from the hip, so as not to call attention to the camera.

### The New World of DSLRs

Technical advances have now made Digital SLR (DSLR) cameras usable on documentary shoots. Most DSLRs offer interchangeable faster lenses, an advantage that

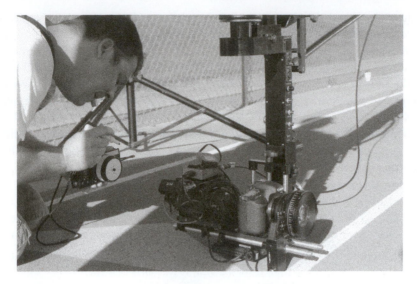

**Figure 5.2** The diminutive body of the DSLR camera is still surrounded by recorders and audio processing devices.
Courtesy CJ Hunt

expands the creative visual possibilities for the documentarian, allowing work in lower natural light and with a controllable depth of field. More specialized wide, fish-eye, or distortion-free lenses with tilt and shift correction can be adapted to control perspective.

Another recording option for DSLRs that have HDMI outputs is to record uncompressed video on portable recorders attached to the camera. This video can then be transferred straight into professional editing systems.

For sound recording, the current model DSLRs, with their miniplug connectors, are still at a disadvantage. Crews often overcome this by reverting to a double system using separate external digital audio field recorders with balanced XLRs that can be monitored by a recordist or attached to the camera. But recoding in double system requires synchronizing your video and audio in post. Software is available to do that, but it adds one more step to the workflow.

Until there are more advances, the crew might question the overall DSLR advantage. Building a rig with a shoulder mount so you can attach a separate video recorder, audio recorder, shotgun mic, and wireless receiver begins to result in a Lego-like contraption that, in the end, isn't any lighter or smaller than conventional HD camcorders. Also, if you want interchangeable lenses, you have to carry them around, something that amounts to extra weight on a field shoot.

In the next few years, we expect the world of DSLRs to improve and a more ergonomic hybrid should appear, but when this text was written, it hadn't happened yet.

### Buy, Rent, or Borrow Equipment

Whether you buy, rent, or borrow, you'll have advantages and disadvantages. You must consider how often you'll be using the equipment and what technical level is needed. If high-end HD is required, then the production is in the realm of cameras and lenses that few can afford. This would mean rentals.

A plan to shoot at a professional level but with medium-cost HD cameras would still require an investment of nearly $40,000. At the low end, it is possible to buy the camera to ensure that it is available for any production need. For low-end HD format, a prosumer video camera that will shoot 1080/60 p at a bit rate over 25 Mbps, priced between $1,000 and $5,000, should give you all the excellent video you need. Although the video on many less expensive cameras is similar, the ergonomics, special features, and quality of the lenses might be lacking. For recommendations, check out the reviews from reputable blogs and ask around.

How many weeks or months of shooting are planned? The cost of renting a low-end camera package might be $800 a week, plus insurance. If shoots are scheduled for only two weeks, then renting is the best deal. Shooting at various times over three or four months might make it more cost-efficient to buy the camera.

## Other Equipment Considerations

You are better off owning a stash of smaller peripheral equipment. Even if the camera is rented, it still is a good idea to purchase a professional tripod, good quality wireless, shotgun, and lav mics, and a transportable lighting kit. Tripods for lightweight HD cameras cost around $1,000, and a usable and durable wireless mic transmitter and receiver can run from $500 to $2,000. You can stock a very usable portable LED Litepanel light kit for around $2,000. Even though you might rent the camera, having the peripherals handy provides greater versatility.

**Figure 5.3** Renting equipment requires insurance and careful testing during the checkout.

Shopping locally always provides consultation and maintenance; however, if a local seller doesn't have it, there are plenty of specialty shops online. A vendor like B & H Photo-Video in New York will carry most professional lines, guarantee their product, and usually ship the same day. They'll also send their monstrous catalog, which is fun on a gloomy day when production is rained out (it can also be used underneath the edit monitor to raise the level of the screen).

### Insurance

For cameras, rental houses will require an extensive equipment floater policy that will cover replacement of stolen or broken equipment. Without this, a producer will have to pay a daily rate on a temporary policy or put down a substantial deposit guaranteed by a credit card. If a credit card has little headroom, the vendor might not rent the equipment. Check ahead of time to see what the requirements are.

Often when seeking permission to shoot at a private location, the property manager might ask if you carry $1 million insurance for liability at that location. You can obtain short-term insurance. Many sites are unwilling to waive that requirement, despite the obvious advancement of human knowledge that will happen if your documentary gets made. Quite often individuals might be covered through employers or universities.

### Borrowing Equipment

Very low-budget docs can be shot on borrowed equipment. As we mentioned in Chapter 3, though, borrowing brings on issues that are anxiety provoking. Halfway through production, the lender might take back his or her camera to shoot another project, stranding you with the option of buying or renting an identical camera or continuing the doc in a different format. Also, major damage to a camera or theft would put you in a delicate situation. Borrowing is a last resort.

## SUMMARY

Preproduction is a confluence of ongoing research and detailed planning for crew hiring, archival acquisition, equipment evaluation, and location scouting. If this process is done half-heartedly, problems will multiply exponentially. Be especially clear on the legal matters.

With all this accomplished, it is time to consider some production situations involving sound and lighting.

### Shaping Your Skills

1. Check your local region to find out about the availability of an initial consultation with attorneys specialized in the arts.
2. Get quotes for a $1 million equipment floater policy designed for your production.

3.  Get a price list at the local video equipment rental house. Generate an item-
    ized equipment list for your documentary's most complex shoot. Calculate
    the cost per day for this shoot, including crew food, possible salaries, and
    travel costs.

## Further Reading

Simon, Deke, & Wiese, Michael, *Film & Video Budgets* (3rd ed.), Studio City, CA: Michael
    Wiese Productions, 2006.

# CHAPTER 6

# Planning for Effective Interviews

In interviewing, there are the studied anticipations, the mapping of direction, moments of arduous encounter, planned retreat, impossible approaches, as well as sublime vistas of personality unfolding.
                    PRODUCER AND INTERVIEWER BETTINA GRAY

The formal interview has always been controversial in documentary. Shunned by some, it is still the meat and potatoes for many filmmakers. It is a vital device that can be pivotal, convey crucial information, develop characters, add authority, and act as voice-under narration for complex sequences. If badly planned, dreary on-camera interviews can bore the viewer to tears and slow down the visual rhythms of your film.

This chapter urges producers to concentrate on priority interviewees, design the interview setting to provide information, and construct questions that provoke useful answers.

## GLOSSARY

**Cutaways shots** Close-up, medium, or reverse shots at the interview location that direct the eye away from the main interview or action.

**Key interview** The prime interviewee, whose authority and voice is pivotal to your argument or your story narrative.

## INTERVIEWS

A sit-down interview is not a natural event. It's not verite. It's a setup. A formal interview's goal is to extract substantive and usable video and audio so the filmmaker can tell the story, convey authority, explain events or procedures, reveal history, or comment on another issue.

## WHY SOME INTERVIEWEES ARE IMPORTANT AND EFFECTIVE

Certain interviewees might become valuable to your project because of their central nature to your topic. The most crucial of these is the key interviewee, a character who usually ends up with the most on-screen time in the final cut. Sometimes this person is interviewed several times during the production. Other times, especially if you expect this person to be hostile toward your story, he or she is held over to the end of production.

Beyond your key interviewee, there is a top tier or A-list. These characters are authoritative because:

1) They are critical actors in the story or provide powerful rhetorical evidence necessary for the program thesis. They are the makers, builders, teachers, artists, engineers, designers, or dreamers that form the story's backbone.
2) They are persons affected by the outcome of events in the documentary.
3) They are recognized authorities, adversarial critics, or known or clever pundits on the topic.

Once you decide that certain persons should be in your documentary, begin preinterviewing by phone or meeting with them, all the while evaluating whether or not they are engaging characters, whether or not they have screen presence, and whether they are articulate. If a top-tier character turns out to be sleep inducing on camera, revise the approach or make plans to visit with this character while in action.

Sometimes, you must commit these interviews to video before deciding which first-tier interviewees shine and can carry an interesting story. I had traveled a great distance to shoot the documentary *Playing With Fire* on fireworks artisans in Peru. Originally I planned to focus on a well-known, traditional maestro, but he was very reserved and indifferent. The program would have been wooden. Then, in the process of shooting other local *pirotecnicos* (the firework makers), I came across Don Cesar and Doña Emilia, both of whom were very cooperative and had a tender charisma. They became my key interviews, which made it necessary to reengineer the focus of the remaining production.

When several top-tier prospects are dropped from the film, producers should go after backup or second-tier interviewees. They usually are:

1) Authorities who manage programs on your topic.
2) People who know someone affected by the documentary's theme (secondary sources).
3) Critics of the topic who have weak credentials.

## Helpful Tactics: A Series of Interviews

Often, when a key or top-priority interviewee is available over a long production period, a producer gets better results with repeated interviews.

Editor Maureen Gosling was the sound recordist when producer and cinematographer Les Blank shot the award-winning documentary *Burden of Dreams* on director Werner Herzog. It was clear Herzog was getting edgier as frustrations mounted during the making of his feature film *Fitzcarraldo* in the Amazonian jungle. Gosling said they both realized the story was Herzog, and although Blank was prone to steer clear of formal interviews, this was different. "He films everything but (interviews). He films what's happening . . . and so we just kept filming everything that was happening and every now and then we said 'Oh, we should interview Werner and see where his head is at right now, because there's a crisis happening,' so we would grab him and ask him questions."

Finally, Herzog could hold back no more. In a long rambling monologue, he let out how he detested his jungle location, calling it obscene and vile. It's a classic rant in documentary history.

## Group Interviews: The Possibilities of a Disaster

There is a great temptation to achieve spontaneity by interviewing two or three persons in a single shot. This is a potent idea that in practice doesn't always turn out well.

The problem is the group dynamic. By nature, people interrupt each other and longtime friends (especially spouses) might abruptly finish each other's sentences, keeping the camera person and sound recordist on his or her toes and often forcing the cinematographer to stay with a static three-shot. If one person monopolizes the answers during the three-person interview, the other two grimace or look uneasy, not knowing what to do. The crew often ends up shooting the wrong person.

We suggest avoiding group interviews as much as possible. If there is no other choice than to shoot a group interview, bunch them close together and try to use multiple cameras. Caution the interviewees not to interrupt each other. While shooting, break away from the master interview three-shot and get individual re-action shots of the group's silent members who might be listening. These can be used for cutaways.

**Figure 6.1** An ambitious four-person group interview suffers when only one person is paying attention to speaker on the right. The others are distracted.

## THE ART OF CONVERSATIONAL INQUIRY

Research is an absolute must for an interview. The producer must dig into the subject's background or use the Internet to review the person's published research, works, and past conversations. If the interviewee has written a book, read it. If that person has made many public appearances on the topic, know what has been said.

### Designing Questions

The interview is a staged event and the producer's goal is to provoke usable responses in various areas. What makes a usable answer? Traditionally, it is a full sentence, rather short, empty of jargon, and one in which the interviewee expresses an opinion, answers the "how" and "why" questions, describes a process, reveals personal feelings, or relates a personal experience.

Construct questions to elicit only one response. A question with three parts, like "How does your group respond to criticisms of your operations and does this bother you and how can you justify the money you've spent?" allows the interviewee to answer whichever part he chooses.

The questions should not be a search for data; that research should have been taken care of in the preinterview. Avoid questions like "How many buses do you have on the route?" Instead ask, "Why would you say you have enough buses to cover the route?"

The interviewer must not pose questions that evoke a yes or no answer. If that happens, follow up immediately with a second question: "Why?"

If the answers wander off the topic of the question, the interviewer should reask the question.

Avoid rambling questions. I was shooting for an interviewer whose first question was two-and-a-half minutes long (I timed it later). When he finished, the interviewee started laughing and said, "I forgot what you have asked." It took more than 10 minutes for the interview to regain a serious tone.

### The Strategy of Identical Questions

For many films, the producer has sought out multiple interviewees from the same topic area. The tendency is to ask each the same questions.

The upside of identical questions is the advantage given the editor to run the answers back to back, setting up a virtual conversation between speakers who might each not even know of the other's existence. The drawback of identical questions is that the rigidity in the questions might not allow the interviewer to guide the conversation to a promising area during the interview.

Producer CJ Hunt suggests a possible solution: Have five or eight similar questions and then let the conversation carry the interview into a free-form direction.

## SETTING UP A VISUAL STYLE FOR YOUR ON-CAMERA INTERVIEWS

For an editor in post, there are few things more maddening than a project with 20 interviews shot by three different cinematographers in four or five different framing and lighting styles. This restricts the editing because back-to-back transitions are too jarring.

Producers who foresee a number of interviews need to standardize the style and framing to achieve a coherent look. This involves placement of the eyes and face, elements of the background, lighting, screen vectors, and mobility.

**Figure 6.2** If an interviewee's eyes are placed on the axis of the vertical and horizontal one-third lines, then no matter how tight or loose the framing, there will be a comfortable look.

### Start by Choosing a Framing and Look That You Like

Often, the interview's subject or theme defines the approach stylistically. Ken Burns has a style that uses a strong key light on the interviewee and a nearly blacked out background. Errol Morris has designed equipment to allow the interviewees to peer directly at the lens. The farm workers in *Fight in the Fields* were interviewed outdoors. This variety is endless, but it is better when it is consistent.

Also, consider the relationship between the character and the interview's location. For instance, if the key interviewee is an outspoken woodlands environmental activist, then exactly where the interview is done could be crucial. The interview for this character might have folksy production values, might include reflexivity (e.g., your voice), might be done in a two-shot, might be shot outdoors at night around a campfire, or might be shot in action while hiking up a trail. Another possibility would be a combination of short interview segments in different outdoor locations.

It is often difficult to avoid cliché interview locations. A respected and somber science authority usually gets a sit-down interview in an organized office or laboratory with highly stylized lighting. A teacher might be interviewed in an empty classroom. A person struggling to adopt a child might be interviewed near a playground. A fisherman's natural milieu is on a rocking skiff on the water. A sports star could appear in an arena, on the playing field, at practice, in the locker room, or at his or her home in front of trophies. Often, there are very few other opportunities available. If you feel this is too clichéd, you might choose a simple outdoor location or, perhaps, an interview in a comfortable room at home. Whatever background is chosen, it is best to avoid a simple white wall. It has no context.

Suppose the only chance for an interview with a renowned expert is at a local airport while she is waiting for a connecting flight. The airport lounge walls are covered with the name of Feldspar Airlines. For this situation, the depth of field for focus must be narrowed to blur the background detail.

Pull the interviewee away from the back wall as far as possible, leaving at least six feet of open space behind the subject. Then force the lens opening as wide as possible (vary the shutter speed to control exposure) and use the longest telephoto

**Figure 6.3** The plain background (left) offers no clue the interviewee is a university professor. Repositioning him (right) depicts him in front of his books, memorabilia, and even a musical instrument.

lens setting while keeping the desired framing. Check the camera's built-in menus for a portrait mode that allows the cinematographer to lock in a wide-open shutter. Using these methods, it is usually possible to defocus the background while keeping the interviewee sharp. If the lighting is too bright, however, this could be very difficult.

### Set the Camera's Eyeline

The camera is generally positioned at or slightly above the eye level with the interviewee. If the interviewee is seated, the camera tripod must be lowered.

There is an inherent visual grammar in our framing choices. If the camera is set high and looks down at the interviewee, it suggests that we have the power position and can view the subject as less than us. By using a low angle, we are looking up at someone greater than us. These conventions have been used for nearly a century in dramatic film, such as Orson Welles's *Citizen Kane*.

When shooting, the old truism is "Two eyes and two ears." If the interviewee turns away even 20 degrees, the viewer sees only half of her face and loses the recognition of her expressions.

Often, the profile shot occurs because the interviewer shifted away from the camera and the subject's eyes have followed. To prevent this, the interviewer must concentrate on keeping the position next to the camera to get the proper angle.

**Figure 6.4** High angle (left) standing over someone at a desk and low angle looking up (right) creates problems with positions of power.

**Figure 6.5** Subject (left) has looked away so only profile is seen. Interviewer should turn the interviewee back toward the camera (right).

**Figure 6.6** It is vital to plan for interviewees looking both left and right.

### Direct the Interviewee to Look Right or Left

Controlling the interviewee's screen direction is important. You need to organize your shots so everyone doesn't speak to the same side.

Some producers plan to reverse the shot in post (that's easy to do), but that backfires if there is any text in the shot that would betray the flip.

What about having the interviewee speak directly to a camera lens? Try it. You'll find it is uncomfortable. Some directors solve this by putting the interviewer beneath the camera lens but you still see the interviewee look away.

Famous documentarian Errol Morris devised a system where the interviewer and the interviewee both faced separate cameras and then the images of the other appeared on prompter prisms placed over the camera lens. As a result, the interviewee was actually speaking to the image of the questioner and, at the same time, directly into the camera. Incidentally, Morris's wife dubbed his device the "Interrotron" to recognize the terror generally associated with being interviewed on camera.

This is now much easier to duplicate. You only need your production camera, a rented prompter prism placed in front of it, and the video signal from an iPad or tablet. The questioner can look into the tablet and its camera can project his face onto the prompter prism. The interviewee then sees the interviewer ask the question and speaks back, looking straight into the camera lens.

## THE INTERVIEWEE'S APPEARANCE

What if you are doing the interview at a powerful politician's home and when the crew arrives, she's wearing a sweatshirt? What if you need a scientist to bolster a thesis and he is wearing a garish polo shirt? Should a financial analyst be wearing a T-shirt?

The time to solve these quandaries is before you shoot the interview. If you didn't address these concerns in phone conversations before the interview, then ask the subject to change once you arrive on location. You must act decisively on arrival or the informal clothing might affect the audience's perception.

During an interview on a serious topic I did with a gentleman in central Mexico, he demanded he wear his Chicago Cubs baseball cap. I argued but finally agreed. When we cut his interview bites against the important political issues in the documentary, his hat looked silly.

On the technical side, there are some very bad clothes for video. Bright, highly reflective shirts or blouses will cause contrast patterns. White clothes in the bright sun will do that, too. Patterned shirts or ties with rows of thin stripes may cause an effect called moiré, which tends to make the picture appear to vibrate.

### What About a Hat or Sunglasses, or a Mask, Religious Clothing, or Hair That Covers the Face?

Because the audience takes cues from the eyes or facial expressions of a speaker, seeing these features during the interview is important.

Hats cause severe contrast problems in the sunlight. They cast dark shadows across the eyes of the interviewees; however, if removed, they might cause the interviewee discomfort, accompanied by a squint into the sun.

Asking someone to remove sunglasses is difficult. Blues musicians and entertainers always wear them. Some people demand to keep them on, especially if lights are set up for the interview. Cinematographer Vicente Franco says you can't push too far. "Sometimes they cannot take their glasses off so I try to walk the light around a little bit or move it up so the incidence angle doesn't create a problem. But the important thing is the story and sometimes it is okay to just let things go for the sake of not jeopardizing the storytelling."

What about religious clothing or scarves that cover portions of the face? Let these stay and hopefully the audience can see the eyes.

Hair that falls down over the eyes is a troublesome problem. Ask your interviewee to pull it back or comb it. Even unruly hair is less distracting when combed.

How about masks or partial masks? For a documentary on Mexican wrestling, *Que Viva La Lucha,* I interviewed each of the wrestlers in his particular mask. It is part of their professional costume and they don't appear in public without it.

**Figure 6.7** Masked faces, although appropriate, interfere with the viewers' interpretation of the speaker.

## CHECK THE LOCATION FOR DISTRACTIONS

The director is in charge at the interview. He or she must assess the location to see how it will best fit in with the overall style the producer is expecting.

Check out the shot in the viewfinder. If there is a need to reduce distractions, crews might want to remove eye-catching posters, reflective glass, anything with motion, old sandwiches, calendars, strange knick-knacks, annoying clothes thrown about, and so on. Dogs and kids should be put in another room. Television sets and computer monitors should be turned off.

I recently edited a documentary where the shooter's instincts in almost every interview were right on—except one. In that case, a monitor that was in the shot behind the interviewee kept switching from black to a corporate logo that rotated around the screen. Needless to say, this had to be keyed out when pieces of that footage went into the documentary.

Often directors add elements to a rather plain interview scene. In an understated way, this works. But if a large poster is added, for example, it often looks contrived. Beware of that.

### During the Interview: Vary the Field of View

It's a good bet that two or three key interviewees will be in the film several times for more than two minutes. However, their actual interviews might go on for 45 minutes. In this case, a single, workable close-up shot might not offer enough variety. The cinematographer should vary the width of the shot several times during the interview, always doing this during a question.

Directors and cinematographers should consult before the shoot on the framing. How tight should the shot be? Does the director want the cinematographer to zoom in to an extreme close-up (ECU) during emotional moments? This framing cuts off the top of the head and the bottom of the jaw and focuses on the

**Figure 6.8** Distractions such as the video screen and hand sculpture can shift the viewer's eyes from the interviewee's face.

eyes. It works if this indeed is an emotional moment. Quite often, though, the interviewee will recover and the tight shot seems overdone.

Cinematographer Emiko Omori resists the traditional ECU for intensity. "A lot of people like super close-ups. I don't. Maybe it is a certain distance I like to keep from the person. . . . Basically, I just like to let things play themselves out. What I do try to do is listen."

Because it isn't wise to stop an interview in progress, the director or interviewer and the camera person should set up signals that alert the other to any change in the framing.

## PREPPING THE INTERVIEWEE

In an earlier chapter we explained that research should be gathered in the first preinterview done in person or by phone. That should have been a long and rambling conversation roaming across many interesting areas. But when the crew arrives on location and begins setting up the equipment, the interviewer should concentrate on establishing a rapport. This will help the interviewee become accustomed to the intrusive camera equipment, crew, and possibly lights.

Greeting the interviewee is the director's job. Cinematographer Emiko Omori says she always tells the crew to stay out of the conversation.

> This is what I require of my crew. I don't chat with the person, I let the director do that. I don't try to make a relationship with the person we are doing a doc on during that time period. Maybe afterwards, maybe at dinner. When we first come in, I always leave it with the director to be the one who establishes the relationship with the person.

During the warmup, the interviewer should avoid the principal interview questions. Many interviewees, if they express something eloquently in the warmup, will never repeat it the same way during the recorded session. If a determined interviewer asks the subject to repeat what he or she said previously, it could cause the interviewee to tighten up or become tense. Therefore, use the warmup to relax the subject and save the crucial questions for the on-camera interview.

Remember that most people are not used to talking to a camera and will be nervous. An accomplished musician who regularly appears on stage before thousands of people told me that being interviewed for a documentary was one of the most stressful situations in life. This makes the warmup a good time to go over several items.

Mention the general areas to be covered. Alert the interviewee that you might reask a question several times because it is important. If the subject is media savvy, the director or interviewer could ask the subject to try and include the questions in the answer. So, if the question is "Why did you fire the two employees?" he or she would not give a single-word answer (e.g., "Incompetence"), but rather say something like "I fired the two because of incompetence." Some subjects will get it and others won't. Don't push the concept if they have trouble with it.

## DURING THE INTERVIEW

### The Turning Head Syndrome

Interviewees often look to the skies or turn their heads during an interview. Sometimes, they actually move out of frame. What can you do about this?

First, don't use swivel chairs or rocking chairs. Next, make certain that the subject's body is facing the camera and that his or her knees are turned toward the interviewer. If the interviewer allows the interviewee to turn any part of his or her body away from the centerline during the warmup, 50 percent of the time he or she will turn it again when the camera is running. In the editing room, this will be a nightmare.

### Listen Carefully, Reask Questions If Needed, and Don't Step on the Answer

Listen during the interview. If the interviewer is attentive, the interviewee might reveal something more interesting and meaningful than the answer to the original question. Be prepared to abandon the two-page question list if the interviewee becomes energized. Being open to discovery will allow the subjects to tell their story, express their point of view, and offer an important critique or golden anecdotal illustration.

If the interviewee is wandering off topic or only half-answering the critical questions, then gently bring him or her back on topic. It's the interviewer's job to return with answers in planned areas.

Finally, don't interrupt by speaking over your interviewee. Novice interviewers often comment "Oh yeah," "I agree," or Good point" before the interviewee is finished with a sentence. This "steps on the answer" and often ruins the best moment of a quote. Be patient and keep your mouth closed, no matter how exciting the answers might be.

## POST INTERVIEW

After the interview on camera is finished, allow the interviewer to continue the conversation with the subject while the others break down the gear and return the scene to normalcy. All interviewees should be thanked for their participation by note or e-mail.

## SUMMARY

Designed and managed correctly, interviews can be extremely valuable resources in a documentary. Selecting the most striking key interviews, constructing productive questions, and controlling the nuts and bolts of the interview frame and location will give the best outcomes toward an engaging program.

Now that the interview plans are set, it is time to consider the sound, light and production needs.

## Shaping Your Skills

1. Find a person to interview and limit the session to five minutes. Before you start, write a list of four objectives for your session. You would want answers to "Why this happened?" and so on. Record the interview on video and transcribe it. Determine if you steered the conversation, if you listened to the answers, and if you have any usable answers.
2. Form a crew and stage five setups for the same interviewee. Each time, evaluate the location background for distracting items and lights.

## Further Reading

Cunningham, Megan, *The Art of the Documentary,* San Francisco: New Riders Press, 2005.

# PART III

# Production

# CHAPTER 7

# Sound Considerations

Courtesy Maureen Gosling

> We are looking at one piece of film that many people in the
> world have seen ... Baghdad being bombed at night. ... I'm
> making a documentary film so I'm really focusing on this
> footage ... and I hear car alarms going off. Well, if you are a
> sound editor, this is a delicious moment of understanding the
> sound of the real world.
>
> PRODUCER GARY WEIMBERG

Too many video and film novices concentrate on the visual and slight the audio. This thinking is dangerous. Audio from the field is half the story. In sequence-driven films, sound's subtleties can be used for energy, pacing, or carrying story narrative. For issues documentaries, well-chosen resonant audio clips edited together form the rhetorical story framework.

Every effort must be made to get clean sound on each location shoot. The crew needs high-quality microphones and thoughtful techniques.

This chapter discusses field audio when using the sound recordist or when a cinematographer is working alone.

## GLOSSARY

**Ambient audio**  Background natural audio in any location shoot.

**Cardioid**  Mic with a heart-shaped or close-in pickup pattern good for interviews in noisy areas.

**Fishpole** or **boompole**  The handheld portable boom that telescopes to six or eight feet for recording on location.

**Foley**  The process of manufacturing sound effects to add to the mix in your documentary.

**Lavaliere**  Also called a lav; the small, omnidirectional or cardioid mic that clips to the lapel in an interview. It is usually cabled but will work with a wireless receiver.

**M & E tracks**  Audio tracks on edit masters that have ambient sound and music but not spoken dialogue or narration.

**Phantom power**  Power for mics that is carried through the mic cable from recorders, cameras, or outboard battery packs.

**Shotguns**  Unidirectional mics with a narrow, cone-shaped pickup pattern that can be aimed at sound sources.

**Signal to noise**  A ratio that expresses how much noise or hiss is on the tape; higher numbers mean cleaner audio.

**VU meter**  A volume unit meter. Its readouts describe the strength of the audio signal and warn about overmodulation and distortion.

**Wireless mics**  Microphones that transmit the audio by local radio signal from the subject's transmitter to a receiver on or near the camera.

## THE VALUE OF GOOD AUDIO

Sound, even routine background sound, is a critical element that carries important nuances of a documentary story. The quavering emotion in the human voice, the violent sounds of the battlefield, or the simple undercurrent of day-to-day events can add many shades of meaning to visuals. Poorly recorded, mushy field audio can force editors to modify or eliminate crucial interviews or sequences when the material gets to postproduction.

If there is money available, a documentary project should have a sound designer who shepherds the audio throughout production and post. The designer will designate how the sound will be recorded on the field camera, will specify how the field recordings will be transferred to the editing programs' numerous audio channels, and will guide the audio sweetening and final mixes. The designer can also construct the audio for the deliverables to theatrical, television or cable channels, or festivals.

## THE SOUND RECORDIST

For field shoots, a professional sound recordist is a must to ensure that clarity, recording levels, mic selection, and mic placement are perfect. The experienced audio person also knows the dance that must be done with the camera person, following the cinematographer's lens while staying out of the shot and still getting the maximum angles for boom recording. The recordist should provide high-quality microphones and should carry a belt-pack mixer that allows careful monitoring of the incoming signal. Recordists will also establish a means of transmitting the sound to the camera for recording.

Recordists can be very inventive on their own. Often, recordists will venture out, gathering environmental sounds that can be added in the edit room to enhance the experience.

For industrials or feature narrative films, there is usually time to survey a location in advance. For documentaries, however, the crew often arrives at the site for the first time on the day of the shoot. Anyone working field audio must be ready for every possible roadblock in gathering clear, usable audio.

Environmental noise is the first concern. The deep frequencies of traffic, equipment motors, playground chatter, loud conversations, amplified music, intermittent aircraft flights, work crews, and wind are in the same range as human voice and are destructive to any recording. Directional microphones and custom windscreens can minimize these problems; however, these cannot be removed in postproduction. If the unwanted audio distractions continue, the recordist must suggest waiting or moving the location to a quieter place.

During the shoot, the recordist is vital in placing wireless mics on critical characters or in aiming the shotgun microphones on booms at an angle that minimizes environmental interference.

When special situations arise, such as recording music, the recordist's knowledge of mixes and individual instruments can make or break the audio quality.

**Figure 7.1** Sound recordist David Silverberg uses his experience in positioning the boom mic for this music session. Editor Maureen Gosling explains, "He has the mic kind of high because the accordion is loud … and he has the mic away from the accordion because he wants to hear the guitar better and the sticks better. In a circle around the mic. That's how he likes to record musicians … acoustically around the microphone."
Courtesy Maureen Gosling

Maureen Gosling, an editor who is also a field sound recordist, explains that the cinematographer and the recordist must be in sync.

> You get familiar with what the frame looks like. This is a musician we know she (the cinematographer) wants to get close-ups on his face … upper body shot. Once in a while … she points the camera down at his feet and the sound guy can point the mic down by the feet, always keeping an eye out where the camera is going … and trying to get it up before she moves up. And he had a radio mic on the musician. David likes to do both … to have the option. If there was traffic, probably his mic on his body is going to be better. But sometimes I like the boom mic better rather than a lav.

## SEEKING CLARITY IN LOCATION SOUND

Natural sound segments are long, meaningful sequences of raw field visuals with clean, understandable field audio. This could be crucial action, an emotional conversation or argument, or even one long running shot during which the protagonist character explains a critical point. They are as good as gold. With the sync visuals, these provide enough recognizable information to substitute for narration and carry the story forward for several minutes without breaking for interviews or narration. Separated from visuals, they can often be pieced together to provide sound under, an audio bed for other footage.

Shorter natural sound shots are also useful as establishers for the beginning of a sequence, as transitional elements to shift topic subtexts or to introduce new segments within the longer story. Long stretches of natural sound segments can placed throughout narrated documentaries to let them breathe, giving the audience a chance to reflect about what they just experienced.

Rich natural sound is the direct result of smart field production. To make these segments most effective, crews must cooperate to capture not only the visuals, but also the clear and easily understood audio without distortion, competing ambient sound, or confusing speech.

### Additional Audio: Environmental Sounds

Anyone recording sounds on location, whether it's a recordist or a multitasking cinematographer, must also look for wild sound. This requires concentration to isolate the particular sounds that are indicative of a location, job, or environment. Recordist Maureen Gosling says this often goes beyond gathering sync sound with the video.

> Well, I made sure that the sound recordist gets some extra sound. In this case, she was recording on tape, instead of video that everybody does now … and so there were certain times when she would get up before everybody else and she would go out and record the sounds of birds in the morning. Or you know, record some water trickling by. I mean there are certain sounds that are individual to the town of Juchitan (in Central Mexico) where we made our film and I wanted to make sure that got in there.

Because these wild sound segments might not be synced with recognizable video, the sound person should put an audio slate at the head of each recording, saying something like "Wild sound of creek by main square, July 3rd at 5 pm."

### Music From the Field

The use of music to add pacing and moods to documentary is as old as the medium. Documentary crews are always trying to find new and unusual songs.

It is very important when recording music in the field for the recordist and cinematographer to work together. They must confer so the camera operator lets the camera run during the entire song without stopping or pausing.

Don't forget to have the musicians sign releases for their performance. Producers should also ask about the publishers of the song. This is covered extensively in Chapter 11.

### Safety Sound—Room Tone

Recordists should capture one minute of natural sound (often called room sound, room tone, or safety sound) from any location where sequences are shot and interviews are done, including indoor and outdoor locations. This will provide ambient sound if there is a recording failure or might cover situations when camera talk is removed and the ambient noise is damaged. It is also absolutely necessary for the audio post editors when they are making an M & E track for distribution.

To do this, the recordist must alert the crew to stop talking before putting the camera in record. Sometimes this is done while setting up camera technical operations such as color balancing.

## THE ONE-PERSON CREW: DOING CAMERA AND SOUND

As a one-person crew, producer and shooter Ken Kobre was on location in five countries with photojournalists covering a range of stories, including wild demonstrations and crowded international sporting events. Did he miss having a sound recordist? "Every moment I was out there," he said. "I found it particularly challenging when you are trying to do interviews in the field … just thinking of questions while your eyes are watching the monitor to see if the audio levels were good."

Kobre says our digital world ensures it will be common for a no- or low-budget documentary to send a single cinematographer into the field without a sound recordist. This is a burdensome duty for the camera person, who is concentrating on the need to capture usable sequence shots and provide good material for the editor while placing and testing microphones, monitoring the audio levels, and listening through good-quality headphones for audio clarity. When the action heats up, and the so-called one-man band is running, the sound levels might be be overlooked or ignored. In these cases, certain mics, like a camera-mounted shotgun and a good wireless set, are vital to ensure usable material.

**Figure 7.2** Producer and shooter Ken Kobre operating as a one-person crew while shooting on location in the Middle East.
Courtesy Ken Kobre

The one-person crew must use a wireless on the main subject, but it is also good to record audio at the same time on a quality short shotgun mic. This usually means the shotgun is mounted on the camera and it becomes a drawback because the solo camera person most often turns the camera to focus on another scene, an action that turns the microphone at the same time and often away from the sound the camera person wants.

Another disadvantage to the one-person crew arises when there is a high level of background sound. An audio recordist, working independently of the camera, can angle a microphone so it avoids a noise source behind the interviewee, but a solo camera operator has the fixed shotgun atop the camera and seldom can make adjustments. In those cases, the editor might be able to isolate the audio onto the best channel in the editing room, double that, and eliminate the offending audio track.

## MONITORING LEVELS

Camera persons can see the incoming audio on readouts in the viewfinder or flip out screen, where newer LED bar graphs take the place of the older analog VU meters. In the following illustration, both channels are recording good audio signals with plenty of headroom before they hit the right-hand distortion alert, which is usually red. In digital audio, the signal must never distort in production, because it cannot be removed in post.

Of course, the camera person should also listen to the sound through headphones to ascertain the quality.

If the cinematographer is busy and cannot carefully monitor the readouts, he or she should set the incoming channels at two separate levels to ensure one will be usable.

**Figure 7.3** LED readouts pulsing to 12 give indications of usable audio signals on both channels while still allowing headroom for sudden louder sounds.

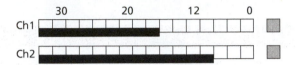

**Figure 7.4** Cinematographer sets incoming audio to different levels to prevent distortion on both channels.

In budget camcorders, options for setting levels are severely limited. Many have automatic gain circuits, and prevent setting the levels manually. Industrial or professional-level equipment usually provides thumbwheels or dials to control sound levels.

## WHAT TO RECORD ON MULTIPLE CHANNELS

Modern cameras can record from one to four channels of audio. They also record mono or stereo signals from unbalanced or balanced cables.

A consumer camera or DSLR with a stereo miniplug input has an unbalanced audio line. These are prone to added line noise and interference caused by fragile connectors or unshielded cables. They cannot use the professional mics without an adaptor. Often, a "Y" adaptor allows the camera person to plug two mics into this miniplug input, using the right and left side of the stereo channels as separate tracks. Additionally, aftermarket sound mixers add a small unit under the camera or DSLR to allow manual control over sound going into the miniplug stereo channels.

There is every reason to select a camera with balanced inputs that take a three-wire cable (with a ground signal) and use an XLR or three-pronged connector. Professional audio equipment and mics have these, although newer digital connectors are emerging.

### Two Channels or More

Most prosumer or professional cameras record two channels of audio, allowing room for planning by the photographer.

With two separate inputs built into the camera, ambient sound with an on-camera mic can be routed to one channel and the other input saved for a shotgun, wireless, or lav. Cinematographers can use both inputs for outboard mics, one picking up ambient sound with a camera-mounted shotgun and the other a wireless or a lav. For an interview, both the subject and interviewer might get individual lavs and be recorded separately, or the recordist can use a lav and a shotgun to record the interview, giving the editor choices in postproduction.

Always exercise extreme caution in routing the sources within the camera channels. It is possible to route the CH1 input into both channels mistakenly, blocking the CH2 input.

High-grade broadcast cameras often provide opportunities to record up to four channels of discrete audio. In general daily use, this is a luxury. Using great care with mics, it is possible but cumbersome to record four separate audio signals. If this is the case, the postproduction editor will appreciate the options it provides.

## TYPES OF MICROPHONES

To record top-quality sound, it's important to understand the microphones. As in video, there is a corollary: The more expensive mics from respected manufacturers such as Beyer, Countryman, Sennheiser, Tram, Sony, Audio Technica, Schoepps, or Lectrosonic generally do a better job. Price is not the only consideration, though. Each microphone has certain range characteristics for the bass and treble sounds. Experiment with different mics by replaying the recordings through a quality system.

Mics can be either dynamic or condenser. The dynamic mics are essentially receivers and don't boost the incoming audio. They are great for picking up nearby sound and are usually indestructible. Condenser mics, which use a battery in the base or connect to phantom power through the cable, boost the audio signal to a set level. That's good and bad news, because the condenser could also raise the general ambient room noise, hiss and all.

The pickup pattern is also a consideration. Omnidirectional mics often record annoying chatter known as camera talk. A better mic for an interview is a cardioid mic, so named for its heart-shaped pickup pattern that is designed to draw sound from the immediate position in front. Lavs can be either omnidirectional or cardioid.

Directional control results from plugging in a mic. This could be anything from a handheld omnidirectional dynamic "stick" mic, to a boom-mounted, handheld, or camera-mounted shotgun, a wireless, or a lav. Each mic has special characteristics in terms of how it responds (see the next section) and how it should be handled. Even with those options, a camera person must know how to route the sound once it gets to the camera.

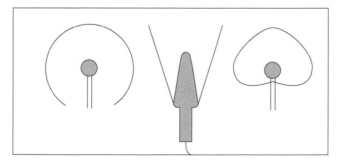

**Figure 7.5** Omnidirectional (left), unidirectional (center), and cardioid (right) pickup patterns.

### The On-Camera Built-In Mic

On-camera built-in mics are usually omnidirectional and pick up any audio from any direction. The better ones are okay for ambient sound, but they are almost worthless for interviewing people. Use these mics as a last resort.

### Shotgun Mics

The unidirectional mic, known as a shotgun, has a narrow, cone-shaped pickup pattern that extends out in the direction in which it is pointed. They come in short and long versions.

The sound recordist usually carries the shotgun unidirectional mic in a shock mount on a pistol grip or portable extension called a fishpole or boompole. Shotguns can be mounted atop larger cameras or on the shoe attachments of smaller cameras, but if shotguns are handheld without a shock mount, friction on the mic's barrel creates unwanted sounds.

A word of caution: Unidirectional mics do not, despite what you've seen in the movies, have a supernatural ability for recording conversations hundreds of feet away. They might also dramatically amplify sounds behind the speaker's location, such as in Figure 7.7, where the sound from the soda machine directly behind the woman interviewee will interfere.

### The "Lav" or Lavaliere Mic

For interviews, crews attach a tiny lavaliere or lav mic. Most lavs are condensers and need either phantom power or batteries. More expensive lavs are cardioids; the less expensive models usually are omnidirectional. The lav can be clipped to the shirt, and as long as clothing does not obstruct it, it will pick up clear audio without much ambient noise. Good lav mics can pick up excellent audio through clothing as well.

**Figure 7.6** In tight quarters, the handheld short shotgun in a pistol grip shock mount is extremely effective.

**Figure 7.7** The shotgun mic on the boom with a gray zeppelin windscreen will pick up the interviewee and the noisy vending machines behind her.

When attaching a lav, place the microphone outside the clothes and directly below the mouth. Hide the cable by tucking it under or inside shirts or jackets. If the subject is wearing a turtleneck collar or T-shirt, run the cable over their shoulder and clip the mic near the front. Do not let the cable dangle.

When using a lav, be careful with placement. Make sure that it doesn't rub against skin, beards, or jewelry. In illustration Figure 7.9, a necklace brushing against the lav could destroy valuable audio.

### Wireless Microphones

The wireless is the documentary maker's dream. These systems eliminate cables and provide clear audio at a distance. The wireless or radio mic uses a lav cabled to

**Figure 7.8** A dangling lav cable is distracting.

**Figure 7.9** The tiny lav mic might strike the wearer's necklace if she moves.

a small transmitter or a bulb attached to the end of a stick mic or shotgun. These send the audio by radio signal to a receiver mounted on the camcorder.

The transmitter clips onto a subject's belt or is placed in his or her pocket and, in most cases, the audio is generally clean. Although wireless systems have improved in recent years, they still have limitations due to distance or outside signal interference. In any type of active field video recording, a wireless mic is a necessity.

## Using Many Different Mics Will Drive Your Editor Nuts

Field audio of the same event and interviewee might arrive at the editing room recorded by three different mics in three separate locations. One interview might

**Figure 7.10** A wireless mic transmitter is usually attached to the belt or placed in a pocket. The receiver (right) sits atop this particular camera but attaches to the back of others. Bulb transmitter (not shown) can be used attached to a shotgun mic.

have been recorded in a car, another in a hollow-sounding room, and a third beside a noisy freeway. When the editor tries to finesse these together as voice under, it is a brutally difficult task. Try to record the same interviewees with the same ambience.

## DAMAGED SOUND AND POSTPRODUCTION FOLEY WORK

Producers who view dailies of field footage should also evaluate the audio quality. Video with damaged or degraded sound should be turned over to audio engineers immediately for testing on laboratory sound programs.

When the field production sync sound is damaged, documentarians must reshoot or look for other ways to fill the gaps for critical pieces. This could mean orchestrating new interviews to replace the damaged answers, the capture of wild location sound to stand in for the damaged material, the use of foley or manufactured sound to fill in unrecorded elements, or the construction of voiced segments to substitute for missing sentiments.

In the past, certain organizations had written policies forbidding the use of non-location sound. Old CBS News policy forbade using any sound other than that which was recorded at the location. However, that policy is debatable. For many producers, the question goes once again to the overall truthfulness of the representation.

Producer Ellen Bruno, whose documentaries chronicle the rugged life of villagers in politically troubled countries, often finds it too dangerous to pull out the camera and record someone's story. But she knows it is imperative that the audience hears that story.

> What often happens ... a lot of the material I get is not recorded so I have to figure a way to get that material in there. And what I have done in the past is that I've synthesized a lot of stories I have heard and a lot of material from interviews that I haven't used and created a voice, really, that is a constructed voice and then based on this material and I've had people speak that voice, creating a character, so to speak, a universal character within the film in a way. I tried that a few times ... I'm not doing that anymore.

## LEGAL CONSIDERATIONS WHEN RECORDING SOUND

Because the technology has improved, it is now easier to secretly record someone's audio. This brings up several legal roadblocks.

Crews may not use extraordinary means to record someone's private conversations. That means high-performance shotgun mics that pick up at a great distance might be construed in court as an invasion of privacy.

Second, telephone conversations cannot be recorded without alerting the other party. In many states, that is against the law and could even be a felony. Surreptitious recording with hidden microphones is an "extraordinary event" and could land the producer in court. Don't do that unless everyone is ready to fight the legal battles that will ensue.

Your subjects have an expectation of privacy. However, any time that the subjects know the camera is recording, they must assume that it will pick up anything they are saying. If you tell people you have stopped recording, you have given them back that expectation of privacy; if you violate that by secretly recording, then you could be at risk.

## DON'T LEAVE HOME WITHOUT IT

This is a suggested list of items for an audio kit:

- 2 lav mics (can be used with wireless; check for clips)
- 1 unidirectional shotgun (short one)
- 1 wireless mic kit with both belt and bulb transmitters
- Microphone manuals
- Windscreen covers for all the mics
- 1 fuzzy or zeppelin for the shotgun on windy days
- 1 pistol grip with shock mount for handheld shotgun
- 1 fishpole boom for the shotgun
- Camera mounts for the wireless receiver and the shotgun
- 2 XLR to XLR 20-foot cables (best quality)
- 1 XLR to XLR 6-foot and 1 XLR to XLR 1-foot (for camera mounting)
- 1 set of high-quality headphones (full ear cover)

Note: Don't buy cheap cables. Get the best you can afford.

## SUMMARY

The importance of recording clean audio on every location shoot cannot be over-stressed. Crews must choose the right mics for each location. The natural sound segments are powerful and can be used to carry the principal story.

Documentaries are often assembled from natural sound segments alone, without narration. For all these uses, it is crucial that videographers pay attention to the sound quality.

### Shaping Your Skills

1. Attend a lecture or a panel discussion in a large hall. Attempt to get clean audio from platform speakers using different mics. Find out what you need to patch into the audio system.
2. Attempt to interview someone for two minutes using only the mic on the camera. Try five locations with different intensities of ambient noise. Decide if the audio is clean enough to use.
3. Interview a person on a noisy public street using a shotgun mic. Then use a lav in the same location. Review the audio to test the value and effectiveness of each mic.

# CHAPTER 8

# Natural and Portable Light

My way of lighting and seeing is realistic; I don't use imagina-
tions. I use research. I go to a location and see where the light
falls normally and I just try to catch it as it is or reinforce it if it
is insufficient.

CINEMATOGRAPHER NESTOR ALMENDROS

Anyone shooting documentary video must be a master of natural light—the illumination available in any location—and an artist with portable lighting carried to
locations. It's important to adapt shots if the natural lighting is working against the
camera. Cinematographers must also exercise deliberate control when adding
artificial light.

In this chapter, we show how the producer, director, and camera person
should plan for the control of light.

## GLOSSARY

**Back light**  A source of light that comes from behind the subject, usually used to separate the subject from the background.

**Boost/gain**  A camera adjustment that intensifies the video signal in low light.

**Camera light**  A small fixture and lamp mounted atop the camera body. It illuminates an area directly in front of the camera.

**Chimera**  A collapsible softbox that fits on a portable stand and diffuses the light on location.

**Diffusion material**  A metal, gel, or paper material that can be placed over a light source to soften the effect of the direct source.

**F-stop**  A number that represents the size of the lens opening. A smaller number means the lens is open wider and admitting more light.

**Falloff**  The visible lessening of light intensity on any object.

**Fill light**  A secondary light source used to take out shadows.

**Key light**  The principal light instrument for any scene.

**Light-emitting diode (LED)**  A promising light source that is cool to the touch but can mimic color balances needed for video.

**ND**  A neutral density filter, internal to the camera or screwed onto the end of the lens, to lessen high-contrast situations.

**White balance**  A correction made in the camera to adjust the video to the particular color of light that is prevalent at the moment.

**Zebra**  A video pattern in the viewfinder that indicates when incoming light spikes over acceptable standard limits for video intensity.

## LIGHT AND CAMERAS

This is the era of amazing low-light camera technology. The circuits in the newest digital video processing chips will boost the available light until it appears brighter than the unaided eye might see. But even with this technology, working cinematographers still have daily battles controlling light intensity, contrast, and color. These struggles have gone on since photography began and have generated strategies to compensate for the difficulties.

## CHOOSING NATURAL LIGHT: PROS AND CONS

There is a divide in the documentary world between the natural light practitioners and the crews who bring along portable lighting. It's roughly equivalent to the eternal quarrel among boaters—the sailboat advocates against the power boaters. In both cases, each side has a valid argument.

Natural light advocates stress the simplicity of their approach and how it contributes to a style. Producer and cinematographer Ellen Bruno works alone and in dangerous situations. "I never use artificial lighting and so that is very restrictive in terms on my personal aesthetic ... I prefer a much grainier broken down look ... what video does in low light ... I love the way it breaks apart."

A pragmatic approach comes from cinematographer Emiko Omori:

> There's only so many things you can deal with on a two-person crew. The first thing that goes is the back light, because I hardly ever use it anyhow. It's a lot of trouble to put up and I've never liked them. So for me, it's location, location, location. You find a beautiful way to shoot with available light. Now that it's me shooting, I take one chimera (a softlight) and I hardly ever get that up ... because you don't have time.

Investigative producer Jon Dann, who works under contract from networks, says when he hires a documentary crew, he partially selects them for their ability to shoot the lighting style of his commissioning program.

> They know that I know that a two-cam interview with a major correspondent needs a two-hour set up and ... that if I give them enough time, that I'm going to get a particular shot ... a look. Am I looking for the *60 Minutes* (style) that has depth but no light to dark ratios? Very realistic. Very meat and potatoes. Or, are you looking for a *Dateline* look, that might have slashes, shadows and more drama ... or an MTV look with slapzooms that appeal to someone 13 years old.

The pros and cons of artificial light equipment are worth considering. Crews that set up production lights get sharper, more consistent color and resolution. The downsides are the complications from the added equipment and the uncomfortable and intrusive nature of the large crew and lights needed for the setup.

Available light enthusiasts stress the low-tech nature of their approach and the soft glow of natural illumination. They note that their presence is not as intimidating as with a roomful of light stands and lamps; however, in achieving this look, they often sacrifice the ability to shoot in darker places and capture the delicate detail needed to justify certain locations. Finally, using available light means a more intense struggle to overcome contrast and color balance problems.

## LIGHT BASICS

### Directing Attention with Available Light

Often, available light can be used dramatically to focus the attention within the frame. Determine what is the object or portion of the picture that is of utmost importance. See if it can be isolated in the most intensive light. Ideally it should cover a good part of the frame, and when possible it should have more light than the remaining elements.

### Using Light and Shadows for Focus and Depth

Light, when carefully managed, does more than increase the image's detail. Controlling light allows cinematographers to intensify the sense of depth, add interest to a face, or focus attention by concentrating on the light's focal point.

Carefully observing the available light in strong compositions can contribute to emphasize the image's spatial depth. Diffused, even lighting can result in a flat, low-contrast image, a two-dimensional scene that lacks depth. Contrast lighting contributes to the perception of three dimensions and depth in the shot.

**Figure 8.1** The eye is directed into the center by the shape, lines, and the light in the picture. The initial focus is the first circle of children, and the next is the torsos of older people seeing the children at play.

**Figure 8.2** Using natural light to avoid a flattened look to an image.

The angle and intensity of the light illuminating the main subject of interest will bring it to the forefront. Both light and shadow in relation to the background will define the contour of the subject making it stand out, separating it from the background, and defining dimension and perspective in the image.

### The Color of Light

Think of light as a combination of colors. Without getting into a detailed discussion of color temperatures, the most noticeable tints are the bluish outdoor and the yellowish indoor incandescent varieties. Difficult documentary situations arise when locations are lit by combinations of the blue outdoor sunlight and yellow indoor lights.

Mixed light sources at a location might include sunlight coming through a window, a fluorescent light hanging on the kitchen's ceiling, and a couple of lamps with normal 60-watt light bulbs. Then, if your subject moves around, he or she will change colors by getting closer to each light source. Video shot in each of these microlocations will not match up in the edit room.

Cinematographers can solve this dilemma in several ways. One is to pour artificial lighting on the situation until it overpowers all the other lights. Another way is to continually adjust the white balance settings on the camera, setting up a consistency in the shots.

## White Balance

The human eye naturally corrects for the color of light but video circuitry must be told what to do. To adjust the color of light, most video cameras have white balance circuits. These automatically provide the camera with a base setting for white or allow a manual setting based on a reflective level of a white card. Careful white balancing will standardize the colors for video shot in different locations, ensuring some consistency for postproduction. Although cameras can make a continuous automatic white balance adjustment, it's possible to do this manually each time the light changes, when the crew moves to another location, or when someone shuts off the camera to change the battery.

To manually white balance, fill the lens with a white card and push the white balance button until a blinking square set above a v glows steadily in the eyepiece monitor. Sometimes, if the camera is seeing a bluish picture, it can warm it up by cheating the white balance with a bluish tinted card. Crews also cheat the white balance with slightly beige cards to provide better skin tones.

Remember to locate the white balance card at the focus point of the scene (that could be an interviewee's nose), rather than next to the camera. Make sure the white balance card is solid white and not too reflective.

## Controlling Exposure Levels

Our eyes are quick when adjusting to high or low light intensity; cameras are not as versatile. They need a sufficient intensity to shoot; generally the more intense the light, the better the video in color and contrast range.

Individual cameras have reputations about their capabilities. Generally, if a particular camera is known as a bad low-light camera, it means that the picture loses the contrast range, vivid colors, or sharpness where the light is dim.

The first step is to evaluate the conditions of available light. A useful tool is the zebra pattern, a viewfinder alert that indicates when the incoming light is spiking over the preset level. Before shooting, the cameraman can set the zebra as high as 100 percent of needed exposure or as low as 70 percent. Some cinematographers recommend the 100 percent level when shooting outdoors; if you see the zebra, then you close down the lens. Inside, set the zebra to 70 percent. This indicates enough intensity to light up the picture.

Lenses usually have manual adjustments to open up and close down the lens. The sizes are expressed in f-stops. The lower the number, the more light it allows in. For instance, a maximum opening of f-1.2 allows in more light than f-2. If your lens only opens to f-3.5, you might have difficulty with intensity.

When adjusting exposure, be very careful that controls are in manual. Shutter speed should be 60th/sec and the boost should be 0 dB. Often the camera circuits will automatically adjust the shutter speed or boost as you adjust the aperture.

The boost or gain is a feature that allows the camera person to intensify the video signal in low light until most detail in the shot becomes visible. Raising the gain (usually in increments of 3 dB) adds noise or grain to the video so only use the added boost when it's necessary.

Outdoors, except in the early morning or late afternoon, the sun's intensity might cause patches of dark shade and sharp falloff. Indoor locations complicate the problem. Some rooms, which appear to be lit well, have very low intensity with moderate falloff, causing a flat look and ugly shadows.

## Contrast

Heavy contrast makes life difficult for the camera person. Savvy still photographers attempt to capture the full range of contrast, getting detail in the dark or black areas. Video cameras can make this difficult, however.

Crews who prefer shooting with available light will welcome overcast days, when the outdoor light is diffused through haze, clouds, or fog. They also revere the so-called golden hours, just after sunrise and just before dusk, when contrast has dropped and the light has a reddish hue, which gives the scene the "golden" look.

**Figure 8.3** Overhead sun causes ugly shadows and forces subjects to wear hats, which further complicates your shooting. The falloff has a sharply defined line, as seen in the man in the middle.

**Figure 8.4** Bright sun causes parts of this scene to disappear into shade.

Some cinematographers believe that the hours from 10 a.m. until 2 p.m. are so difficult for shooting that they should be reserved for other pursuits. Says producer Ellen Bruno, "I find myself shooting pretty much in the morning and late afternoons and late evenings and pretty much taking a siesta midday and or then take enough time to hang out with people and get to know people. I know from trial and error that if I get some of that stuff (high-contrast noon-day video) back in the editing room I just won't use it."

### Managing the Contrast

Outside, use a neutral density (ND) filter to reduce the contrast. Some cameras have the option of a double ND filter for particularly bright days. These are valuable, but remember to remove the ND filter indoors.

Even with the ND filter on, the zebra alerts might appear and the cinematographer will need to manually cut down an intense, overbearing light source or reflection by closing down the aperture, moving the camera location, or tightening the shot.

To see detail in the shadow areas, set the sensitivity by zooming into the full shadow, then locking the aperture when the camera exposes for the shadow. In these cases, the background in the picture will "bloom" or skew to the bright side.

With a stationary object, one way to beat contrast is to use reflectors. These come as fold-up units or hard cards and are colored in white, silver, and gold. Beware of other colors. The basic rule of reflectors is that they tint the light with their own color. White reflectors will reflect a softer, pleasing white light. This kind of reflector functions nicely as a fill, because it doesn't change the key light color (from the sun). A silver reflector gives off a sharper, brighter light, and can appear streaky. Gold reflectors work well outdoors, reflecting sunlight quite effectively.

**Figure 8.5** The crew holds folding silver and white card reflectors to battle noonday contrast extremes while retaining good color balance.

The handiest little tool in a light kit can be a 4 × 3-foot piece of white foam core board (purchased at any art supply house for about $5) that will serve as a reflector. This can also double as a white balance card.

### Use a Building or a Large Sign
All is not lost if no one brought a reflector. Look around; it is possible to use the large surfaces of white or adobe-colored buildings as reflectors. Believe it or not,

**Figure 8.6** Often one subject in a conversation is in deep shade and this cannot be easily solved with reflectors.

**Figure 8.7** To balance exposure, the crew should move the location to a position where the light allows similar exposure for both.

they work quite well. Put the subject near the building and turn them to face the building. The camera goes between the subject and the building.

### Uneven Contrast Situations

Natural light can be made to work. If at all possible, try to shoot the subjects consistently in either the light or bright areas. Avoid having two subjects interacting if one is in the light and the other in the shade.

## SHOOTING INDOORS WITHOUT PORTABLE LIGHTS

After battling the strong contrast from the sunlight, shooting indoors should be a relief. But that's not usually so. Indoor lighting can be uneven, discolored, and flat. It can put grim shadows on faces, make eyes ghastly, and make skin pallid.

Most modern offices are lit by fluorescent lamps built into the ceiling. These are generally weak, oddly colored, and do not provide sufficient light. They can cause ugly shadows on the subjects' faces and a sallow look. If these must be used, then position the subject so the overhead fluorescents strike the subject's face at a 45-degree angle.

Windows in a room are a delight when you live there and an irritation when you're shooting. Windows let in the blue light and create areas of high intensity that overwhelm weak yellow indoor house lamps. Take care to position the camera somewhere between the window and the subject. Avoid flat lighting by turning the subject until there is falloff on the face.

**Figure 8.8** Shooting at a desk with windows in the background causes serious contrast problems (left). By moving the interviewee and repositioning the camera so it is between the desk and the interviewee, the available outdoor light pours through the window and provides luminous natural glow, much like a huge softlight (right).

### Avoiding Strong Background Light Sources

In many locations there will be very intense, annoying background lights that spike over the natural illumination. These come from household lamps, equipment alert lights, or reflections from much stronger light sources on mirrors, chrome, or shiny furniture.

On an indoor shoot for one interview, the setting sun caused all sorts of problems. The subject was a university researcher at her desk in her office. We had closed the blinds behind her. However, as the interview wore on, the sun dipped low in the sky and suddenly appeared on the blinds, making dancing abstract patterns. Now, every interview shot would have a different design on the backdrop. We had to stop the interview and find large sheets of cardboard to place behind the blinds.

## PORTABLE LIGHTS

Adding artificial light can raise the video levels to stimulate vivid colors, resulting in better skin tone. The most exciting development in this area is the evolution of LED light elements. These lights use low energy, can be color balanced, and are mostly lightweight flat panels with different dimensions that can easily be set on a hot shoe/tripod mount or light stands.

LEDs use minimal wattage with an output greater than their equivalent conventional lights. Besides their portability, most run on AA batteries, rechargeable lithium-ion batteries, AC, or 12V adapters plugging into an automobile-style source plug. Many of these light fixtures are 5,400K daylight-balance and come with built in dimmers and color calibration filters to control color temperatures (5600–4200K–3200K). LED fixtures are designed to mount soft diffusers or color gels for lighting expression. Very few of these lights have conventional barn doors, so you might have to resort to flags or black foil to control light falling on the subject.

**Figure 8.9** New LED lights are a boon to field production. They provide variable color temperatures and are cool to the touch.

On big-budget shoots, professional gaffers might bring a truck full of gear, but mobile documentary crews need transportable lightweight kits. These might include (a) softlights—large boxy diffusers that light without shadows, (b) focusable lights—500- to 1,000-watt lights that can be spotlighted or widened, and (c) broads—a long, thin instrument that puts out diffused light.

**Figure 8.10** Collapsible softbox (left) focusable light with barn doors (middle) and broad light (left) are the workhorses of portable lighting.

### Strong Key Lighting Adds Dimension

With portable lights, a cinematographer can add structure to the framed interview by increasing the intensity of the key light and using a backlight to separate the subject from the background.

If the key is too weak, then the shot is very flat, despite all efforts to get depth in the frame. When the key is strong, it makes the interviewee stand out. Be careful when shooting only with natural light from windows or room lights, because you might have flat lighting and lack of emphasis in the shot.

## FOR INTERVIEWS: THE CLASSIC 3-POINT LIGHTING SCHEME

It's always good to be prepared. Carry at least two working artificial light sources, preferably ones that can be aimed (spotted or flooded) and some diffusing material to soften the light. With larger crews, more lights can be added.

The most common diagram for lighting a single subject is the three-point model. A key light is the most powerful and principal source; a fill light is about 60 percent of the key's intensity and is used to knock down or create shadows, and a backlight at about 90 percent of the key's intensity is used to create a separation between the subject and the wall behind.

If you are not using new LED light fixtures that are power misers, then you need to be careful where you hook up the older portable lights because they draw a large amount of power. Be cautious when plugging in more than 1,000 watts of quartz lights into any common 15 or 20 amp electrical circuit. The lights themselves won't overpower the circuit, but other machines in other rooms might be tied to the same circuit, which could lead to blowing the breaker.

In a private home, the kitchen usually has more and separate power circuits than any other room. In more modern kitchens, the four-plug wall receptacle above the countertop often has one circuit in the upper plugs and a different one in the lower plugs.

Nonetheless, unless the crew carries a full light kit to every setup, three-point lighting is a rarity. Working efficiently with what's available, photographers who set up portable lights usually begin with one diffused light as the key and then add a diffused light as a fill. Sometimes the key light can be gelled to a blue cast and window sources used for fill.

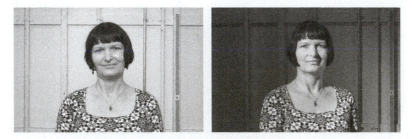

**Figure 8.11** High key lighting draws attention to the interviewee (right).

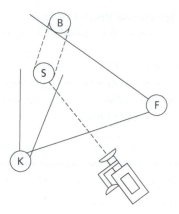

**Figure 8.12** Three-point lighting diagram. S is subject; B is backlight (90 percent of key intensity); K is key light (100 percent); F is fill light (60 percent of key light intensity).

### Bouncing Lights

Often, to simply raise the level of illumination in a room, it is possible to use one portable lamp and bounce the light off the wall or ceiling. Bounce it at the juncture of wall and ceiling, or at the corner where walls meet, and you'll get a softer light.

### Camera Light

A camera light is a fixture atop the camera and is used for a close-in fill. It will show up as a hot, specular source unless it's controlled by built-in diffusers or by adding diffusion material to the barn doors on the light fixture. Flip-down filters attached to the fixture can change the light color from indoors to outdoors.

### Safety Issue

Liability problems could occur when you bring along portable lights; they can be dangerous. Older quartz lights are white hot and often unstable on their stands. Cables snake across the floor. If you do not secure the cables with tape and brace the light stands with sandbags, someone could trip over the cable and pull the

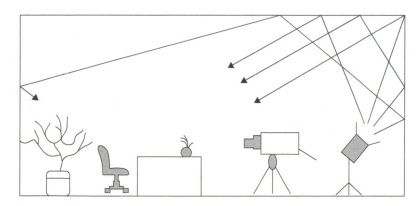

**Figure 8.13** Turning the light away from the scene might allow you to bounce light off walls and corners.

lights down. Also, if you tape cables to interior surfaces and the adhesive tears up the paint, you might have to pay for the damage. Clamps fixed to wall supports can also damage a surface.

On one shoot, a student crew attached a light support clamp to the bars of a false ceiling. In the middle of the interview, a portion of the ceiling collapsed under the weight of the lamp (we have it on video). No one was hurt, but a few dollars exchanged hands to fix the ceiling.

## DON'T LEAVE HOME WITHOUT IT

For shoots without a hired gaffer, I carry this kit.

- 1 focusable light with 500-watt lamp and stand
- 1 small focusable light with 250-watt lamp and stand
- 1 broad with 500-watt lamp and stand
- 2 50-foot AC power cables
- 2 3 × 2 AC adaptors
- 2 umbrella diffusers
- 1 chimera collapsible softbox with mounting ring
- 1 extra lamp for each fixture
- 1 rollup container with sheets of diffusion material
- 1 rollup gel kit that contains full and half blues
- 1 wad of black foil and black gaffer's tape
- 2 sheets of 4 × 3 white foam core bounce cards
- 1 pile of wooden clothespins

## SUMMARY

Light is a minefield for beginning photographers. Like audio, it must be studied and understood before it can be brought under control. Cinematographers must know about light color, intensity, and contrast. They must be aware of the special care needed for both outdoor and indoor situations.

Portable lights can help establish good video levels and skin tones for interviewees. Outdoors, crews must also plan to use ND filters, reflectors, or other strategies to defeat contrast and shaded situations.

### Shaping Your Skills

1. Interior lighting situations can be troublesome. Take a camera package and find a smaller office with a window behind the desk. Practice shooting an interview in a mix of indoor and outdoor intensity, while managing color and contrast.
2. At noontime on a sunny day, take a camera outside and work in both sunny and shady areas to shoot an interview with good skin tones and good background video. Take along a reflector and use it to defeat the contrast.

3. Enlist the aid of two friends. Have them engage in a walking conversation and attempt to follow them with the camera, moving from a sunny outdoor situation through a door into a hallway and then into a completely enclosed room. Do this on automatic and manual settings to see if you can effectively handle intensity and color problems.

## Further Reading

Ferncase, Richard, *Basic Lighting Worktext for Film and Video,* Boston: Focal Press, 1992.
Salvato, Larry, & Schaefer, Dennis, *Masters of Light: Conversations with Contemporary Cinematographers,* Berkeley: University of California Press, 1986.

# CHAPTER 9

# Field Production: Shooting the Documentary

Cinematographers often use high-end production rigs for big budget documentaries.

> And I have a mantra that I say to myself when I am shooting:
> One shot is never enough. One shot is never enough.
> PRODUCER/CINEMATOGRAPHER KEN KOBRE

Production is an organized adventure to gather all the valuable, intimate, and meaningful scenes, sequences, interviews, and characters on video before the budget runs out.

The director and cinematographer plan the translation of the documentary theme into visuals that the editor can use to tell the story. The production crew works as an ensemble under the producer and director to solve the challenges and mechanical pitfalls that bedevil any video shoot.

Production could last as short as a weekend or could go on for years (and usually does), ending only when the hundreds of hours of footage are turned over to the editors.

This chapter examines the director–cinematographer interaction and suggests how attention to aesthetics and smart shot framing will ensure a robust variety of clips for high-quality sequences for postproduction.

## CRUCIAL PERSONNEL

In any location production shoot, documentary crewmembers have definite position responsibilities. These include the following:

- A director (if not the producer) who carries out the producer's vision while on location. The director defines the visual approach to the sequences and shots. He or she must keep an active mind to consider all the possibilities to create sequences, imagining how these shots will fit together in the mind of the editor as well as blending the styles of previous and subsequent shoots. The director should have good social skills to keep the subjects relaxed while conveying a sense of trust.
- A director of photography (DP) or cinematographer who will translate the producer or director's approach, style, and conceptual vision into video or film. During prep, the DP orders all the tools for production and tests and maintains them. On a shoot, the DP or cinematographer works closely with the director to be one or two steps ahead of the situation and take advantage of the best light, framing, proper exposure, and choice of main subject and background. A DP must be skillful with natural light and an artist when portable lights are needed.
- The sound recordist is in charge of audio quality, microphones, and their placement. The recordist will decide where to route the audio on the recorder.
- The gaffer maintains and rigs the portable lights.
- The production assistant (PA) is a gofer who handles pick-ups and delivery of people, video equipment, materials, and any miscellaneous needs.

## THE DIRECTOR AND THE CINEMATOGRAPHER MUST WORK TOGETHER

By the time the crew begins shooting, the producer and director should be confident of the documentary's style, possible sequences, and effective characters. Then the producer, or the director hired by the producer, discusses these plans and needs with the cinematographer. The relationship between the director and cinematographer must be based on respect for the artistic eye of each.

Producer Lourdes Portillo says her process involves screening other films and then a give and take about the style.

> I think first I get the idea of what we are going to do and then I discuss it with both of them . . . the sound person and the cinematographer. More the cinematographer first. I say, "I want to make a film about electricity and I think it should be this and this. What do you think?" And then he says, "Well I don't know. You should look at this film." And then we have a big conversation . . . it takes a long

time and then it settles down to a style. We agree . . . we have a tendency to agree anyway . . . but we bring a lot of stuff in and when we are ready to shoot, we already know what it is. So, it is not like . . . let me look through the lens . . . I never look through the lens.

Maureen Gosling, working as director on a film with cinematographer Chris Simon, says the give and take is a must. "So before we go on the shoot, we talked about everything. We said we want to shoot this or this and I would make a list and she would respond and say, 'Let's shoot this and this,' and so on. 'Here's my two cents,' and then we'd make a list."

Director Gary Weimberg agrees.

I believe in the collective process. On a big show, it is very important to have a real collaborator as DP. Kevin O'Brien and I have worked together on at least a dozen films (some my own, some I edited) so I have seen literally hundreds of hours of his stuff. I know how he visually thinks. We have developed "the dance" between director and cameraman so we can sort of be one multieyed monster connected by cables but moving together through space and time. As he shoots, my job is to stay alert to what he is doing, to help if I can with ideas or equipment. For example, I have the tripod ready to hand him before he asks, because I see he is zoomed long and needs more than a handheld and anticipating that need and also I am looking for what is beyond the viewfinder. I look 360 degrees and he looks through the camera. It's a wonderful thing.

Cinematographer Vicente Franco says the director must communicate his or her needs.

**Figure 9.1** Cinematographer Kevin O'Brien and director Gary Weimberg work closely together as they shoot basic training for the documentary *Soldiers of Conscience*.
Courtesy Luna Productions, photo by Ian Slattery

My role as a cinematographer is to display visually what they (director or producer) have in mind for the story, knowing that as a cinematographer or DP I am actually directing part of the time, whether I like it or not, because I am continually deciding on framing, on composition, and the relationship between the subjects. So in order to make sure that I am not really doing my film but that I am doing the director's film, I need to understand their vision. Whatever it takes.

Franco says the documentary director needs to steer clear of micromanaging on the shoot. "I prefer a person (director) who has a conversation with me and communicates with me and then he or she lets me do my job. Definitely, I don't want anybody behind my back . . . kind of trying to direct as the action is going on." Franco says any corrections need to be addressed at the end of the day.

Look at what we have done and discuss it. If I'm not taking the approach that the director wants for his or her film, then we can revise it. I worked with one (director), whose name I won't mention, who tells you that you put the tripod here and not a foot to the left. That is a real indication that you don't have the trust of the director. That's not an enjoyable way to work and it's an indication that my ability to see the shot is not being respected. So, I shouldn't be there.

In any case, the director and the crew had better be ready for anything once they reach the location. Every shoot, producer Ellen Bruno says, is a "journey of discovery." Even though the location has been picked and vetted as a good bet for sequences, almost anything can happen. Cinematographer Franco agrees, saying that any crew coming to a location should not just shoot the same old stuff. "They should keep their eyes open and keep their minds open."

## PRODUCTION CREWS: HOW LARGE?

Producer Ellen Bruno tells about going to her first dangerous shooting location as part of a crew of four.

It is not practical nor desirable to be traveling to these places talking to people about intimate stories with three extra people hanging around me. It just doesn't work so since that time, I've gone from a crew of four to just myself and I've shot and recorded sounds and edited myself. It allows for more comfort and intimacy and just being able to move. I can throw everything in a backpack and get on the back of a motorcycle and go through the back roads of Burma and nobody would know who I was or what I was doing and it gave me a lot of freedom.

Going it alone is difficult but not unworkable. However, the usual documentary field crew is made up of a producer/director, cinematographer, and sound recordist. Leaner production teams allow a degree of intimacy with the subjects and adapt easily to cramped conditions. Those producers argue that the focused work ethic of a small crew leads to better footage.

Depending on budget and work rules, this crew can grow until it is intrusive. I once accompanied a CBS network documentary crew of eight on a New York shoot, including the cinematographer, the camera assistant, the sound recordist,

**Figure 9.2** Cramped locations often make for difficult interplay with the microphone boompole.
Courtesy of Kauthar Umar

the gaffer for lights, the producer/director, the on-camera host, the production assistant, and the driver. They dragged six boxes of equipment to the location and set up what looked like a small studio for an interview. Needless to say, it was intimidating for the interviewee.

### Production Crew Must Work as a Team

Even though the director calls the shots, the crew must be efficient, technically proficient, and trained to respond as a team in complicated locations. Most cinematographers refer to this as a dance, with crewmembers watching the camera person's lens so they can shift out of the shot.

Often they must act independently if an unexpected situation arises. In this way, the sound recordist might turn the audio boom and redirect the mic to get the voice or incoming comments (useful in that golden moment) or the camera person might pan to capture an action that exemplifies the opinions of an interviewee.

The crew cannot thrive if there is dissension. A crewmember who badmouths others or second-guesses the director must stop it or leave the crew. Producer and editor Maureen Gosling says long days on the road can make the crew restive.

At the beginning there's the honeymoon—everyone is excited, everyone is happy, everyone is totally getting along with each other. At a certain point, that starts to change and right in the middle there will be conflict and tension because people are getting tired and not getting a break and are around these people too much. This happened with *Blossoms* when we had a moment when people started getting cranky but then we got through that and by the time the filming was ending, we were back up again and we were excited.

## VISUAL GRAMMAR

Producers, editors, and cinematographers also communicate through a common cinematic grammar of individual shots each recognizes.

Cinematographer Emiko Omori says that "You really, as a cinematographer, need to understand the principles of filmmaking . . . the wide shot . . . the medium shot . . . the close-up . . . not that you have to follow those rules all the time."

When a camera person is at a location to shoot a sequence, he or she must consider the plight of the editor months later. Cinematographer Vicente Franco says it helps to have been on the receiving end of the visuals.

> Because as an editor of my own documentaries I know what you need in the editing room to put these things together . . . so when I am shooting, I am always thinking of the editing room. So a list and part of my responsibility or role is to provide everything that they are going to need in the editing room to put the story together . . . and that helps me a lot as a cinematographer . . . that I have editing skills.

Producer Ken Kobre's mantra about "one shot is never enough" is a good start for new shooters. We suggest that when a novice cinematographer shoots sequences, he or she set a rule to get at least two of each of these shots:

1) Wide shot (WS) establisher
2) Medium shot (MS)
3) Close-up (CU)
4) Extreme close-up (ECU) of the subject and ECU of interesting details
5) Reaction shots
6) Reverses, high-angle, and low-angle shots
7) Trucks, pans, tilts, and zooms if called for
8) Point-of-view (POV) shots

An interesting variety of shots serves not only to make the documentary experience more interesting, but also gives the editor useful tools to compress time and dialogue.

The wide shot or panoramic shot allows you to show the location in the frame; however, it is not a free pass to give the audience the Grand Canyon.

A reaction shot is a tight close-up of the face of someone watching the action. For any sequence with an audience, it's good to have four or five of these. The camera person needs to turn away from the action to catch the faces.

**Figure 9.3** Although the wide shot (WS) flattens the image, horizontal lines in the frame and foreground and background items create visual depth.

**Figure 9.4** The medium shot (MS) adds more context about the relationship of the subjects.

**Figure 9.5** The close-up (CU) provides more details and brings the viewer into the subject's intimate personal space.

**Figure 9.6** The extreme close-up (ECU) adds detail but also serves as a transition between shots with the painter's face.

**Figure 9.7** Popular Mexican wrestler Tiger receives medical attention after being knocked unconscious during a fierce match in the documentary *Que Viva La Lucha*. This is the setup for the reax shot.

**Figure 9.8** Two of the many crowd reaction shots used to depict the stunned and anxious fans after the wrestler is hurt.

### The Revealing Reverse Shot

Shooting requires maximum concentration behind the lens to be in tune and follow in the frame. Often the camera person needs to move behind the action to give direction in the video. This is the reverse shot and it adds great depth to the frame by showing a foreground and background element.

## THE CAMERA AND LENS IN MOTION

When the camera is physically in motion alongside the subject, it is called a trucking shot. These are tricky to keep steady and it helps to have the director or production assistant close by if the camera person is backpedaling across rough terrain.

**Figure 9.9** Reverse adds information. In this wide angle, the natural lines of the scene lead the viewer's eye toward the direction of the action. The casket in the foreground is the initial point of interest. After that, the viewer's eye sees participants in the midground and the desolate street in the procession's path.

Using the lens to add motion is problematic. Panning, moving the lens across the scene, or tilting, moving the lens up and down, should be used to depict intentional movement from one subject to another. Zooming in can intensify the focus and pulling back can show the relationship of an individual detail to the wider scene.

However, pans should be short, covering no more than one-eighth of a circle, and the pan shot needs to begin as a still picture, pan slowly, and end as a still for 10 seconds. The same suggestion applies to zooms and pullbacks. Additionally, the zoom and pullback are difficult to keep steady, even from a tripod. Finally, editors find these lens motion shots difficult to work with in a sequence because the shot usually needs to be held until it ends. Sometimes, that might be as long as 20 seconds.

A tilt is a vertical motion of the lens moving from one focused shot to another above or below it. These are effective in shifting the audience's attention from one close-up to another, say from a paper on a desk to the eyes of the person sitting at the desk.

A point-of-view (POV) shot shows what the subject might be seeing without the subject in the frame. It is very useful in editing any sequences with action.

## FRAMING SHOTS WITH INTENTION

A documentary should be revealing and should provide an intimate experience. As a viewer I want the cinematographer to bring me as close to a subject as possible. This sense of closeness is essential to engage the audience.

The particular shot's field of view represents the viewer. So, if there is a succession of wide shots, the viewer can only feel as if he or she is standing on the sidelines. It the producer uses a lot of close-ups, the viewer senses he or she is inside the personal space of the subject. For documentaries, then, the cinematographer must be bold. If you are going to shoot, get closer than you think you have to be. A colleague called this "getting in their faces." Any decision to keep the camera at a distance from the subject lessens your chance to provide this inclusiveness for the audience. Good telephoto lenses are very important in cases when a close-in crew would simply be too intrusive.

### Let the Camera Observe the Action

Documentary crews attempt to capture the action within the screen frame. In other words, frame it and wait for the action to happen. Don't continually readjust the framing by zooming or pulling back while recording. This will handcuff your editor with short, unstable shots. Omori says a cinematographer needs to be watchful. "Wait for something to happen. You have to be patient. If you are impatient, you will miss the shots. With video, there is no excuse about waiting. Coming from film taught me to be thoughtful and plan."

**Figure 9.10** Top: Framing is too wide with too much activity. It gives the audience too much leeway to let their attention wander. Bottom: Using the close-up reframes the activity and brings the viewer intimately into the action.

### Use the Frame as an Enclosure to Intensify the Action

The image is what provides the visual text. When shooting, frame only what you need for the shot because your editor cannot crop it (not with quality) in post. Framing the shot tightly will keep the viewer's focus on the important action and seemingly bring the audience into a more intimate association with the subject.

Concentrate on the edges of the frame to enclose the action. Shoot as tight as possible to avoid unwanted elements that weaken your focus on a specific subject group. In the examples shown in Figure 9.10 & Figure 9.11, the extreme wide shot has three activity groups and sets up a perceived distance for the audience. When the camera person reframed the shot to a close-up, viewers are brought more intimately into the action and can focus on one group.

## THE EYELINE OF THE CAMERA LENS

This revives the continuing argument about larger, shoulder-mounted cameras versus the lighter, smaller cameras that are held in front. The lens of the shoulder-mounted camera is at eye level; however, the smaller cameras, when off the tripod, are often held out in front and one or two feet below the subject's eyeline. If shooting with a small camera, using a shoulder brace or rig will bring the lens back to eye level.

## PAY ATTENTION TO THE ACTION VECTORS WITHIN THE FRAME

When shooting an action that repeats itself, you must be aware of how the action will appear in the frame. If the cinematographer crosses the street to change camera positions, this will reverse the apparent motion vectors across the frame. This error is called crossing the axis.

**Figure 9.11** The lens of a shoulder-mounted camera generally sits at eye level of the subject.

**Figure 9.12** When a lightweight camera with a flip-out viewing screen is used, there is a tendency to fold it below the eyeline.

**Figure 9.13** These examples depict a cinematographer "crossing the axis." A bicyclist moving in the same direction (top) appears to be on a collision course because the camera has crossed the street and is shooting from the other side. To soften this effect, a nonvector shot moving toward the camera could be cut between the top two shots.

**Figure 9.14** Angle/Angle: The straight-on shot (left) flattens the image and removes any depth form the frame. The angled shot (right) uses perspective lines to add depth to the image.

In the case of Figure 9.13, if the tripod position moved from one sidewalk to the other across the street, the bicyclist, although always moving in the same direction, would appear to crash into himself. A third shot, in which the rider comes directly toward the camera, can provide relief in this case.

A solution to crossing the axis is to flip the video image in postproduction so that the vectors go in the other direction. However, flipping the picture will make any text in the frame read backward.

### Adding Depth to Flat Objects

Most common objects or buildings are symmetrical in structure; moving the camera position to the left or right changes the perspective and adds depth along what is called the z-axis, or the apparent depth in the frame.

Buildings are the best example. Shoot the arches in Figure 9.14 straight on, and the shot has no depth and looks flat. We suggest following an old rule called "angle/angle" (an angle from the side and an angle from below). Doing this adds perspective to the image.

### Using a Frame Within the Video Image

The cinematographer should look for natural frames that exist within the frame to focus the viewer's attention (see Figure 9.15).

### Framing for Backlight

Usually, a strong light behind your principal object works against you. There is no way to get detail, and characters and buildings become silhouettes. However, in some cases a silhouette can be a striking image, conveying an abstract sense of motion or design or time of day and relieving the intense concentration on action. This should come in the area of beauty shots.

## USING MULTIPLE CAMERAS AT A SCENE

A producer planning on multiple cameras for a single shoot should ensure that they are exactly the same model and that the settings are uniform, including white balance and audio recording. Using different models makes intercutting difficult

**Figure 9.15** Frames within frames. The side pillars and adobe walls reframe the images in a Mexican town plaza.

**Figure 9.16** Using a silhouette: Women go to collect the fish caught by the village's fisher-men. The shot often suggests the beginning or conclusion to a particular sequence or day.

because each camera brand has its own unique personality in terms of image quality and aesthetic color and sharpness, so mixing models might cause the images to clash later in postproduction.

There are many benefits of multiple-camera shoots. One is a supply of prime footage for the editor to match cut sequences. Also, the producer will have three

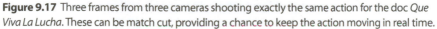

**Figure 9.17** Three frames from three cameras shooting exactly the same action for the doc *Que Viva La Lucha*. These can be match cut, providing a chance to keep the action moving in real time.

separate audio recordings from which to choose the clearest. Finally, using this approach for an action-driven scene will allow the editor to bring the viewer closer to the emotion and the experience.

To avoid shot duplication, the director should define the wide, medium, and close-up shots, assigning each to a particular camera. All communication should be carried out with hand signals planned before the event, because these public activities tend to be extremely loud, and talking on a cell phone, walkie-talkie, or yelling can be difficult.

I found the easiest way to keep sync and make the work easier in post was to start each shoot with a visual hand clap for all cameras and then never stop them. Video storage is cheap and the extraneous material can simply be discarded before post.

## PREPARATION AND SCHEDULING

To organize a comfortable shooting schedule, a producer must consider locations, distances and transportation, meals for the crew, maps, and specific contact numbers and addresses.

It takes experience to forecast the length of time the crew will need to spend in the field. Depending on the location, sound, and lighting conditions, a 30-minute interview might take anywhere between two and four hours, including setup and breakdown.

A simple shoot at a weekend festival might take two hours for setup, three hours at the event, two hours to get reaction, and another hour to break down. Shooting days with multiple locations can easily exceed 12 straight hours.

The logistics of setting up a tight schedule often run afoul of unforeseen delays, so it is good to have a "plan B" ready when the principal shoot bombs out. This way the crew can at least shoot B-roll, capture cover or generic images, shoot beauty shots, or record wild sound needed in the documentary.

When possible, the producer should do a location survey with the DP to determine lighting and ambient sound conditions as well as optimum shooting times.

### Prepare Recording Media Ahead of Time

Any raw field stock, whether it is film, tape, or flash card storage, should be labeled in advance of arriving on location. It can be too hectic on location to organize this. Also, the cinematographer and sound recordist should check out and test all equipment to see that switches and menus are set to the proper positions.

### Be Cautious of Overambitious First Shoots

The first shooting days on any doc must be minor interviews or secondary sequences. This will give the new director and crew ample time to develop a rhythm, make a few mistakes, and create a system of communication. Postmortem discussions with the crew about problems can lead to smoother shoots in the future.

### The Empty Schoolyard: The Band Is Gone

Double-check all schedules to be certain that shoots are planned for days and times when there will be activity. There have been shoots when the documentary crew arrives only to find that everyone else is gone. School kids might be on a vacation day. Artists and musicians did the preconcert sound check two hours early and no one told the crew. The buses left for base camp early and now the offices are empty. The office staff is at lunch. The procession was yesterday. The troubled parents only bring their kids to the clinic on Tuesdays and today is Thursday, so there is nobody in the classroom.

## Remain Calm When the Excitement Hits

Unplanned events and unexpectedly chaotic shooting situations often cause even the most senior shooters to become excited. The result can be hours of field tape that do not translate into good edited versions.

It commonly happens to a novice camera person at a fast-moving event or a riot situation. There is so much excitement and surprise that the camera person becomes frantic trying to capture everything, moving from one scene to another and ending with very short shots that are useless to an editor.

Calm down. Focus on one sequence at a time, following the action in search of a beginning, middle, and end. Don't stop or pause the recording. Be patient.

Although you might miss some of the other exciting moments, you must choose your path and make every effort to cover it well while building a sequence. As a rule of thumb, try to hold each shot at least 10 seconds; counting is a way to keep your focus on usable shots. Remember that the speed of the cinematic action will be determined in the editing room and not the camera.

During the shooting of a documentary on fireworks makers in Peru, we finished a morning assignment and I was resting in my hotel room. I could hear the fiesta outside in the street with music, people, and fireworks. Then I heard Keith, my co-producer, screaming on the patio of the hotel, "Get the camera and come out!"

I grabbed the camera and found myself in a noisy crowd, angry because the town's borrachito or drunkard had burns from firecrackers that caught on fire. The police and other community members were in a loud dispute about whether the town's drunk or the character featured in our film, the fireworks maker, was responsible. The police took both to the station, where the argument continued.

In this case I had to position myself with the camera right in the action, keeping in mind the different lighting conditions, and framing in the shade or the light, getting close to the subjects to record the best audio. The entire sequence ended up being a single shot that lasted 22 minutes, concluding with the authorities taking the burn victim to the hospital and allowing the fireworks maker to go free.

During the shooting I had to consider the editorial coverage, reaction shots, reverses, and details, constantly evaluating if a particular scene had a sense of completion, always thinking not of the visual coverage, but audio as well, as I was only using the built-in camera mic.

## The Final Production Reality: Exhaustion

Any project that requires traveling for long periods of time will lead to major fatigue. Scheduling a day or two between long production days is crucial to allow the production team to recover the necessary energy to stay in focus. A tired crew will develop annoying attitudes, affecting the outcome of the shoot. Technical mistakes will be more frequent. Taking the time to rest on long shoots and travel must be planned into the production schedule to get the best possible results.

Production is exhausting. Says producer Maureen Gosling:

> I've been on shoots . . . the ones I've been involved with . . . and everybody's so into it and you don't take a break. And pretty soon everyone is falling on the floor. They can't stop. The momentum of an event is happening and you just push yourself

and push and then you are a wreck later. But sometimes you do it because you'll never get this opportunity again and everyone is exhausted and starving and needs margaritas and beer at the end of the day.

## SELECTING ADDITIONAL EQUIPMENT

In addition to the principal camera gear, audio equipment, and lights, there are a few tools we would suggest are essential on location.

A quality tripod with good fluid head is absolutely necessary for every location. Even if the cinematographer intends to shoot the action handheld or use a monopod, the tripod will save tired forearms later in the day. Extras might include a set of baby legs (a tripod-like stand barely a foot high), a monopod, and a smaller vibration-dampening rig.

Bring either an interchangeable wide-angle lens or a high-quality wide-angle adaptor. This brings a more intimate dynamic to close-in shots and smoother handheld movements.

Include a checklist of all the gear. This is necessary because if you are missing a simple $3.50 blue gel to color balance tungsten to sunlight, that could ruin a shoot. Be sure someone goes through the checklist everyday both before and after the shoot.

Carry as few equipment cases as possible. The camera case, audio case, tripod bag, lighting kit, and gadget bag are the essentials. Having other paraphernalia can get in the way of your ability to work fast and find exactly what you need in a hurry.

There is a complete list of our favorite tools at the end of this chapter.

**Figure 9.18** Smaller cameras often require a mounting rig that steadies the camera on the shoulder.

## DON'T LEAVE HOME WITHOUT IT

If I have not hired a camera person with his or her own equipment and I am shooting, I bring the following:

- A professional camera with XLR connections
- Two extra camera batteries (total 10 hours charge)
- AC battery charger
- The manual for the camera
- A wide-angle adapter with lens shade
- Two cases of high-quality recording cards (premarked)
- A hot-shoe adaptor to allow two mounts
- One handle adaptor rig for mounting small camera lights
- One 10-watt camera lightpanel with diffuser and battery
- Reflectors or white cards
- Lens cloth
- One tripod (professional) in a strong soft case

Once on a location, quite often there is a great need for some odd tools or items that are not available everywhere. These items should go in the gadget bag:

- Swiss army knife or any other multiple tool
- Gaffer's tape (gray and black)
- Sharpies or other indelible markers
- Pens, notebook, and index cards
- Clipboard
- Scissors
- Flashlight (small but with powerful light)
- Pair of leather grip gloves
- Clothespins
- AC adapters
- AA, AAA, and 9V batteries
- One 25-foot AC cable
- Various hand tools, needle-nose pliers, Phillips screwdrivers of all sizes, box cutters
- Drinking water, cell phone, and credit cards

## SUMMARY

Production is the delicate ballet of collaboration. It takes a carefully chosen and balanced crew to shoot consistently good footage. Camera persons must be constantly aware of how they are framing a shot, and learn to use natural perspective, lines, contrast, and lighting in the frame to direct the eye of the viewer.

## Shaping Your Skills

1. Make a list of all possible equipment you might need if you are shooting a local band playing before an audience in a nearby auditorium. Would a multicamera shoot be appropriate?
2. Shoot a sequence with activity that has a repeated pattern—ideally, something like baking bread. Do the required series of shots from both the tripod and handheld. See if you can frame only what you need and direct the viewer's eye to the image.

## Further Reading

Compesi, Ronald, *Video Field Production and Editing* (6th ed.), Boston: Allyn and Bacon, 2006.

Rabiger, Michael, *Directing the Documentary* (4th ed.), Boston: Focal Press, 2004.

# CHAPTER 10

# Producing for Small Screens and Mobile Devices

As the number of screens in people's lives increases, we have more opportunities to fill them with unique and compelling stories.

PRODUCER AND DIRECTOR BARBARA KOPPLE

In the past decades, documentary producers had theaters, television, cable, film festivals, universities, and DVDs as distribution channels. Then the Internet spread, with its interactivity, streaming, and easily accessed video sites. Combine that with technological advances that gave us smart phones and e-tablets and a new distribution paradigm had emerged—watching programs on mobile devices.

Yes, the future of small screen distribution is promising, but producers and directors must be aware that there is more to the mobile screen audience than shortening the TRT.

This chapter is about strategies for producing short, effective videos for the Internet. Distribution will be covered more extensively in Chapter 14.

## GLOSSARY

**Letterboxing**  Horizontal black bars at the top and bottom of the screen when positioning a 16 × 9 image on a 4 × 3 screen.

**Mobile distribution**  Getting your doc, an abridged version of your doc, or the trailer on some network tied into the world's 2.5 billion smart phones or tablets.

**Nonexclusive license**  A media license that allows the producer to sell similar rights to others.

**Pillarboxing**  Vertical black bars that appear at the right and left side of the screen when positioning a 4 × 3 image on a 16 × 9 screen.

**User-generated content (UGC)**  Refers to short videos on websites that distribute free content, such as YouTube, MySpace, WorldMadeChannel, and others.

**Viral**  Web term to describe the spread of information in a nonlinear fashion across sites.

## THE EVER INCREASING NUMBER OF SMART PHONES AND TABLETS

For the documentary producer, it could be a new multiplatform world. A recent Pew Research Center study confirmed that more than half of American adults have either a smart phone or tablet like an iPad. That study separated out two audiences: older users who use mobile devices to supplement their newspapers and television sources and younger users who rely completely on the mobile devices for information and visuals. This newer audience is immersed in participatory cultures and social media connectivity and reaching them presents a challenge for traditional documentary makers.

### These Changes Require Fresh Ideas

The traditional distribution venues, where the documentary audience is willing to spend an hour or so watching the documentary in a darkened room, should remain for many years, but new mobile device and Internet opportunities are growing fast and are uncharted territory.

Even customary outlets for documentary producers have seen the light. Commissioning programs such as *Frontline/World* and others are experimenting with documentary segments constructed only for the Internet. These update earlier stories or excerpt sections for playback on user-generated content sites. They do not appear on everyday television.

## A PRODUCER'S CONSIDERATIONS

Web video producer Russell Johnson says the goal is not to just shorten your documentary, but to recognize that Internet exposure demands a new conceptual basis. Your video offerings must be engaging and designed for effective presentation on the small screen.

He also stresses that the Internet is an interactive platform. "You want people to react to what you've done," he says. Your audience is not sitting a distance from the screen, but is most likely within touching distance. They might, at the mention of ideas for themes, be encouraged to abandon your program and skitter off to another.

Producer Johnson says another exciting advance now is the Web's transparency for video. "Video is searchable, not just by the keywords you enter, but by meta-tags embedded in the message or by audio tracks," he says. This means that producers who seek exposure on the Web have to be extremely aggressive in setting up clues to be found when someone searches for a topic. "You can tag things to be found."

Refine the documentary's keywords. Unless you are Ken Burns or Michael Moore, your name or your production company's name might be unknown. So the keywords of your uploaded doc material should reflect the subject matter and value of watching the video.

## SHOULD YOUR HOUR-LONG DOC BE ON THE WEB?

For the producer, Johnson says, Web video is useful and cheap. Producers can post raw field footage, link any site to the film's trailer, or edit together short minidocs to stir interest. But Johnson isn't sanguine about streaming the entire documentary on the Web. "Unless it is a public service program, doing that will be just like giving it away. Once it is out there, it is gone," he said.

Sites for the independent producer can be used in a traditional sense: for publicity, program sharing, and distribution.

There are free sites with limits on size and program length. These are good for publicity and experimental documentary design. YouTube is the giant in this field and can guarantee a large audience if your promotional outreach goes viral. Some producers use Vimeo as a sharing location.

There are also sites that direct viewers to your program so that they may stream it or purchase a DVD, including Amazon, Netflix, or iTunes.

Some producers gain exposure by giving away free access. An advocacy doc that kindled the Internet's fascination with conspiracy theories, *Loose Change,* a commentary on the 9/11 tragedy that cost $2,000 to make, was put on the Internet in 2009 for free at the same time DVDs were sold. Director Dylan Avery claimed 4 million downloads, and his company is still selling DVDs.

## TRAILERS AND WEB BUZZ

Trailers on the Web are now a common exposure for documentary makers. But trailers produced for television or theatrical distribution should be redesigned and reedited for Internet distribution, reworking the aesthetics and keeping them concise to match up with short attention spans and crowded viewing areas. They can be posted on user sites like YouTube and Vimeo and then linked to the film's website.

As we mentioned in Chapter 4, there are both fundraising trailers and audience interest trailers. Customary trailer content that is fast-moving, nonlinear, and up-tempo still works, but producers should alter it for Internet-only presentation.

Two important factors are the $16 \times 9$ shape of the screen and the size and quality of any graphic text blocks. All graphics need to be large and bold. Any text on the screen should be kept to 15 characters across. The audio tracks must be simple and loud enough to overcome competing ambience.

### Getting the Web Buzz Going

We cover more on publicity in Chapter 14, but it is wise to remember that Web content spreads "virally." Before you post the trailer, spread the word by sending Facebook, Twitter, and e-mail links to everyone you know and notifying blogs and websites covering your subject matter. With an estimated 65,000 videos uploaded a day, the chance of your documentary trailer making it to the popularity summit might be small unless you stoke the fires of curiosity that will spread your production across the net.

If producers want the audience to act on something in their YouTube or Vimeo documentary trailer, it is best to put the Web address in graphics across the bottom of the frame somewhere in the video.

For the listing, make the one-sentence description of your documentary as concise as possible. YouTube will show less than the full sentence, often, of the video page.

YouTube selects a thumbnail to represent the video posting from the precise center of what is submitted, so put a symbolic shot there, if possible. The site will give you two additional choices if that shot is vague or nonrepresentative.

## SOCIAL MEDIA HELP OUT

For the documentary producer, social media sites like Facebook, LinkedIn, and Google+ are a boon for exposure and publicity. These can also direct interested users to the YouTube or Vimeo sites to see the trailer or short informational videos. Your documentary can have its own Facebook page, as well as a website. These can be cross-referenced to other contact lists you have generated.

## IMPORTANT CONTENT CONSIDERATIONS

There are few rules as to subject matter. It is hard to predict what will garner hundreds of thousands or even millions of views. Thirty seconds of a skateboarding squirrel can receive as much attention as a trailer for a documentary about a vital issue.

Producer Johnson says viewers tend to be attracted to the same kind of material they watch on TV: humor, music, movies, and informational documentaries. The audience tends to skew toward a younger demographic that enjoys edgy, subversive subject matter. Documentary topics in investigative areas, explorations in conspiracy and hidden cultures, and stories about new gadgets, scientific novelties, and do-it-yourself subjects are popular attractions, says Johnson.

Johnson also says producers who generate consistently good material are identified so viewers receive a notification of every new posting. Offering a series with a promise of more to come can offer an advantage over a one-shot production.

**Figure 10.1** To introduce a lightweight laptop, producer Johnson designed a story that tied an interesting period in San Francisco literary history—the beat era—with a writer using the machine in one beat coffeehouse that is still in operation.
Courtesy of Russell Johnson

Almost every video will get a few curious viewers. If a documentary producer is aiming for a small audience, the viewers that come to a site might be enough.

Viewers tend to browse rather than search video websites. Searching is not yet very effective in the Web world. Unlike standard websites, video is buzz driven, not search driven. Videos are then shared virally, passed along to friends, colleagues, and relatives. People who go to these sites do so more to be entertained than informed.

## WATCH THE ASPECT RATIO

When posting to the Web, the most popular aspect ratio is 16 × 9 widescreen, but a producer could also select a 4 × 3 aspect ratio. Professor Herbert Zettl, in his highly respected book on applied television aesthetics *Sight Sound Motion,* points out that the 4 × 3 aspect ratio is best for the human close-up, where the face fills the screen with little wasted space. However, 4 × 3 doesn't work well for groups on screen, landscapes, or long shots, such as in the screen captures in Figure 10.2 from a YouTube video of a French bicycle race, in which the town's street details become microscopic when the playback is viewed on a mobile screen.

**Figure 10.2** The 4 × 3 frame allows for more height in the French village bicycle race long shot. However, the details disappear. The close-up (right) is much better suited for carrying information about the bicycle race on the small screen.

**Figure 10.3** Two scenes from a Russell Johnson Web doc on artists at New York's Chelsea Hotel. The close-up interview (left) works but the artist medium shot (right) is about as wide as you can go without losing detail on the small screen.
Courtesy of Russell Johnson

When the 16 × 9 screen is used, Zettl says, the landscape details and two-person conversations have more meaning. Producers should be very aware, however, that the tiny MP3 player screen size does not translate the awe-inspiring energy the audience might get from an IMAX or Cinemascope version of an artist's studio, as shown in Figure 10.3.

Smart phone and tablet screens are not always used in the horizontal; they can be turned vertically, making the film or documentary's image a difficult slog. If a widescreen 16 × 9 production is letterboxed onto a vertical smart phone screen, the details in the image become minute. The same rationale applies to the 4 × 3 aspect ratio screens. When the screen is horizontal, it suffers from pillarboxing with wide black bands.

The aspect ratio dilemma is not a problem for production . Go ahead and shoot widescreen, but center the action and important elements so that they will play in 4 × 3 aspect ratio as well. Then, before uploading, the producer should crop the edges for sites that run the old-style 4 × 3.

## DESIGNING VIDEO FOR MOBILE DEVICE SCREENS

Clearly, the tiny screens on smart phones, iPads, and YouTube-style websites are quite a shift for the immersive energy of documentaries designed for 52-inch living room flat screens or 40-foot-wide theater projection screens. Connecting with an audience through the smaller window suggests a different strategy for programs designed for them.

For the smaller screens, you must consider the noisy venues in which they are used and the reduced picture size and audio quality on the device. The viewing experience on a mobile screen is radically different. It has, as they say, different rules of engagement—that is, how the viewer relates to the device.

For the mobile screen, the conditions of use could be a noisy, crowded room, with a high background hubbub and bright sunlight or overhead lights that diminish the quality of the image. Even with headphones on, the viewer will be hard-pressed to pick out subtleties on the soundtrack. And the size of the screen, in some cases only several inches in width, does not overwhelm the visual field, but instead is only a fraction of what is in front of the viewer.

With these prevailing conditions, viewers might have trouble screening out distractions long enough to watch 56 minutes of a *Frontline* documentary, 90 minutes of a feature-length doc, or even a 15-minute documentary short. The odds are not good. Producers like Johnson suggest documentary segments shorter than 10 minutes.

### Difficult Video Effects

The streaming, buffering, and rendering capabilities of various website codecs are getting much better, but are still not universally primed to present all the intricate high-resolution elements of the videos. On many small viewing screens, the video looks degraded, showing torn frames and missing pixels caused by slow broadband connection speeds, storage, and buffering backups. Therefore, we have some suggestions.

1) Fill the frame. For Web video, fill the screen with large images, medium shots, and close-ups, active gestures, and blurred backgrounds. On the limited size of mobile screens, tiny details and wide shots will be lost. Producers of issue and current events documentaries that feature a series of talking head authorities will find their styles better suited to the smaller frames. Less B-roll is needed because the full face on a vertically formatted or nearly square mobile screen is an effective use of the medium.

2) Avoid pans, zooms, and fast pullbacks. Pans and zooms used to be discouraged for Internet video because the bandwidth and codecs weren't up to snuff. But that has changed. "You just don't have to throttle back anymore,"

**Figure 10.4** Sometimes, it is difficult to make out the details in normal wide shots when viewed on the tiny screens of tablets.

Johnson said. However, from an aesthetics standpoint, quick swishpans or fast zooms still are marginalized on the tiny mobile device screens, because their power to involve the viewer is lost on the tiny units.

3)  Stay away from clever video effects, such as picture-in-picture or split screen. It simply doesn't make sense to further reduce the size of the image by making it smaller. Adding two images to the screen makes the complexity difficult to scan on the small screen.

4)  Make graphics simple and put text in large sans serif fonts. Intricate intertitles or smallish lower third identifiers will be murky on mobile-sized screens and only readable by viewers with extraordinary vision or recently prescribed glasses. Make the graphics simple and large.

In the past, it was unwise to put important images or graphics on the edge of the television picture, because on some screens, the transmission over the air would eliminate them. The usable area was called the "safe" area. Now, if the documentary is not meant for broadcast television, a producer can disregard the so-called "safety zone" and fill the entire mobile screen frame with video and graphics. The picture's black levels (pedestal in TV tech jargon) can be lowered to zero instead of the murky gray 7.5 IRE of broadcast television and the color saturation levels can be increased beyond what would be allowable on a local broadcast station.

## Consider the Color Saturation

Mobile screens can be clear indoors but difficult outside and in some brightly lit public areas, they are almost invisible. To combat this possibility, producers should consider the saturation of colors in segments edited for mobile screens. Bright, primary colors will show up more evenly on the tiny viewing area.

## Audio Considerations Are Crucial

Viewers often use mobile screens in difficult, noisy, cluttered rooms. Detailed, cleverly mixed audio that works in a theater simply won't come across in a coffee shop.

This suggests that every audio track destined for Internet distribution and mobile screens should be as clear as possible. To achieve this, audio should be carefully gathered in the field. Audio, especially interviews, should be recorded with plug-in microphones such as lavs or small shotguns (see Chapter 7). Using an inexpensive camera's built-in microphones is a last resort and should only be used for location ambient sound. These built-ins have condenser automatic gain circuits that boost all speech, background chatter, and room echo to unbearable levels. Add Internet audio compression codecs and you have mushy, almost unrecognizable sound without any clarity.

When audio post is done, producers for mobile screens might take a lesson from audio engineers in the early days of popular radio music. No matter how sophisticated their studios were, they mixed a final program down by listening on a set of cheap speakers one might find in a car, a very smart move. Those who want to distribute on mobile screens should always watch a final video edit in a noisy, badly lit coffee shop.

## FORMATS

Most video sharing sites allow the uploading of various formats. The iTunes store does have particular quirks and dislikes.

Be careful when digitizing in the "progressive download" format, which means that the video starts almost instantly and continues to download as the video plays. The advantage of these formats is that they can be hosted on any web-site without expensive streaming software. Unfortunately, some computers don't play these unless the user first downloads the codec.

### Shooting Formats for Internet Sites

Even though your YouTube video will play sketchy older formats, always produce in full 1920 × 1080 high def and use cameras that shoot at the highest bit rate possible.

The most downloaded or "browsed" videos on the Web are the most profes-sionally produced. Your offerings will be compared to those, and that is why you need high production values.

### Encoding and Posting

For YouTube and other sites, uploaded files have limits. Producers can encode videos for uploading in most popular video formats, except that Windows Media files are not compatible with iTunes.

Test videos after encoding them, both offline and online. Some MPEG4 for-mats cause serious artifacts on moving subjects. Windows Media and QuickTime can produce compact files at very high resolution. YouTube and other sharing sites automatically resize video to their own formats.

## WHAT ABOUT COPYRIGHTS AND PUBLIC DOMAIN?

The Web is a mess of judicial uncertainty on many copyright issues. The sites themselves often escape copyright legalities, but it is left to the producer to take responsibility for what is in a project. Read the boilerplate contracts about "terms of service" on each site before uploading material.

Courts are beginning to sort out the reality of copyright, pirating someone else's work, and what material is available for other uses. Do not use copyrighted music without permission. Check out possibilities for public domain music or original compositions by local composers. There are books and websites with more information on public domain music and archival. A good source is the website at http://www.pdinfo.com/.

### What If Someone Steals Your YouTube Doc?

You really have little recourse. Putting your work out on a free site for the world to see is a little like leaving artwork on a New York City street for people to enjoy.

The viral nature of the Web that generates the buzz then becomes an enemy as your stolen work spreads through forwards, blogs, and other sharing sites.

To paraphrase the classic blues performer Howlin' Wolf, "Once the red rooster is out of the barnyard and on the prowl, there's not much peace."

## SUMMARY

Just where Web video is going is anyone's guess, but the possibilities are exciting and offer new democratic methods of gaining exposure. Producers should keep track of the most productive user-generated content sites for documentary trailers.

### Shaping Your Skills

1. Take a smart phone to a crowded coffee house or café. Attempt to show someone a short doc that you have located on YouTube. Watch for the viewer's frustration with his or her inability to hear the audio or see the video due to lighting issues. Explain what inferences you can draw in relation to trailers you might produce for mobile devices.

### Further Reading

Zettl, Herbert, *Sight Sound Motion* (5th ed.), Belmont, CA: Wadsworth, 2001.

# PART IV

# Postproduction

# CHAPTER 11

# Using Music in the Documentary

Using a local composer cuts costs for documentary music.

> We discuss the film early, early on focusing on what temp
> music to use before he starts and what that should be to reflect
> where we both want to go in the end with his music.
>                     PRODUCER GARY WEIMBERG ON COMPOSER
>                                      TODD BOEKELHEIDE

Documentary producers have always embraced music, whether the songs are pop hits, oldies, or from field recordings, or whether the score was composed for this particular film. Music adds a secondary mood, rhythm, continuity, or presence to the film.

Major distributors, festivals, or broadcasters will ask for the origin and license agreements for each piece of music in the program. For that reason, music can be a complicated and expensive luxury. More documentary makers are turning to local composers and performers for unique music soundtracks. This chapter reviews some suggestions about music integrated into the edit.

## GLOSSARY

**Bed**  Underlying music track that provides a mood, tempo, location, or sync for cutting visuals.

**Cue sheet**  A detailed log of all music, music licenses, and releases in an individual program. Usually required for broadcast.

**Incidental**  Ambient background music recorded during field shoots.

**Mechanical rights**  The rights to the actual performances and recording that produced the music used in the documentary. These might be owned by a record label.

**Publishing rights**  The intellectual rights to the song and lyrics, usually owned by a publisher.

**Sync rights**  A license to use a song as a background for the cutting of visuals. This applies even if the music was originally incidental.

**Temp music**  Any music inserted during rough cuts for style and cues.

**Theme**  A song or music that is identified with the documentary and is usually played at the open or over credits.

## CHOOSING THE MUSIC

From the very beginning, music has played a major role in documentary work. Most producers use music to enliven a program, add a theme, carry a mood, establish the presence of a historic period, provide a counterpoint for transitions between sequences, suggest a tempo, or add emotion.

Music should be integral to documentary planning and should not be an afterthought. Many producers work on the music angle throughout production, whereas others take it up at the beginning of post.

Noted producer Ken Burns often gets the music settled before field production begins. For his historical bio documentary *Mark Twain,* Burns wanted to convey a sense of the period as well as provide a bed to match the cutting in his iconic style. Burns had the piano, violin, and guitar music composed before he shot the visuals. The tracks were either original compositions or covers of popular songs that had passed into public domain. The *Mark Twain* soundtrack was later sold as a CD in stores.

Music can be acquired in many ways. It can be composed and recorded in a studio, taken from other master recordings, captured in the field, downloaded from music libraries or taken from popularly distributed Internet or CD sources.

Whatever the source, most music is licensed by both a publisher who owns the copyrights (publishing rights) and a performer or group who actually recorded the cut to be used (mechanical rights). In most cases, these are separate entities. A license is needed from both to use the music.

## USING PRERECORDED MUSIC

Everyone knows great popular songs that would give a standout presence to any documentary. It might be jazz, an old blues song, something from the Rolling Stones, a rapper's latest, or Beethoven's "Ode to Joy."

Here's the bad news: Licensing popular music does not fit into a cash-strapped indie documentary budget. A producer can minimize the spending by contracting for short-term partial licenses, hoping that if the documentary is purchased by a distributor or programmer, more money can be raised to secure the more involved rights.

The licensing costs paid by the producer are based on these factors:

1) How much of the song is used. For certain purposes, if fewer than 45 seconds is used, it costs less than licensing the whole song.
2) How the music is used. It could be a theme, a sync track, or a bed to establish a tempo and cut visuals. Each could carry different rates.
3) Where the film is distributed. For sale on DVD? In public performances (screenings, festivals)? Or for sale to broadcast? In foreign countries? By limiting first distribution, a producer can limit the costs.

Copyrights and music have a very complex interrelationship. An excellent place to check on additional material is at the government website http://www.copyright.gov/.

### The Duration of the License is Crucial

Music rates are based how long the license will run. The duration could run for a couple of years or for perpetuity. Not planning ahead can be trouble. The wonderful *Eyes on the Prize* 14-hour documentary series about America's civil rights struggles used vast amounts of period music and archival but licensed it for only a short time. When the license was up, the series had to be pulled from public distribution. For 15 years that series languished and could not be screened until foundation grants provided substantial funds to relicense the music for perpetuity. *Eyes on the Prize* is once again available. The lesson is clear: Secure the music licensing for perpetuity if it is in the budget.

## PUBLIC DOMAIN MUSIC

Public domain music includes songs and tunes that have an original sheet music copyright date of 1922 or earlier and have passed out of copyright. A list of many of these songs is available at the website http://www.pdinfo.com/.

A producer who wants to use public domain music is only off the hook for the publishing rights and cannot use any recorded editions of the song because later performances and arrangements are copyrighted. The producer would need to find a musician to play an original cover of the pre-1922 sheet music for the film. So, Beethoven's "Ode to Joy" is available but the music must be performed specifically for the documentary from pre-1922 arrangements.

### Rights Also Depend on Medium, Venue, and Geography

There are clearly defined geographic and market venues for the rights. Producers must be careful to pinpoint these for the channels or regions that match their distribution plans. For instance, if the documentary is to be screened at a festival or to local audiences, rights are very limited and might not cost much. Sometimes, publishers will allow a gratis license for a festival, knowing that if a distributor picks up the doc, the producer will be back to renegotiate for the increase in rights. It works the same if you decide to sell the DVD to the public; you'll need to renegotiate those rights and so on. Once again, be careful to buy rights for the duration of the planned distribution.

### Street Musician Music

Sometimes a documentary crew will encounter a wonderful street musician and record what he or she plays, throwing a few dollars in the hat. That is great, but if you want to use that music, the producer must get a release from that street musician (or local band performing in a club), specifying that he or she signs over all the rights for the performance in perpetuity. Then, the producer must identify the music, if possible, and check to see if there are any publishers with copyrights. If it was written prior to 1922 then it could be in the public domain.

### Hunting Down the Rights Owners

The best way to uncover the rights holder is to look at recording liner notes, contact distributors, check with ASCAP and BMI (two big music publishing groups), or check with the U.S. Copyright Office.

Searching for rights is a tedious process. If there is a substantial amount of music in the film, a producer might want to hire a professional music rights acquisition specialist to handle the search and the license negotiations. This person will find the owners, determine the use, and bargain for prices.

### Begging for Free or Reduced Rates

Publishers are willing to negotiate almost anything. There are wonderful stories of public-minded publishers and performers who liked certain documentary topics and passed the licenses along for reduced rates or even for free. But don't count on that. This type of persuasion takes trust, a common goal, and a lot of e-mails, phone calls, and letters.

One student production group managed to get free festival and local broadcast rights to a popular song, but it took six months of wheedling, begging, and posturing. The gratis licensing, however, only went for local broadcast and cable access and local festivals. They still couldn't sell the program to a national channel without returning to renegotiate.

### Using Licensed Music Without Securing the Rights

If someone recognizes it and asks that the music in question be removed, it will have to be done. The more prestigious festivals are aware of licensing roadblocks and don't want trouble.

For a screening on some version of local access cable, no one might ask you about the music. But for larger cable channels and national PBS exposure, they will want to know everything. Broadcasters who pay for the use of your program are very skittish about music and will ask for a cue sheet. The cue sheet will have to refer to licensing agreements for every appearance of each piece of music. The cue sheet will ask for the following:

1) Description of the work
2) Writers (composers, lyricists or arrangers)
3) Publishers
4) Duration of the cut
5) Usage (theme, background, in concert, etc.)
6) Performing rights
7) Sync rights (paid by another entity)

There is a sample PBS cue sheet available at http://www.pbs.org/producers/redbook/forms/music_cue_sheet.html.

### Broadcasters' License Fees

Broadcasters pay a yearly annual fee to major publishing groups to use prerecorded music. However, that license is for material used on their channel and doesn't give indie producers the right to reuse it everywhere else, such as distribution to other venues or the educational market. Check with the broadcaster.

### So-Called Royalty-Free Music Sellers

These sellers abound on the Internet and offer downloads of both original and prerecorded music for theme, presence, or transitions. Their concept of "royalty free," however, is not always the same as your concept of the term. By those words, they mean that you won't have to pay more for repeated use. You make a one-time payment, something that used to be called a "needle drop" when the world used records made of vinyl.

To use a music library, producers must search through their offerings (a tedious task), get a sample to see if it fits the film's needs, and then pay a download fee for the higher quality cut.

Charges vary based on usage and distribution. If the film only needs a portion of a song and wants it for screenings and festivals, the prices might be less than $100. If it is headed to broadcast or cable, then the one-time price includes an additional fee. The same goes for DVD distribution; there's an additional fee. On the other hand, these companies will provide the producer with a contract and a license to use it.

## HAVING MUSIC COMPOSED FOR YOUR DOCUMENTARY

Having someone score your film is the most cost-effective way for independent documentary makers to acquire music.

Begin by finding a composer. Check with local bands, music schools, or film collective groups. Search the Internet. Check out the credits on local indie productions. Talk to colleagues. It helps to find someone local who has filmmaking experience. Check out the composer's reel. What has he or she done before? Any work on documentaries?

Bring in the composer as soon as possible, or at least toward the end of production. Describe your concept of the music and see if you can reach common
ground. Are you looking for beds to cut to, themes, transitional bright hits, or
mood pieces? In the rough cut stage, ask the composer for a temp or scratch track
to set against the video. This will give the editor some sense of the timing, rhythm,
and flow of each sequence.

Here's how it worked for producer Gary Weimberg on *Soldiers of Conscience*,
co-produced with Catherine Ryan.

> We discuss the film early, focusing on what temp music to use before he starts and
> what that should be to reflect where we both want to go in the end with his music.
> I am a big believer in temp music, both to help the cutting and as a very efficient
> way to communicate to a composer what I think might work. I screen rough cuts
> with him where he responds as a brother filmmaker, not just as a composer. He
> really makes important and if necessary, harsh comments that basically always
> improve the film. I like to call him "Orson" Boekelheide.
>
> Once he starts, sometime after rough cut, we have a wonderful back and
> forth. Me listening and getting to comment on his stuff which he very completely
> mocks up (using synthesizers) so there is no mystery about what he is doing, and
> where we are going. Often I will take those early mock-ups and bring them back
> in the editing room and use them instead of the temp music cues as I continue
> to work.
>
> So, before players are hired/recorded, we both have a complete sense of the
> real score, but then the actual players do their thing and the whole experience
> takes flight. Few moments are as pleasurable as to sit in the biggest recording
> stage at Lucas (Skywalker Sound), listening to nearly 16 string players from the
> San Francisco symphony, with Todd (Boekelheide) an Academy- and Emmy-
> award-winning guy, conducting.

Producer Jennifer Maytornea Taylor says she enjoyed the process of scoring
her film *New Muslim Cool* about Puerto Rican Muslim hip-hop artist Hamza.

**Figure 11.1** Recording the symphonic music used in the documentary *Soldiers of Conscience*
at Skywalker Sound Studios.
Courtesy of Luna Productions, photo by Gary Weimberg

Scoring the film was for me the most fun of the entire project. And it was a way to bring Hamza back as an artist and he and his brother had written a song and they said they wanted to put that into the soundtrack and it was actually the song that you hear when we introduce them as hip-hop artists.

It's a very musical film, but there are couple of tracks which were acquired and there was a couple of tracks that Hamza and his brother did but all the rest of the music and score was also done by our field recordist in Pittsburgh who is also a composer. And he pitched me and . . . and he said "I know Hamza and he likes jazz," which is true.

We ended up with 12 different tracks and he would send me the stem and I did some layering and would combine some others. He drew on all these musicians who live in Pittsburgh and I went to Pittsburgh for the last days of scoring when the bass player came in and then we ended up with the final tracks that Chris and Herman, who was our music producer, produced two times for the film.

### Record the Tracks in a Studio

If you've gone to the trouble to work with composers and musicians to build some original tracks, then record the music in a studio at the most affordable level. Professional recording engineers have a wonderful bag of tricks to give music a robust fidelity that will carry through on all your distribution dubs. They also can provide multiple mixed tracks or specific tracks that can be routed to a single channel of audio.

### Original Compositions and Copyrights

Even using original compositions by local composers does not untangle a producer from the rights jungle. In one section of my documentary on Cambodian political reconciliation, I used about 45 seconds of an original instrumental from a CD written and published by a local composer. He signed a release and each of the three musicians who played on that track for the CD signed a release. When PBS got the cue sheet, they found that one of the musicians was registered in a union benefits program and said there would have to be compensation. Their license took care of it.

## SELLING CD SOUNDTRACKS

Again, this is a different licensing effort and the producer needs to contact everyone again and renegotiate the license fee. Usually, this isn't as difficult as it is expensive.

## SUMMARY

Music adds tempo, intention, and emotion to your doc. The question of what music is best for the documentary and how to get it should be solved before postproduction begins. It must be part of the total sound design. Hiring a local composer is often the most cost-effective way to add music.

## Shaping Your Skills

1. Search Internet music libraries for music to accompany a documentary about (a) hip-hop lifestyle, (b) the culture of the Middle East, or (c) undersea creatures. Locate a track for each and detail the cost and the rights you will acquire.
2. Search local contacts to see if there are composers in your city, town, or nearby region.
3. As if you were addressing a prospective composer, write a few paragraphs about the type of music you'd like for your proposed doc, detailing the use (as transitions, mood, etc.) and the underlying meaning you'd like the score to transmit.

# CHAPTER 12

# Finding Structure for Short and Feature-Length Documentaries

From video frames by Paul Rubicek

> A documentary is a collection of found objects: fragments you've collected, accidents of interview and happenstance, pieces of stock footage that surface in the course of six to nine months of research and production. The puzzle of making those disparate pieces fit into a dramatic structure—one that has acts, one that has an arc of inquiry and discovery—is a very, very difficult thing to do well.
>
> DAVID FANNING, EXECUTIVE PRODUCER OF *FRONTLINE* AND *FRONTLINE/WORLD*

After planning and shooting a documentary, the producer, working with the editor, sorts through hours of field video and extracts the patterns that will tell the story. This is done for a 10-minute short film as well as traditional-length documentaries.

Producer Jon Dann compares this encounter to a gallery visitor making sense of pointillist art: "You are kind of staring at pixels and dots that start to begin to form a pattern and then you begin to identify the pattern from various sources and then from that pattern, a story with a beginning, middle, and an end may emerge."

This chapter begins by exploring the initial steps producers should take to rough out a structure for their field video. It also covers considerations necessary when writing scripts for this structure.

## GLOSSARY

**Deductive design**  Thesis-first documentaries that begin with a thesis statement that will be followed by sequences and interviews that support the thesis.

**Episodic design**  Documentaries composed of a flow of related but self-contained segments or sequences.

**Inductive design**  Documentaries that begin with a series of intriguing sequences, engaging segments, or tantalizing examples that draw in the viewer without stating a thesis.

**Multithreaded design**  Documentaries that unfold several parallel stories at the same time, intercutting between them.

**Observational design**  Documentaries without a thesis statement, narration, or voice under; usually episodic.

**Paper edit**  A structuring device in which crucial sequences are isolated and then repositioned on cards or paper to find an acceptable story flow.

**Prequel**  The opening segment, often before the title, that foreshadows the program with a thesis or tantalizes with powerful sequences.

**Rough cuts**  Intermediate edited versions of the documentary.

**Selects or threads**  A preliminary collection of usable shots in individual scenes, sequences, or themes.

## OVERALL ORGANIZING STRATEGIES

### Unraveling the Footage

Few documentary makers would dare undertake the daunting task that faced Academy-Award-winning producer Connie Fields in 2000. After four years of research on South African apartheid, she returned to her editing studio with 1,500 hours of archival footage, 6,000 photographs, and 135 interviews from nine countries. From that point, it took her seven more years to finish the first of her award-winning seven-part documentary series *Have You Heard From Johannesburg*, which she first released in 2008.

Hammering out a story from massive visual collections is the specialty of historian documentary producers such as Fields or Ken Burns. But most of us won't have to tackle a warehouse of materials. Instead, we might only confront 10 to 50 hours of raw field video, interviews, archival footage, natural sound, music, and stills that need to be culled and shaped to our documentary. In this section, we describe some general approaches that might help your initial organizing efforts.

### The Search for the Dramatic Arc

Shaping the scenes, finding the sequences, and focusing on intriguing characters for a documentary is nothing new. Back in the 1920s, the anointed first documentary *Nanook of the North* presented a story arc of survival adventures as a smiling, affable but clever Inuit hunter and his family endured the bitter Canadian winter climate.

In the decades that followed, documentaries settled into a pattern of realist, journalistic, propaganda, or experimental styles. But 50 years ago, with the introduction of smaller and more portable cameras, filmmakers began to experiment with a less formal and more observational cinema form. This required producers and directors to find and rely on a dramatic arc.

Editor Maureen Gosling says the demand for gripping stories is even more prominent now. "The increasing emphasis on dramatic structure that keeps coming up on ITVS and PBS and all these others, everybody wants it now. It wasn't as critical before but now you figure out how to do it, even with a documentary film where you might not have this climax, this character arc or whatever. Or you try to find the character arc or dramatic arc."

Every producer and every director talks about the arc. It is common to hear a producer say, "I finally found the arc." Often, it doesn't appear until late in the editing process.

Using this dramatic device can often hamper a more free-wheeling, open film, however. When the French documentary *L'Amour Fou* premiered in 2010, it told the story of the half-century love affair between legendary fashion designer Yves Saint-Laurent and his partner Pierre Berge. It was laced with dazzling archival films of Saint-Laurent and the glamour of the couture world in Paris, but director Pierre Thoretton interspersed these engaging films around a dramatic arc detailing the packaging, transport, and final auction of the couple's massive art collection. To continue this framing device through the film required the audience to look at the whole process of air freighting artwork, a distracting element from the more engaging historical archives. One critic suggested that using this dramatic device was akin to building the film around a "yard sale."

## FINDING THE STORY IN THE EDIT ROOM

Producers shouldn't live in a fantasy world. They should make decisions with eyes wide open about what's on those 50 or 70 hours of field material now stored on hard drives. The following steps are suggestions on how to start an organized review.

**STEP 1.** As soon as the field material arrives in the edit room, have the material transferred to hard drives; DVD dubs can be made at that time if needed. Put the master field recordings in a safe place.

**STEP 2.** Review the dailies as soon as possible. If a sequence has severe technical problems with video or audio, have technical experts assess whether it can be saved. If it is badly flawed, don't even consider keeping it in the mix. Set it aside, reshoot, or eliminate it, period.

**STEP 3.** Have someone make shot logs and interview transcripts. Transcripts are annoying to do personally and expensive commercially (transcribers charge about $40 per page), but they are absolutely critical to long-term organization. A 30-minute interview might run for 12 pages.

**STEP 4.** Back up all video files to separate hard drives in case the files become corrupted or the drive fails. (Yes, they do, all the time.)

Logs are keyed to each visual clip or shot and should be annotated with shot quality, length, and location, whether it is on a hard drive or master tape. The logs will give the first hints of standout sequences that are compelling.

Editors and producers can also use bins on editing system hard drives. If the bins have been thoughtfully organized, they will provide a systematic method to allow staffers to become familiar with the footage.

The next phase is to ask questions. After reviewing the visuals in edit bins or window dubs, reading the transcripts, and looking at the logged shots, it is time to begin organizing. Go back to the visuals again and again.

1) Look for standout sequences. These must be intriguing, well shot, and strong enough to develop topics and characters. Give each sequence a name and make a list.

2) Assess the quantity and quality of footage of the key character portrayal. A producer will need sufficient story material and sequences of the protagonist to rely on this personality to carry the story line.

3) Do this for each of the main characters.

4) For an issues doc, the producer should check the visual footage that corresponds with interesting transcript segments. This will confirm that that powerful transcript statement will work in the film.

5) Decide early whether a single strong story dominates the raw footage or if there are multiple threads of the same quality, a condition that might suggest an episodic plan.

6) Test to see if the chronology of the story will work as a backbone for the film. Assess the visuals that make up the payoff sequence to judge if the field tapes actually contain that strong visual story. In a recent documentary that I edited, I backtracked from a recognizable payoff sequence to find the story. One scene in the film was about an artist up for an industry award. A very able cinematographer doggedly stayed with her every second as she waited in the wings at the awards ceremony. She ended up losing and his video captured her disappointment, her tears, and her early departure from the ceremony. In this case, the story's payoff was solid gold. From there, we backtracked to see if the initial scenes were equally as well documented. They were, so we could cut the final scene first and then returned to the early footage to construct the story's beginning.

7) Evaluate the sequences for consistent style. Perhaps a more capable cinematographer shot outstanding footage while other crews only captured mediocre material.

8) If there was a host, did the director succeed in getting genial and vibrant on-camera work from the personality? If not, there might have to be a decision on reshooting or junking the host format.

9) In an issues doc, begin a search for a sequence or interviewee who might deliver the thesis statement. Decide if every subtopic was covered with consistent thoroughness. Decide if some interviewees will need to be covered with b-roll because of image quality or problems with engagement.

Finally, if the visuals are inconsistent, poorly shot, or uneven, then a decision will have to be made to reshoot.

### Using Selects or Threads to Simplify the Project

To evaluate the visual quality of your clips, have the editors assemble selects or threads of shots and characters. These threads or selects will collect all shots of a certain location, time, event, and so on. The editor can isolate these selects and dub them off to a DVD, giving the producer or writer a chance to review all the possibilities without bothering the editor.

Selects are very helpful on the visual side. A producer can evaluate the 10 different wide shots of the building's exterior. The striking quality (or lack of it) for each shot can indicate whether it will serve as an iconic beauty shot. If one shot jumps out, make notes based on bin name. This will prevent overusing segments that do not have strong visual support.

## STRUCTURAL MODELS

The narrative models in the next section are by no means the only organizational structures that exist. These are generic outlines that represent select traditional approaches to the documentary. We encourage filmmakers to experiment and to find exciting innovative ways to arrange the powerful elements of their field material.

### Short Documentaries Under 12 Minutes

Until the mid-1960s, theatrical or broadcast documentaries were mainly feature length, but producers began to note the power of shorter segments. In 1968, CBS television began a program called *60 Minutes,* composed of short 6- to 12-minute segments. No one gave *60 Minutes* much of a chance and early on, the network kept switching its timeslots, expecting it to go away. Nearly 50 years later, it is still on the network, has won more Emmy awards than any other program, has spawned uncountable copycat programs, and by ratings total is the most successful program in television history. In 2013, it still does its short 6- to 12-minute segments in exactly the same format as it did in 1968. How can it get away with staying the same?

The answer is this: *60 Minutes* found a variety of structures for the short documentary that worked. It built these correspondent-hosted magazine segments, as they called them, around single topics in current events, international politics, unusual locations, or celebrities in the arts. It hired an army of producers who researched the topics, found the B-roll, and even conducted most interviews. It then brought the on-camera reporters in during the last week to do the key interviews and wraparound standups and voice the narration. It didn't compromise on production quality or equipment.

What can we learn from *60 Minutes*? After all, not all short docs will be narrated and, in fact, most won't. The key lesson is this: A single, concentrated topic, presented with uncompromising film work, beginning with your most engaging video and focused on a single controversy, character, or challenge, will be successful.

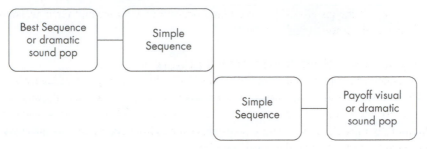

**Figure 12.1** Short-form documentaries thrive in innovative formats but usually force the most striking visuals to the forefront.

Here are some lessons from their work.

1) Short documentary pieces can offer clever and sometimes experimental nonlinear styles, but they still should be focused on well-chosen visual stories. Legendary *60 Minutes* producer Don Hewitt was once bitterly criticized for a hidden-camera investigation of a cancer clinic. He responded that the hidden-camera footage was valuable because television was a visual medium and people believed what they saw more than what they were told. He said there was no other way to document it.

2) Don't hold back. Lead with your most engaging visuals. When structuring the short documentary, it is absolutely critical to assess what engaging video you have and how this will draw the viewer into the story. For the short format, always, if at all possible, move your golden moments to the front. After that, you can begin an interplay of nat sound sequences, interview segments, and archival.

3) Keep any on-camera talking heads short and to the point. Unless the topic is a portrait or character study, long talking heads will break up the rhythm of the piece. Keep them concise and focused. Use active rather than sit-down interviews.

4) Don't rely on music to carry the piece. The *60 Minutes* short docs use music with great care. An overpowering music bed under the story will distract from the high quality of your video work.

5) Be innovative. The short magazine format allows for more nonlinear structure. Although an overall dramatic arc is nice, it isn't always necessary for the short doc.

6) Avoid forcing your short doc into a prescribed TRT. Instead, cut the short doc for what it is worth. Producers working on 30-, 60-, or 90-minute documentaries are often forced into widening the topic and extending production to fill those time periods; you don't have to do that.

### Longer Traditional Documentaries: 30–90 Minutes
#### *A Thesis First Model for Issue or Informational Docs*

Most journalistic or issues documentaries are deductive, starting with a powerful thesis clearly outlined at the beginning and followed by sequences and authoritative

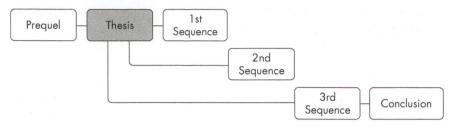

**Figure 12.2** The thesis first deductive model tells the viewer what's coming and then backs it up with support from authorities and sequences.

interviews that offer support for the argument. Good examples can be seen in the style of most PBS *Frontline* docs.

The thesis statement does not have to be spoken by a narrator but might be developed in a number of ways. However you do this, the audience will know what is coming.

The film's topic statement could be in the title, such as *Harvest of Shame,* or *Who Killed the Electric Car.* It could be expressed in narration spoken by a host: "Tonight we will tell you a story about conspiracy at the highest levels," in skillfully produced intertitles or by leading the prequel with a key interviewee's short, punchy statement that "Global warming is the most pressing problem facing humans today." Whatever mode is used to deliver the thesis is almost unimportant; in this type of documentary, the audience knows what's coming for the rest of the running time. Viewers then expect a rhetorical exposition of effect and cause and solid support for the thesis from the array of experts, witnesses, sequences, and B-roll. They might also expect to hear counteropinions from experts making the case for opponents of the topic.

In many ways, the solemnity of an issue can tempt the producer to veer from the documentary's visual storytelling power and construct a program that resembles an argument that might be better presented on a printed page. Critics call this "complain and explain" documentary or the "parade of talking heads."

We caution that creativity and storytelling are needed for issues, science, and historical docs. Be extremely vigilant about basing the entire program on a cavalcade of bites from talking heads interspersed with formula B-roll illustration segments. Also, be cautious that one or two interviewees don't reappear too many times in the structure.

### The Inductive Model Unfolds and Tantalizes without a Thesis Statement

The sampling model is the opposite of the deductive model. It is inductive and most suited to the storytelling power of narrative genres like the journey or walled city documentary. For this design, the producer avoids any thesis statement and instead opens with a series of fascinating sequences that capture the viewers and slowly draw them into a compelling story.

The purest sampling structure is observational—with no hint of a thesis at the beginning, no foreshadowing, no narration, and no conclusions at the end. It offers the viewers an open text; they can draw whatever conclusions they wish.

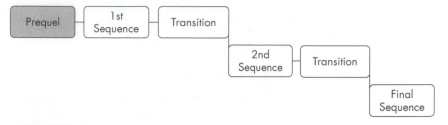

**Figure 12.3** The inductive model presents episodic sequences without telling the audience what the documentary's thesis is about.

To see a good example of this, watch any of the great Frederick Wiseman's studies of American institutions, films such as *High School, Titticut Follies, Welfare, Model,* or *Central Park.* Hidden behind nonengaging titles are fascinating sequences.

Many docs use a hybrid sampling model, engaging the viewers with strong sequences but also interjecting foreshadowing about the nature of a journey by slipping in carefully constructed visual sequences such as getting on a train, starting a campaign, or setting off on a walk.

The foreshadowing might be expressed in a bold manner, with an on-camera host opening the program by saying, "Will the researchers ever find a cure?" Or the key character in a journey doc might narrate in a voiceover saying, "I was returning to my father's homeland to find out if that culture still exists." In whatever form you choose, the foreshadowing sets out the path for the drama in your documentary.

This can be even more subtle when the foreshadowing is done with understated hints, obscure visual clues, or a short bite from a less prominent character who says, "Oh yeah, and by the way, whoever wins the Oscar for best film has reached the top."

In my documentary on Mexican masked wrestlers, *Que Viva La Lucha,* one foreshadowing clue came when the main character offhandedly mentioned he hoped to someday wrestle in Japan. The concluding documentary scenes were of his matches in Japan.

At the end of the feature-length *Buena Vista Social Club,* some of the Cuban musicians fly to New York to play at Carnegie Hall, a goal mentioned obliquely earlier in the film.

In *Wild Parrots of Telegraph Hill,* director Judy Irving follows the travails of a man who becomes caretaker and advocate for a flock of wild birds that roost in a densely urban neighborhood. The sequences of the birds and the caretaker's living quarters are enough to encourage interest. The foreshadowing leaves no doubt that the birds' survival is in danger and of great concern. Finally, as a treat, director Irving delivered a second surprise about the caretaker at the end without foreshadowing. We won't reveal that one; you'll have to see the film.

### Using the Three-Act Model Derived from the Theater
For profiles, biographies, or complex issues, the theater model gives the producer more options. It uses a structure of basic storytelling honed over years by dramatists tussling with the problem of keeping an audience's focus on a multidimensional

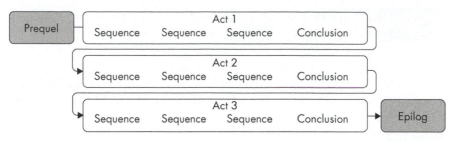

**Figure 12.4** The theatrical drama model. Each act or segment contains its own parade of sequences, conflicts, and conclusions as the story progresses.

story. To do this, subdivide segments of the hour running time into acts. Within each act, there is an opportunity to develop scenes and shorter dramatic arcs.

The classic theater design, then, begins with an opening gambit called the prequel that is followed by three acts with scenes and individual dramatic arcs that provide a rising or falling tension within each scene. It ends with a strong payoff and then the epilogue.

The key to this theatrical structure is its ability to provide tension or a shortened dramatic arc within each act or major segment of the doc. This works well in stories with multiple strong characters who are facing challenges, in biographies that stretch over extended periods of time, or in issues docs that have multiple subissues.

### An Interwoven or Parallel Sequences Approach

Sometimes, when the most intriguing sequences are not central to the film, a more intricately layered model can be used to open the work. In this case, a feature-length doc might launch with three or four sequences running in parallel and intercut together with abrupt transitions, moving like dimensions in a symphony, some rapid and loud, and others soft, slow, and playful. All are united by an underlying melodic line (the character or protagonist) who appears and reappears in various sequences when the switch is made from one to another.

Consider this model if there are four or five extremely powerful but totally separate sequences that engage the viewer, need little explanation, and share characters or events common to all.

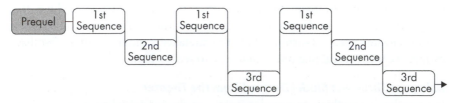

**Figure 12.5** The multithreaded opening of *Buena Vista Social Club*, directed by Wim Wenders, begins with a golden moment, then intercuts in parallel fashion, sequences including topic history (Seq 1), a concert (Seq 2) and a recording session (Seq 3).

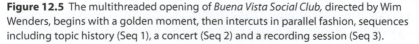

For an example, look at the opening sequences of *Buena Vista Social Club*. It begins with the interwoven sequences, but as the story progresses, it settles into a series of musician profiles that leads to a payoff when the troupe ships off to New York to play a memorable Carnegie Hall concert.

A word of caution: The interwoven multithreaded doc is hard to maintain for an hour, so in most cases, it is used for effect at the beginning and is abandoned for the body of the program.

### Lead with Your Strongest Sequences

What if the overall organizing structure is not immediately evident in the first rough assembly after production has ended? What if the payoff and challenge that inspired the original idea never really developed? This happens all the time and it demands adaptation.

The producer and editor should begin testing new schemes by making rough assemblies of the first rough cut sequences, the new framework to a subtle but yet unrecognized storyline. Perhaps everything in the documentary happened over the course of a day or a week, during several months in winter, or before the monsoons came.

Producer Catherine De Santis discovered a solution when finishing *I Do,* her doc on couples, marriage, and commitment. She was struggling with a story structure that wasn't working. The rough cuts didn't flow; she was staring at a collection of unconnected sequences looking for a unifying force. On the night before a fine cut was due for a screening, she took a chance and began attaching the sequences to a series of folksy observations dispensed by a single character, a veteran city hall marriage license clerk. It clicked, and with the clerk as the backbone, the story tumbled out.

## PAPER EDITS

### One Way to See the Structure

When the organizing schema is starting to jell, you might want to try a paper edit. This is the documentarian's version of the storyboard after the fact.

Producers need to find a visual organizing strategy for this. Start by reviewing the transcripts of your interview segments (whether they are formal, sit-down interviews or longer exchanges in the field) and isolating the segments that reveal important points of the story. Then you can start assembling these on a blank computer page, inserting the different topical bites into some order. Or, you can use the old way (which still works), which involves cutting the most powerful bites out of transcript copies and laying them on a blank table. I like the table because you can see more geography at one time.

Arrange the scenes first and then attach sequences to each scene. Put them in any order that makes a modicum of sense and don't worry; you'll be moving them around as you seek a structure.

After that is done, begin attaching the most powerful and telling sound bites with particular sequences. Don't stop until everything has a place.

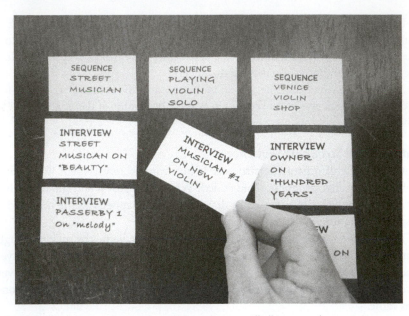

**Figure 12.6** For some, using cards, a tablet or laptop will allow a producer to move around scenes and sequences and visualize the story flow.

This paper edit layout provides a visual depiction of how the documentary might flow. It might also reveal if there are enough sequences to structure the doc and how all this fits into the projected TRT. To do this, give each sequence a ball-park estimate on time. One sequence, perhaps at a community meeting, might have enough natural sound segments and discussion to last for 4:30. Another sequence with interns might top out at 1:30. Continue doing this until the new plan fills approximately one and a half times your goal for the project.

Now, evaluate how these placements reflect the story line or dramatic arc that is in your head. Move these parts around until you see a natural unity, a narrative that will bind all these parts together. In our example, because the overall framework is no longer the mural chronology, you might shift to the community's concern and fight for its public space. Once that is complete, transfer the parts and their flow to a written document and you have the basic beginnings of a script.

### An Editor's Point of View on the Paper Edit

A producer's efforts to prepare a paper edit can greatly assist in post. Editor Maureen Gosling explains how this works.

> Recently, I edited a film for a young director. She had done a lot of work already, and so it made my job easier. She had already done paper edits and she had digitized parts that she had wanted from all this footage she had shot over a year, And she gave me that. And it had references to the footage so I could just look in the bin but she told me about and I would go to the bin and cut it in. So, we started

with her paper cut and we went from there. And usually, when it's on paper, it doesn't work the first time. Then I worked with the material and then she would come back and give me feedback and it just kept going back and forth and it kept getting more refined as we went along.

## IF A SCRIPT IS NEEDED

Documentary producers, you could say, are gunslingers: They shoot first and ask questions later.

In narrative fiction filmmaking, there is always a script before shooting. In documentary, there seldom is a script. In fact, some documentaries end up at festivals or on DVD without ever having a formal script. If needed, it can be transcribed later.

Producer Ellen Bruno's own approach mirrors this strategy. She calls it making films from the heart.

> What I basically do is go around and collect the images and situations that are resonating with me and which I think have got to contribute to the telling of a particular story because it is part of my experience and is touching me deeply.
>
> So what I do is collect experiences, collect sounds collect rhythms. It could be the pouring of tea in a little tea shop in Burma and I see it every day 10 times a day and it is one of the simple rhythms of daily life and it takes on a significance for me. And so, I go and collect this material and take it back to the edit room and so that's where the real challenge is in the sense of making it into some sense of something whole.

She said she might take anywhere from three months to a year to craft the story.

However, there are some documentary modes that lend themselves to pre-scripting. In science, historical, or issues films, scripts can be useful. Investigative producer Jon Dann, who usually works under contract with a network program series, says scratching out an early script saves him time that might be wasted during the latter production. "The complexity of doing an investigative story is so labor intensive that you wind up going through so many dendrites that you can eat up your time . . . but you almost want to create your structure from the very beginning. I would actually start writing at the beginning . . . because if you don't, you spend a huge amount of time getting details and information that are not central to your story." Dann says that an initial script is only a jumping-off point and that it always changes as he and the editors collaborate through a series of rough cuts.

Dann's scripting is a means of organizing his ideas and controlling the scope of the production shoots. Like many producers, he understands that there is no clean transition between production and postproduction. Editing often begins during production when it can delve into complexities and expose missing elements, which in turn prompts more production shoots or pickups. In the documentary *Soldiers of Conscience,* produced by Gary Weimberg and Catherine Ryan, the editing-production-editing-production cycle continued for over a year.

### Working with a Script Allows a Scratch Track

If the basic format for the film was an on-camera hosted program and it was shot that way, then the producer might have been writing scripts all along. A major portion of the story flow has been recorded as the field production before the editing starts. After the paper edit, it's time to start writing a narration script for the host to fill in between the on-camera segments. The editor will surely want this as he or she begins cutting.

If there is no on-camera and only off-screen narration, the first step is to review the selects with the editors. The story is only as good as the visual sequences and B-roll, whether the information is revealed through characters' bites or the narration. If production was shortened due to scheduling or funding problems, the program might be thin on field material.

Let the editors work on crucial sequences first and then begin a rough assembly. Place crucial pieces of natural sound into the mix. Wait to write narration until after a review of the rough assembly.

## WRITING FOR THE EAR

### Your Script Will Be Spoken, Not Read

This is particularly important. This script is for conversational speech and not for the eye. The script has to complement visuals, not describe them, and must fit time-wise into the segments of visuals. The prose sentence structure learned in school will not work. Regular print text is not going to work. Even breezy magazine-style writing will not work. Think dialog. Think that viewers will be focused on the visuals and might not even hear the narration.

### Scripts for the Ear and for Video Support

Scripts are written to support rough cuts. The writer needs to assess how much information the video and natural audio are already providing and how much of the story is told without any narration. The script shouldn't describe to the audience what they are seeing. Instead, the writer is adding bits of information outside the visual/audio sequences. The short sentence structure and dialog phrasing is there only to support the video.

Do not write continuous narration, called wall-to-wall in the business. Breathing spaces are needed in between the short bursts to allow the audience to absorb the material; otherwise, the constant barrage of facts can run counter to your purpose.

Narrators will speak what you write. If a print writer is hired to do the script, this can cause problems, as editor Maureen Gosling recounts about the narration she and Les Blank sought for *Burden of Dreams.*

> We needed to explain things for which we didn't have visuals. That was an interesting process because we had a writer who was a very good print journalist and writer but he had never written narration before and it was a challenge for him because he would come up with the elegant statements . . . but they were tongue twisters for a narrator because they had too much alliteration . . . or too poetic. He was constantly writing it for himself and not for the film, and I was telling him,

"Look, it has to fit in here . . . in this spot." Once in a while, I could adjust the film to his narration because it gave me an idea, but he was trying to write it as a nice piece of writing without realizing that it had to fit, timing wise and within reason . . . and content-wise in that spot.

## Script Mechanics

There are many different looks in script design. Some are elaborate and others are sketchy but the crucial requirement is that the all script parts can be traced to the original location of material.

The script example is only one of many and puts the visual cues on the left and the audio text on the right (see example that follows). The visuals can have time code or bin location and the soundbites need a time code for quick identification. We suggest that the producer, the writer, and the editor pick a format that works and use it consistently.

Narration is aimed at the ears, not the eyes. Here are some guides to writing for the ear.

- Before you start, listen carefully to narrated documentaries you admire.
- Mimic the short sentences, pauses, and phrasing.
- Write short or compound declarative sentences.
- Write in the active voice. Put whoever does the action before the verb. This makes for more powerful sentences.

---

| | |
|---|---|
| WS of room (01:06:25:10) | THE ART COMMISSIONERS KNEW THIS TUESDAY MEETING WAS GOING TO BE UNUSUAL. |
| SEQ OF CROWD GATHERING :05 | **(NAT SOT OF CROWD)** |
| CUS of crowd | SUPPORTERS AND OPPONENTS OF THE CONTROVERSIAL MURAL HAD TURNED OUT. . . SPOILING FOR A SHOWDOWN. |
| MS of artist at mic | . . . AND ARTIST DAN ORNATO'S TURN TO SPEAK SET IT OFF. |
| Use sequence of battle (01:12:14:10) | **(NAT SOUND OF RUCKUS)** |
| BITE OF ARTIST (01:21:14:10) USED AS VOICE UNDER | **"I don't expect these right wing fascists to understand true art. they want their precious walls to be blank."** |
| MS of cops | AFTER 30 MINUTES. . . THE POLICE HAD RESTORED ORDER. |
| MS & CUS of people leaving :10 | **(NAT SOT OF CROWD)** |
| (01:14:13:10) | BUT NOTHING WAS ACCOMPLISHED. SO, ADJOURNED. |

---

**Figure 12.7** Example of one script format. There are many ways to show the text versus video.

Example:
- Weaker (Passive voice): The meeting was disrupted by the protestors.
- Better (Active voice): The protestors disrupted the meeting.

- Use simple, precise verbs and adjectives. Skip multisyllabic words designed to impress the audience.
- Eliminate introductory phrases, clauses, and nested phrases.
- Let the video tell part of the story. Watch the sequences before you write each segment.
- Don't describe. Explain!
- Test your script by recording scratch tracks and playing that against the video. Keep repeating this process until you have the effective narration to enrich the program and add clarity.

### Options for Adding Information to Nonnarrated Documentaries

Many documentary makers are determined to avoid the unseen narrator, the so-called Voice of God narration. This can be done in simple ways.

One is to use intertitles or text that flashes on and off the screen against a black background. Suppose some complex cultural or historical information needs introduction. Intertitles can easily be added to the film and faded in and out. Their drawback is that they change the style and pacing of the film (see Figure 12.8).

There are certain guidelines for intertitles. They should be short, have no more than 20 characters across (this makes them large enough on the screen), and not use more than six lines. Also, there is some graphic sense to using a reveal, where a second line of an intertitle is added and the first remains.

## USING DIRECTED VOICE-UNDER INTERVIEWS TO AVOID NARRATION

Another solution to avoiding narration is to string together parts of interviews that express the story line or information. A caution here is that much of the natural sound on the footage has background noise mixed in with speech. When played as voice under other visuals, it can be jarring.

A better solution is to enlist an interviewee to provide exact explanations of complex visuals and then use it as voice under visuals. Start by cutting the sequence

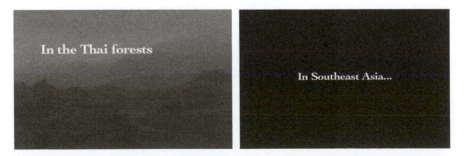

**Figure 12.8** Intertitles can be placed over simple visuals or isolated on a single color frame.

that needs an explanation. Then, request an interview with one of your documentary's characters who has a good screen presence or voice. By showing this person the edited sequence and leading him or her with designed questions, a producer can record an impromptu narration track.

How does this work? When Indian-born filmmaker Ananda Rahti wanted to describe the intricate cultural background for the symbols of a Sikh wedding ceremony, she avoided a narrator by cutting the sequences, then showing them to the bride's sister, who talked at length about the wedding and the meaning of the customs. Her completely informal voice became an unstructured narration with a natural feeling to it. As for the edit, it was precise and complete and easy to layback against the pictures.

## SUMMARY

The key to finding a story arc for the film is to stay conscious of what is and what isn't in the footage. Then begin the paper edit, work with the editor on the major sequences, take that to a rough assembly, and continually adjust the sequences if they seem bulky or out of order. Depending on the documentary's genre and style, a narration, subtitles, or voice under might be needed to explain certain sequences.

### Shaping Your Skills

1. Pick a major documentary and watch it twice. During the second viewing, outline the major tensions, characters, payoffs, and dramatic arcs the producer used to maintain the story flow. Describe how the process used is either a deductive or inductive storytelling technique and whether or not it worked.
2. Write a practice narration. Read it onto a recorder. Play it back and criticize the sentence structure if it sounds like prose. Then redo the copy and enlist a volunteer to read the corrected copy. Compare the narration for style and effectiveness.

# CHAPTER 13

# Editing the Documentary

Your footage becomes your world and the footage becomes
where you are getting your ideas from.

EDITOR MAUREEN GOSLING

Editing is not a science, it's an art; so there are many different approaches to this final segment of the documentary journey. Even with a script, editing a major documentary is a bit like assembling a 1,000-piece puzzle from 10,000 random parts without any initial idea what the final picture will look like. The editor must select the elements that bring energy to the story and exclude the ones that do not belong.

This is an intellectual, critical, and creative process. Experienced editor Maureen Gosling suggests: "I think that it is as complex as building a freeway or a building . . . you know figuring out all the little pieces, because in a building you have to think about the plumbing, the electricity, the materials . . . everything has to fit together . . . and making a film is like that. It's very complicated."

This chapter offers real-world organizational examples, suggestions, editing shortcuts, and handy techniques to sidestep pitfalls. The goal is to keep you sane while you edit a gem of a documentary.

## GLOSSARY

**Audio post**  The work done on the audio tracks after picture lock has been reached. For post, the tracks are separated from the video to upgrade the fidelity, amplitude, transitions, and clarity. They are then resynched to the video. Also known as sweetening.

**Bins**  Organized subcategories of clips in editing programs.

**Fine cut**  A second-to-last edited version of the program that has all of the graphics, dialog, and music.

**Match cut**  An edit that joins clips from different camera shots that are similar enough to give the appearance of continuous action.

**Online**  The master edited version, complete with all graphics, sound sweetening, color corrections, closed captioning, and adjustments for technical parameters. The online master is used for distribution dubs.

**Picture lock**  The final version of the edit before the audio is stripped off for post and the color correction is applied.

**Rough assembly**  The first combination of roughly edited sequences and other elements to evaluate the flow along the expected dramatic arc of the storyline. Has no narration.

**Workflow**  The most efficient method of integrating various formats into the post process without disrupting editing.

## THE EDITOR'S WORLD

In many cases, the editor has not been on the location shoots, so the visuals arriving in the edit room on the field clips become all he or she knows of the story. In the feature-length documentary *Detropia,* the editor faced a mountain of field material—500 hours of shooting. Co-producer Rachel Grady said they had a monumental challenge. "We didn't have a script. The editing room is where the story was written."

## THE RELATIONSHIP BETWEEN THE PRODUCER AND THE EDITOR

The editor is responsible for the look, feel, and visceral sense of the documentary. He or she will assemble pleasing combinations of various shots, hone the flow of sequences, add symmetry to the pace of ideas, manage the audio and video workflow, and produce constantly improving versions on schedule.

The working relationship between the editor and the producer should be respectful; otherwise, there will be a disaster. Exactly how much creative control the editor is given in shot selection and content trimming is the issue that must be discussed prior to any cutting. Does the editor have the freedom to experiment with sequences? Does the producer expect to be sitting behind the editor for the entire edit? Will associates be brought into the edit room for decision making? Does the producer want to do some hands-on editing?

I began one project in which procedures were not settled beforehand. On the first day, the producer, his associate, and his partner all showed up in the edit room to sit behind me. As I attempted to show some of the sequences already in progress, the producer announced that I shouldn't bother and that I was to restart the cutting right then and there, and that each person in the room would comment and make suggestions shot by shot. Four people, two of whom had not seen the logged video, suddenly were making decisions about each shot. This did not last long.

## THE SIGNIFICANT MOMENTS

Editors are always combing the field video for standout segments and sequences. Editor Gosling says that during the initial process of analyzing the video material, "the significant moments are easier to find than the structure. It becomes evident when your images look great . . . when a person is very expressive and says a meaningful point concisely with clarity and emotion . . . or when your camera person captures a built-in sequence in camera to give a sense of being there. The most challenging aspect is that you have the story but finding the structure is the real challenge and it is both a rational and intuitive process."

## THE NEED FOR A FRAMEWORK

Every editor creates interior sequences while searching, with the producer, for the overlying dramatic arc. On my documentary *Free From Babylon* based on a naturalist and self-made alternative architect "Treehouse Joe," the documentary

**Figure 13.1** *Free From Babylon*'s principal character, Treehouse Joe, built a number of unique structures.

opens with a shot inside a circular round clay house under construction. That introductory shot defined the circular structure that would carry through the entire documentary.

From there I chose to cut to his three previous architectural experiments, all of which were created with recycled materials: a cabin, the treehouse, and a four-story pagoda. Each of these is interwoven with Treehouse Joe's personal story and his philosophy that celebrates the collection of ideas in the same manner Joe collected materials to recycle. At the end of the documentary the viewer completes the circle by being brought back to the present experimental building in the first images, but now the sequences are showing the completion of the clay house. This unusual structure became clear after a series of rough cut versions, and required deleting an entire interesting scene that did not quite fit into the story.

Maureen Gosling uncovered an interesting association when she edited producer Les Blank's *Sprout Wings and Fly* on a fiddle player from Appalachia, Tommy Jarrell.

> I noticed in the footage that all of the elements were represented. Earth. Wind. Fire. Air. It's not something that everyone would notice, but because it is such a universal paradigm—symbol . . . that theoretically it should work. So, instead of ending with death, I started with death. And he's sitting in a cemetery and he's playing a song and he's telling a story about this old guy cutting his toe off . . . and there's humor, too. But it immediately talks about the issue of death with this older person. Then the next step is water . . . and it totally fits with he's making moonshine and they go to a stream and it is beautiful and he's pointing out how clear the water is in this creek. And he's talking about the connection of making moonshine and making music and then he starts to play music that sounds like water. And it fits perfectly. And it was a banjo . . . and it was this totally beautiful lilting song and it totally fit and then it transitioned to nature and to some cherries on a tree and then next thing you know, we are talking about love and fire and so the fire stuff starts to come in and so the end is kind of cathartic and there's young dancers dancing. They are clog dancers and they are very energetic. And he plays this incredible song—John Brown Dreamed That the Devil Was Dead— and it was totally a transcendent song and it took you up and so the film starts with this earthy sort of thing and at the end, there's this wonderful light release. And it worked. It worked.

### Consider the Viewer a Newcomer to the Story

Editors are restrained by other factors in choosing structures. They must consider that the viewer is seeing the story for the first time, a realization that helps dictate the appearance order of elements so that they make sense. Maureen Gosling says that in her *Blossoms of Fire* documentary on Zapotec culture in the town of Juchitan, Mexico "one of the topics that I thought needed to come later was the whole acceptance of gays and lesbians in Juchitan, because once you get to know the town, then you can talk about that. Because if they came too early, then some people may not want to keep watching . . . it was a pretty provocative part of the film and I wanted to save it, to build up to it."

A similar problem cropped up for Gosling on her new documentary about the life and vision of Arhoolie Records founder Chris Strachwitz and his adventures searching out America's roots music. "He makes connections between Zydeco, Tex-Mex, the Blues and Appalachian music in one sentence. . . . That's his personality. But first you have to know what Blues is . . . you have to know what Cajun is . . . so we have to introduce the topics early and then later on, when he starts talking about the connections, you'll know what it is. Right now, it's kind of this vague thing in my head and then we'll have to try it out to make it work."

### Establish a Style of Editing

Editing is built around shot selection, placement within film grammar, tempo, the use of music, and relationships. Clever editing can hone sequences that trigger strong emotion while delivering information in an artistic manner.

Perfecting the art of editing can take months and years. The subtle artistry in finding the right combinations of wide shots, medium shots, close-ups, or reverses, POVs, and two-shots that express action, relationship, intimacy, or intention is best learned through repeated work and studying how others did it.

Award-winning producer Ellen Bruno edits all of her documentaries. Her approach is very personal and her objective is to process the experience herself so she becomes the conduit. Working at her own pace, it sometimes takes up to one and a half years in the editing stage.

In *Satya: A Prayer for the Enemy,* about the resistance of Tibetan nuns, she creates a poetic multilayered portrait of the spiritual and political inner and outer world of Tibet. "I think my films are political because I'm the vehicle and the way that I process information and the way I am moved and touched by things in this world on a very personal level and a very heart level."

Bruno chooses an editing strategy of longer shots to make her audience pause and think.

> Intimacy can be developed by shot length, too. You know, you draw people in and you say . . . okay, this one isn't going away and you allow people to have a different experience that is not just an image. It could be a person or it could be a piece of nature but whatever it is, you go a bit deeper into it. It becomes a combination of my experience that is coming in and what is going out the other side in this form. So, yes, my experience is very much part of that and of course, everything is filtered through my experience.

Editing styles can add subtle differences to particular films. Some documentaries, especially the *Frontline* series, are based on current events and have an upbeat pacing and narration; others, like the documentaries of Ellen Bruno, are artistic collections of poetic images that tell the story. There is the deliberately paced multihour *Farmers Wife* from David Sutherland, the folksy emotional style of Ken Burns, the edgy films from Barbara Kopple, the thoughtful observational camera of Fred Wiseman, or the skewed, fast-paced MTV *Real World* style of editing. Studying previous documentaries might suggest a style for any particular project. There are few new styles—just new versions of old tunes.

# PREPARATION FOR THE EDIT PROCESS

Editors need to view all of the footage—every single shot. Some prefer to digitize the video themselves and organize it with keywords to be able to access it when is needed. That way they can simultaneously test the footage for technical quality and content. If the sound is bad and the picture is fine, keep the picture and vice versa. If there is a poor-quality image but the ambient sound is interesting, keep it. It's all about potential uses for certain shots.

### The Luxury of an Assistant Editor

An assistant editor, if the budget allows, can free up the editor for more crucial content decisions. The assistant editor should handle mundane operations such as digitizing, logging, reformatting, carrying out logging and bin structures, making global changes to the rough cuts, and running gofer jobs to pick up stock, elements, equipment, sandwiches, and so on.

### Standardize the Workflow

This is the time for the producer and editor to set a standard workflow that will ease the input problems. The workflow must take into account that there might be multiple formats of source material. What will be done with an older $4 \times 3$ format or black-and-white archival video to make it fit it into the $16 \times 9$ screen ratio? What will you do if someone shoots 1080/24p and then borrows a camera and shoots 720/60i and finally buys a new camera that shoots 1080/60p at a bit rate of 80 Mbps? Which machine hardware and which software will be used (Avid, Final Cut, Premiere, or others), including which edition of the software (release 5.1, etc.)?

Consider storage. You might have up to 50 hours of video. Designate which hard drive will be the home base for clips and program changes. Use and maintain backup hard drives. You should resist suggestions to let someone take the backup hard drive and begin working on other edits. Massive incompatibilities will result.

For audio, standardize workflow for stereo or mono recordings, which audio goes on which channel in the timeline, how or if the levels will be changed during digitization, and which audio tracks will be used for narration, music, wild or imported sound, and manufactured foley effects. You also have to isolate two channels exclusively for a rough mix scratch track for the editor. You should also plan on an M & E track that has music and ambient sound but no dialog.

Our current multiplicity of digital formats creates massive confusion if the workflow is not established ahead of time. I edited and co-produced *Deadline Every Second,* a look at international photojournalists, with producer and shooter Ken Kobre. The project started as a short documentary to be used in conjunction with a textbook. Kobre had fascinating access and total cooperation from a major news photo agency and as he wound his way around the world, shooting in six countries, it became apparent we had a dazzling gem of a major film.

Gradually, the project compiled 70 hours of field material, all shot on digital chips and needing conversion to an intermediate format. Ken converted some and sent me the material on hard drives; the others I converted from the chips. It wasn't until well into the two-year project, when doing a rough assembly of sequences, that we discovered he was using an older version of Final Cut Pro and was up-converting to a different intermediate format. That first assembly of the doc caused major compatibility problems. I had to go back and reconvert the material and reedit the sequences.

This was not the only example of our lack of foresight. The digital world re-quires massive storage. I was editing on my laptop. We started out with one exter-nal 2 TB hard drive, which soon blossomed to four 2 TB hard drives, all daisy chained together, along with another 2 TB drive for the edited material. Each drive needed a separate 2 TB drive for backup. During the editing, two of the drives failed completely, necessitating a scramble to find what hadn't been backed up. In the end, we had a total of 12 2 TB hard drives for the project.

My older model laptop looked like a mother sow suckling her piglets. Its on-board memory pushed to the limit, its older processor was working furiously. My desk was covered with the five humming drives, the laptop, and a large viewing screen. If I rearranged any of the cables, things didn't work as well; I didn't dare disassemble the spider web of machines.

The surprise was that it worked. I cut a complex hour documentary with six video tracks and 15 audio tracks on the tiny machine. Once it had gone to the postproduction lab for color correction and audio post and the fixes had been reat-tached, *Deadline Every Second* became QuickTime file that went to other labs to build HDCAM U.S. and European masters. It has played on American, European, and Australian broadcast systems, and has been shown in London, Paris, and Athens, as well as major U.S. cities.

At that point, I liberated the laptop from its prison.

## Set Deadlines and Conditions

Everyone needs to agree that a final online with full color correction and audio post must be ready on a specific date. Without this time-certain nature, edits seem to go on forever, involving everyone in the project for extended periods of time.

The drop-dead date is usually when you have to turn over a master to a festi-val, distributor, or duplicator. Don't forget to factor in the color correction that might take a week and the audio post that might take weeks or a month.

Be realistic about how long this edit will take. If it's a feature-length project and goes through a number of rough cuts, the edits and reedits might extend over a year. Pressure mounts and the working days get longer as the deadlines near. It is important to set humane work schedules ahead of time. Creativity might drop off if editors have to work through weekends and holidays. Clear agreement on these issues will prevent bad feelings later.

### Remember There Will Be Rough Cut Screenings

Occasionally, the producer needs to show rough cuts to a small audience of major funders, possible distributors, or future contributors. Editors need some time to clean up the rough versions because people outside the industry do not understand messy cuts, dips to black, ill-mixed audio, or stuttering transitions.

## BEGINNING POST

While crews are still gathering video in the field, the editor can start roughing out sequences based on completed events.

This early beginning has its benefits. If these sequences need additional video, the editor can write out a shopping list. Early work on the sequences can also benefit the producer. The editor might find a key segment or interview to be unusually weak and lacking any visceral power. This might conflict with the producer's initial plans to give the underwhelming segment a feature position in the program.

Discovering deficiencies might also allow the producer to reverse course and spend the remaining production budget going in a new direction. During production of *Reading Between the Rhymes,* a documentary on hip-hop culture in education, the postproduction team advised the producer that the footage was suffering from a regional focus. The producer, with little money and only two weeks of production time still available, made a decision to fly the crew 3,000 miles to a national hip-hop gathering, a tactic that resulted in powerful new sequences and gave the program a much needed national scope.

### The First Moments

The first moments of post can be overwhelming. Maureen Gosling says if you wade in and make some progress that the patterns will begin to appear.

> We started out with 200 hours on this film and we cut it down to 25 and now we are going to cut that in half. And now the cream is starting to rise. We are starting to get the good stuff and we are starting to make sequences and then groups of sequences are starting to work with each other and that is going to suggest modules or beads on the necklace and start thinking that this would be good in the middle of the film or this would be good to start the film because it introduces this character or this is a great ending.

### Transcripts

As we mentioned earlier, make transcripts of all or at least the important sound footage as soon as possible. When there are 50 hours plus of field video, it is easy to lose track of where the good interview segments are hidden. Not having transcripts can easily delay postproduction for weeks.

Sending out tapes to a transcription service can be expensive (you pay by the page). If you elect to do the transcripts yourself, it takes about six times real time per hour of video. So, for that one-hour interview, you'll spend six hours transcribing. No kidding. Be forewarned.

A word of caution: Exciting transcripts don't necessarily translate into exciting visuals or golden moments. All you get in the transcript is a clue to the content. The producer should ask the editor to put the chosen bites into selects or threads for viewing. Seeing is believing.

## Logs

Daily production reviews have various names: the rushes, the dailies, or the field tapes. Watching them immediately gives you a vague sense if something is missing and should be reshot. However, there is no substitute for logging shots.

Logging each clip (shot) with its time code start, an organized name, short description, and a rating (great, okay, poor, no good, shaky, dark, etc.) is a terrific idea. The name given to each shot will be critical when sorting the clips to find a particular one from a particular shooting day or location.

There are many different procedures for logging. Some editors use photocopied sheets and write in longhand. I've found using a laptop makes the results easier to read. Some logs are done from window dubs of the master field recordings and some are done after editors have made subclips of longer field tapes.

## Bins and Clips

Bins are collections of clips that relate to each other. There is no need to set up all the bin names before you start logging, just general ones. I've found that new sub-bin categories come to mind as you log. For instance, in a program that featured a story on media production, we started with a bin called "office" that contained noncritical general office interior shots. But we found 60 to 80 clips in that, which is too many to sort through handily. So we subdivided the "office" bin into "people" and "details" depending on whether someone appeared in the shots, and then subdivided the people into key characters and minor players. It's common to repeat people under thematic bins, and their own interview as a way to access subjects.

We also had an original bin "ext" for exteriors of the building. But we eventually made up a sub-bin within "ext" labeled "ext-ext" for shots that included nearby buildings shot through the windows. Within that sub-bin, we had another sub-bin for "morn" and "night" for the mood these shots evoked.

The individual clip names have to be obvious to the editor and producer. In a recent edit job, we had 50 field tapes of 40 minutes each shot over a five-day period by two camera persons, for a total of more than 1,400 individual clips. These included 10 major interviews, the activities of perhaps 20 characters that appeared at different times during the five days, plus all extraneous cutaways, exteriors, and general office background shots. It took one solid week to finish the job.

Be careful that your clip naming methods are organized. Software will sort alphabetically, so if you want something to pop up first, give it a name that starts with an "a." On this project, because all the field tapes were shot with identical hour time code identifiers, we noted time code in only minutes and seconds. To identify a particular tape, we embedded a notation in each clip name with the date shot and cassette # for that day.

The initial word is crucial. We named each shot generally by event "full staff meet" or character initials "RC," followed by a shot description, then the date and source (21#2 represents the second chip shot on the 21st), then an abbreviation to indicate the camera view, notations of trouble or quality problems, and finally a rating, for which I used the "+" key (+ meant a good shot; +++++ meant a memorable shot). Using this scheme, we would have a clip name that looked like this.

04:06 SF discuss in office with RC, 17#2, strong video on WS

If there was no major character in the shot, the event or location became the name.

04:05 Tues Meet . . . discuss deadlines, 18#5 . . . WS (low audio)

With this organization, I could pull this shot and know when it was recorded (at the Tuesday meeting), what was happening (they were discussing deadlines), what field source it was on (on source chip 18 of the fifth day), what kind of a shot it was (wide shot), and that the audio was low enough to note.

The assistant editor, if there is one, should be in charge of organizing the schema for the logging and for making these into quickly accessible documents. Although most of the searching is done on the video screens, the logs should be printed and put into a three-ring binder. I've seen different editors use colors, marked binders, or word search computer files for organization.

## PROJECTS WITH SCRIPTS

On some projects, there might be a script. If it is a hosted and narrated doc, then the editor's job should be much easier. There is a plan and you can concentrate on the sequences and illustrative B-roll. However, if the script is too specific, editors like Maureen Gosling get restive.

> I felt this was going to be paint by number but then so I told him (the producer) what I wanted to do before I followed the script. And so, he wasn't used to doing it that way. And he found there was a way to combine our two styles. At the beginning it was a bit dicey but then we found a way to work together and so when he did give me a script, it felt kind of nice because it felt like I had something to start with and then I could take off from there.

For producers working on a narrated doc without a host, it becomes a bit more difficult. Someone on the edit team will have to record a scratch track of the first version of the script. The editor also will need a temp music track to set the tempo for certain scenes. This will allow you to put together sequences and lay shots in a rhythm against the rise and fall of the narrator's voice.

## PROJECTS WITHOUT SCRIPTS

Cutting a documentary without a script is the norm and not unusual. Many documentaries evolve as the producer and editor experiment with shot placement and position in sequences and strong bites.

When working without a script, the editor might start cutting key sequences. These will give a sense of where the strengths might be. Daily communication is important. Occasionally, when the editor isn't aware of what the producer is thinking, the editor might spend hours cutting a sequence that the producer would never use in a million years. Other times, the producer will ask that sequences be recut and reorganized over and over again. In this kind of cutting, it is wise to save each day's edition of the timeline as a separate file, so it is always easy to return to what you had in the past.

This nonscripted editing works best if the story is centered on the quality of the natural sequences, such as in the journey documentary. For current events or science documentaries that are constructed around rhetorical arguments or evidence-supported theses, it works better to have a solid guideline.

In projects without scripts, there must be more constant discussions between producer and editor. I've witnessed or been involved in many tortured arguments about which interview segment is strong enough to displace the others, or which sequence carries the story. I've even seen an argument that evolved into an impromptu wrestling match between a producer and editor over the use of certain shots in the sequence (they went back to editing after we pulled them apart).

## SHOT SELECTION

An editor must look at every shot and evaluate every clip. Editing begins with careful selection of these units. From a field tape that gives you 10 wide shots of an outdoor location, just three seconds of one will be the best. What makes one better than the other? The choice clip might be better framed, have more coherent colors, have clearer audio, be more stable, or have compelling action within it. Some will automatically stand out, but in other cases, the differences might be subtle.

Editors working with a cinematographer who is skilled and artistic and knows his or her trade will have an easier task.

### Find the Establisher to Open the Sequence

Build around the purpose of this sequence. Maybe it is to transport the viewer from one point to another. Or to demonstrate the humanity of a character. Or to provide evidence for a rhetorical argument. Or just to provide a cutaway from a particularly boring interview.

Knowing the use will allow you to choose an appropriate establishing shot. The establishing shot opens the sequence. Traditionally it was a wide shot but now almost any shot that sets the tone, whether wide or close-up, will work.

### Tempos and Rhythms

The length and placement of shots establishes a tempo for the sequence. If there is no music bed or spoken segment to cut against, then the rate of cuts must have some inherent logic. History and archival material are cut more slowly, stories on art might linger over the shots, journey docs might have a tempo from the mode of transport, and band biographies might mirror their music beat.

If there will be a score, this is the time to put in temp music. Get the composer to fabricate some on simple instruments to set up rhythms for the editor.

### Don't Use B-Roll as "Wallpaper"

To be effective, true B-roll is selected to illustrate narration or the voice of an interviewee. These images are very specific to the words spoken. As the speaker discusses an event, time, process, thought, or abstraction, the rise and fall of his or her voice suggests the visual cuts. Cutting B-roll without knowing the length of the spoken sentences can be artistically rewarding but might mean you'll recut it later when you have a specific timeline or confirmed audio. As such, save the B-roll segments for later.

The danger is to simply cover the shots to avoid staying on a speaker's face. By doing this, you are using wallpaper, a derogatory term describing the random inclusion of unrelated video to cover timeline space. Wallpaper shots often lead to confusion and are an insult to your audience.

### Cut the Prequel Last

Don't cut the all-important opening sequence, often called the prequel, until you are very near the fine cut stage. Building the prequel works best when the editor has had some time to become familiar with all the visuals.

### Suggestions for Using Zooms, Pans, and Tilts in Shots

Some editors argue that camera or lens motion in the shot adds life to your editing. It must be used intelligently. The most effective motion is one that has intention to draw the eye from one subject to another. Good examples of this are the familiar tilt up from the reading material to the eyes, short pans from one reaction CU face to another CU, or a rack focus shot that takes the viewer's concentration from one spot to another.

If there is motion in the footage (camera pans, tilts, zooms), be sure that the motion reaches a conclusion or stops before you cut to another shot. If you want to cut on motion, then follow it with another motion shot that continues the same vector, either moving in or out along the z-axis, or right or left across the screen. Make sure the motion is comparable to the first motion (if not, you might use your editing software to alter the speed of the second shot). Finally, if you are using only one motion shot, then try to follow that motion shot with a nonmotion or neutral vector shot.

### Lead Audio with Video or Video with Audio

It's an old trick. The video for the next sequence actually starts one second before its audio and thus covers the end of the audio from the previous sequence. You can do the same with the audio: Sneak it in a second before you cut to the video that accompanies it. Either way, it could make for a more seamless transition and keep the audience's attention.

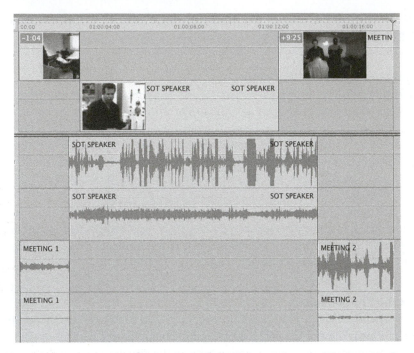

**Figure 13.2** In this case, the sequence "MEETING 1" video continues while the audio from SOT Speaker comes in. Then the video from "MEETING 2" appears before the audio from "SOT SPEAKER" is finished.

### Allow the Sequences to Breathe

Do not be afraid to build in pauses, rests, and spaces to slow down the pace. Sometimes, after a particularly gut-wrenching sound bite, pause for a second to allow the viewer to process information either intellectually or emotionally. If the video is jerky and the speaker's lips continue to move after you have cut the audio (lip flap), then freeze it or slow down the clip speed.

Viewing a documentary that is tightly cut without breathing spaces can be frenetic and anxiety provoking.

## THE STAGES OF THE EDITING PROCESS

### Rough Assembly

When the first sequences are cut, it is time to begin a rough assembly. Open a new timeline and place the sequences in order as a series of blocks. Watching this will allow you to review the overall flow and effectiveness of the program's dramatic arc.

### Rough Cuts

The basic working stage is the rough cut. It defines the vast middle of the editing process, which is the period for constant recuts of sequences or reordering the various sequences and sound. The rough cut has very little in the way of graphics, has a scratch audio track, and has very rough audio mixes on a separate channel to judge placement of visuals.

This is a difficult period when many changes are made. One suggestion is to work the rough cuts in scenes that are approximately seven-minute segments, only assembling them into a longer program when someone wants to review it.

The rough cut also lacks finished music, which is a critical problem when it is a major portion of the fine cut. The composer or music director must generate a track similar to the one used, so there is a reference when cutting.

### Integrating Graphics, Animation, and Text CGs

All of this happens as you get nearer to the fine cut. Often there are issues with graphics (size, shape of pixels), archival film or tape (format, size) or animation from high-end programs (After Effects, etc.). Always check playback on a high-end monitor and attempt to play back sections with these inserted elements. Any problems should be dealt with immediately.

Text CGs (lower-third names, title, intertitles) should be a coordinated graphic scheme. The producer and often the graphics designer must approve the fonts, sizes, and location.

### Subtitles

If the program is in two languages or if there is a difficult regional dialect, then subtitles will be needed. These are far more complex to do than anyone might suspect.

Subtitling multiplies the viewer's stimulation; therefore there's a complex interplay among the visual cuts, the audio track, and the subtitles. The subtitle should run no more than two lines and be economical in word usage. It should be on the screen long enough to cover the phrasing it translates but not long enough to jeopardize the engagement of the viewers.

In my experience dealing with multiple languages in documentaries, I prefer a process of interpretation to literal translation. Often, literal translations become incomprehensible because of differing language, grammar, cultural expressions, and idioms that need an understandable equivalent in the subtitled language.

Here is a basic technical warning: Make certain that you can read the subtitle, especially against white backgrounds. Choose a clear, easy-to-read font like Helvetica and use a full black outline or a 90-degree angle drop shadow. Occasionally, subtitles have been effective when placed in the letterbox band below a 16 × 9 format. Allow at least a week to do a decent job.

### Works in Progress: Screenings and Feedback

Several times, after you have reached the rough cut stage, the producer might want to have a screening. These require at least a day of prep so you can make the rough cut presentable. Editors hate to play rough cuts for small groups because the audio quality or color correction can diminish the editing effort. But Maureen Gosling says they are valuable.

All directors who I work with, we always have work in progress screenings . . . two or three . . . and you invite a mix of people and you invite film people and nonfilm people . . . you invite people who are versed in the topic and then people who have no connection to the topic. So you get a good variety of responses. The film people will notice certain things and they can get specific with you about something that isn't working cinematically. The people that know the topic will let you know if something is explained properly or if there is a detail missing and if something is being explained right or if there is a factual error. And then the nonfilm people and those not familiar with the topic are just going to see it as the general public and be able to tell you that they didn't understand this or that the dramatic impact for me was such and such a scene and why was that so early and depending upon how articulate they are you can really get a lot of good ideas.

Now when I first started editing, I got upset when people critiqued and criticized my work. It was very upsetting 'cause I thought it was perfect and so it's always hard to do a feedback screening. You feel vulnerable and you feel put through the wringer but the next day or the day after that . . . you say "Wow . . . there's some ideas in that" . . . and then there might be a lot of work to do because you realize . . . "Oh my god, we went off in the wrong direction" . . . but I would say that most of the time you start going in another direction and it's even better.

## Fine Cut and Picture Lock

Once you receive approval on the fine cut, the concluding version is called picture lock. At this stage, there are no more changes to shot length in the documentary. Now the video and audio get extra work.

Picture lock is when the video is stripped off and sent for color correction. Unless you are very skilled at this, don't be tempted to do it yourself. Color correction is an art, and an experienced colorist can do wonders for badly balanced video color.

At the same time, the audio will go to a postproduction lab where it will be transferred to specialized programs like ProTools to repair any problems with clarity or fidelity. Before it goes to the audio specialists, embed two frames of video and two frames of audio tone into the leader ahead of the first video. This is called a sync pop. Put this marker (both video and audio) approximately one second before the head of the documentary. If sync problems develop during the audio post, the manual sync pop will allow the relinking of the tracks.

A sound designer or audio post specialist will also be able to help if you want to or need to use foley effects to enhance your sound tracks. Foley sound is any effect that is constructed but intended to replace natural ambience or everyday sound that might have been muffled or garbled in the original recording. An example might be the sound of someone walking down a hall.

Using foley effects can also be an ethics question. For some, the addition of artificial sound lessens the documentary's claim to be an authentic re-creation of the scene. For others, the difficulties of recording sound under documentary conditions almost demand that some expected but noncontroversial sounds need to be there and might not have been captured.

### Take a Short Vacation

The audio is off to post and the video is off to color correction. You've been working like a dog on this for months. Take a break. Fly to Cabo. Exhale. Go to the lake. Backpack. Get out of town.

### Online

The online is the last step. This is where the newly corrected audio is remarried to the color-corrected video. Now you have an online, the basic edited master ready to be duplicated for delivery to distributors. There will be further steps, such as second audio programs (SAPs) or closed captioning done at a postproduction house, but all of these will come later and will depend on distribution needs.

### Your Program's Edit Masters

You should make at least four master copies of the final online version and archive these in different locations. Forget the expense and put it on the highest quality media available. You might also chose to put them on different media, with one on an industry-standard tape, such as HDCAM, and the others on keepsake hard drives. Back up that hard drive with others that will remain untouched.

The original footage should be kept in a separate location. As tech formats begin to change, you'll need to update the master to newer formats.

## SUMMARY

Good postproduction takes careful planning, as well as transcription of all audio and logs of all shots. The progress through the first sequences, the rough assembly, the rough cuts to the fine cut, color correction, and then the online can take months.

### Shaping Your Skills

1. Shoot a 10-minute field video of a particular event and include a two-minute interview. Now, log it, transcribe important audio, and cut a 1:00 sequence without voice under, and a 2:30 segment using bites from the interview as a voice under guide. Finally, cut in some music to see if this alters the tempo.
2. Get a raw field tape for a sequence that needs complex audio work and additional music. Cut a sequence with an eye toward the use of a soundscape as the bed for the visual.

### Further Reading

Murch, Walter, *In the Blink of An Eye* (2nd ed.), Los Angeles: Silman James Press, 2001.

# CHAPTER 14

# Starting the Buzz and Going to Festivals

I was from the prehistoric age. (Now) If you have a film and
you're talented and someone is not seeing it, it's your fault.
DIRECTOR SPIKE LEE

Finishing the documentary's online is not the end. If that took a year of difficult work, there's still a long road ahead stirring up a buzz in the community, creating publicity materials and websites, packing the doc off to film festivals, getting critiques, and stirring up interest. The producer can choose to self-promote or turn it over to publicists and festival specialists.

## GLOSSARY

**IMDb** An Internet film industry database that is accessible to the public and will
provide the background information of your film.
**Launch** A carefully orchestrated program to promote the finished documentary to the
public.

*(Continued)*

## GLOSSARY *(Continued)*

**Screeners**  DVD or other alternative copies of your documentary that are sent to festivals or persons interested in the film.

**Withoutabox.com**  The major Internet database for film festival entrants. Works with 850 festivals worldwide.

## PUBLICITY AND EXPOSURE

Many finished documentaries have one or two public screenings and then die a quiet death on a shelf in the editing room. If producers want to avoid this end, they must take active steps in the area of promotions and festivals.

There are always two paths: Do it yourself or turn it over to specialists who will charge you for their services. Independent marketing consultants Lyla Foggia and Kelly Neal estimate that a documentary might need a unit publicist ($2,000+), a website designer ($4,000), and a graphic designer for publicity materials and poster ($5,000+).

When producer Ken Kobre needed to launch his documentary *Deadline Every Second,* he hired a publicist and coordinator. She set up museum and university screenings, made advances to affinity organizations in each city, stimulated publicity, and organized the showings. These efforts were very successful.

Hiring a specialist might seem like an expensive luxury to cash-strapped filmmakers, but not going in that direction often causes regrets. Producer Barbara Grandvoinet, who attempted on her own to publicize her documentary *Children of the Trains* through websites, says that if she had it to do all over again, she would hire someone with experience to do the publicity.

## SCREENERS

A first objective is to get the finished doc out to persons interested in the program. After the technical evaluation, burn at least 20 DVD screeners with the program on them. These can be done on a home system or at a dub house. Buy distribution cases and make colorful labels with all the needed information for a professional presentation. These can be handed out to persons who are interested in the program. For a film festival or film markets, take scores of these screeners along.

Don't paste a paper label directly onto the DVD. These can gum up DVD players. Instead, get labels directly printed onto the discs.

## PRESS KIT

Along with the screener, the documentary needs a press kit or, at least, the parts of one. A press kit used to be a professionally printed folder that contains information about the documentary, the issue it covers, the highlights, the crew, and some striking production photos that can be used in brochures or festival programs. Now, it is also available on the Internet with downloadable packets of information and photos.

Each press kit page usually carries a standardized logo image and perhaps a freeze frame or two in the heading. You can use both sides of these sheets.

Here's what should be available for a press kit:

1) A one-page synopsis of the doc (two paragraphs will do).
2) One page with a treatment style storyline.
3) One "Highlights" Page. Use a bullet-point layout for eight or so brief phrases extolling unique and powerful features.
4) One page with festival notices, awards, critical reviews, newspaper articles, and screenings. Continually revise this as needed.
5) One page with bios of the producer, director, cinematographer, and anyone else involved who is a standout (it could even be the narrator). Use photos of each to personalize this page.
6) One page with credits for the documentary.
7) Three or four high-quality production photos on photographic paper as well as a Web link where someone can download more high-res photos. These should include single shots of the documentary's subjects as well as shots of the crew in action. (Be sure to include photo credits with the production shots.) The more striking these are, the better chance you'll have to get them into newspaper stories or festival brochures.
8) Copies of your poster. Some film festivals will request two large display posters. These should be more elegant than simple copy store reproductions.

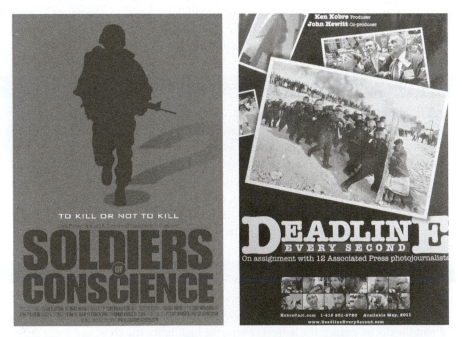

**Figure 14.1** The larger 36-inch color poster format can feature multiple text segments or be a single iconic graphic to represent the documentary. They are expensive to print.
*Soldiers of Conscience* poster courtesy of Luna Productions, design by Deutsch Design Works, Didem Carissimo.
*Deadline Every Second* poster design by Ben Barbante

## WEBSITES

For websites, there are the industry databases and then there is your own documentary site.

For the industry, producers should put their doc information onto IMDb, a popular site that is a catalog of most dramatic and documentary movies. It will include your synopsis, reviews, awards, the crew positions, and information about distribution, copyright, and so on, and a link to your trailer and website. It allows cross-references to films, so users searching for documentaries might happen upon yours.

### Role of the Film's All-Important Website

Your film needs a website that incorporates the name of the documentary and a capability to post links and updates to it. The website is a unique exhibition space. Viewers can access links to the trailer and other chapters of the film. Interactive elements can be added to solicit e-mails, seek funding, or gather comments. Well-chosen keywords and links could allow it to become viral and spread exponentially in many directions. Website hits will demonstrate the possibility for an audience who might be eager for information about the topic.

Web pioneer video producer Russell Johnson warns that your site will mean little unless you take an active role. "You have to really do some outreach, blogging your video on other sites. It's increasingly hard to be discovered on YouTube. The really successful Web videos almost all have professional PR people pushing it out to other sites."

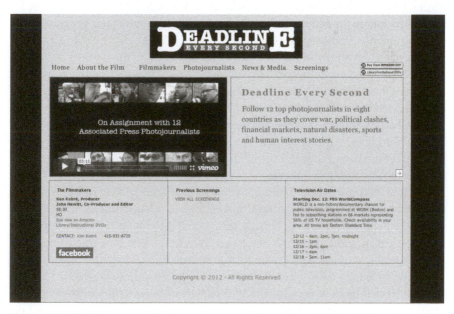

**Figure 14.2** Web home page for documentary *Deadline Every Second* provides users with access to the trailer, press kit, and other access to retail opportunities.
Website design by Ben Barbante

During the rough cut stage, short segments from the doc (webisodes) can be posted online to stir up interest. It is difficult to say if this is effective, because sequences and the story arc might change, and what is posted might not make the final cut.

Interviews from the doc can be excerpted and added to the website. Comments from a recognized personality in the field could get some buzz going. Be sure that your signed releases allow you to use these subjects in the film's publicity.

## USE SOCIAL MEDIA FOR PUBLICITY

The Internet world changes constantly and new popular sites pop up almost every day. Producers searching any of these sites need to navigate to the producer's tab and usually this requires registration.

## ROLE OF THE WORLD'S FILM FESTIVAL CIRCUIT

Certainly, winning some award at Telluride would be a good kickoff for getting the word out about your doc. And, of course, all filmmakers dream of tromping through the snows at Sundance. Or Banff. Or Berlin. Or Amsterdam Doc/Fest. Or Tribeca. And you might get there, if you try hard enough. However, a reality check might find you at the Chicago Peace Documentary Festival, the Padre Island Festival in Texas, or any of the multitude of good local festivals that don't have headline status.

The goal of the film festival circuit is exposure, getting critical notices, and winning awards; it is not about financial return. Producers can spend a lot of money to prepare for and enter these festivals with the hope that it generates recognition and distribution possibilities.

There are currently hundreds of film festivals in the United States and hundreds more in international settings. Not all of them feature documentaries; in fact, many have such narrow entry requirements that documentaries are not a priority. Read the entry submission information carefully. Ask around.

The best all-around source for film festival information and entries is the website Withoutabox.com. We have spoken of it as your festival entry database, but it also has vital information about festival submissions and specialties, and will alert you by e-mail to upcoming deadlines.

Not all documentary festivals are equal in clout, but getting into one allows the producer to affix that recognition surrounded by a laurel wreath on the film's website or publicity materials. "Official selection of the Hot Springs Documentary Film Festival" is good; better yet would be "Winner of Best Documentary at the International Documentary Film Festival, Amsterdam."

If the documentary is selected, festivals can be demanding. Big-name festivals like Sundance might ask for specialized distribution copies in film or the high-def projection video 2K or 4K format (it costs $8,500 to convert a feature to 2K) or pricy posters and press kits that can run into the thousands of dollars. If you are featured, the festival might send you plane fare and put you up in a hotel, but only if the documentary is screened with the regular program. Otherwise, you'll have to pull out the credit card to attend and answer audience questions.

### Should You Enter Film Festivals?

Yes and no. There are a lot of entry fees and rejection letters, but the recognition can be valuable. Festivals are juried and getting in generally means that the film was selected for the quality of work—a good sign. Don't hesitate to get photos taken at the festivals of you with festival organizers, you pontificating at panel discussions, you speaking to the crowds, and you (if it happens) accepting your awards.

Information for individual festival deadlines, which come up all year long, can usually be found on their sites or Withoutabox. Don't enter festivals with specialties that are different from the documentary's topic. If it says a "festival of South Asian documentaries," don't try to argue that the Philippines are close enough and it should be included.

When a filmmaker is selected for the Katmandu festival, should he or she go? It might cost up to $3,000 to spend some time watching other people watch the documentary. If they are giving your film an award, it might be nice to show up. Do not be put off by small crowds. Some festivals cannot manage the publicity they should be doing.

A suggestion for gaining access to festivals is to have your TRT fit their needs. Producer Barbara Grandvoinet had trouble getting her 40-minute *Children of the Trains* into festivals. "They only have so many hour slots. So now I have two versions, one of which is short of 30 minutes. They can program several of these into a slot. Even better, if you have something that is 5 or 10 minutes long, they can use these in many places. You have a better chance."

## LOCAL SCREENINGS CAN FUNDRAISE FOR DISTRIBUTION

Raising money (but not bundles of it) by throwing fundraising screening parties requires organization and a mailing list. These gatherings require a substantial time investment in building an invitation list, location scouting, snack food acquisition,

**Figure 14.3** Large personal screenings are good places to answer questions and ask for money to help with the next step: distribution.

drink buying, and technical prowess (you might need to haul around a video projector and screen).

Good venues for screenings are museum spaces, exhibition halls, community halls such as scout buildings, schoolrooms, church assembly rooms, or even local savings and loan community rooms. You need to do publicity, set up a program, put out an attractive display of food, charm everyone with a short speech, show the doc or a trailer, and then pitch for support your distribution efforts. You might need the dollars for rights acquisition or for high technical expenses.

Still, you can't be bashful at these screenings. As one fundraiser explained, at some point, you have to come straight out and ask for their money. They can pledge, write checks, put loose change in jars, or whatever.

## PREMIERES AND LAUNCH PARTIES

Not a fundraiser, but a public showing at a premiere is a great launch vehicle for exposure. It needs to be done in a comfortable location: a local multiplex, a local theater, a school auditorium, or some available arts group or museum space with good projection facilities and comfortable seats.

Producer Ken Kobre launched his documentary *Deadline Every Second* with premiers at the Corcoran Gallery in Washington, DC, Columbia University in New York, UCLA in Los Angeles, at the City Club in San Francisco, and at venues in London, Paris, and Athens. Each was followed by a panel discussion that included one of the photojournalists who were the subjects of the documentary.

Sometimes there is a local film or production collective that holds screenings or has facilities for screenings. Contacts must be made weeks or even months in advance, so the groups can do scheduling. With good creative publicity, you can get a decent audience. The most gratifying part of these is the warm applause when the credits roll, although the postshowing question-and-answer sessions have produced some baffling moments. When we were doing Q & As after a festival showing of our Cambodian political doc *Landmines of the Heart,* there were some otherworldly moments. We'd say "Any questions?" A hand would go up. We'd recognize the person and she would launch into a five-minute diatribe about her own feelings about the topic. No question. It can be baffling.

## SUMMARY

After the difficult work of production, the more frustrating job is stirring up public notice, gaining exposure, and distributing the documentary. Whether choosing self-distribution or turning the program over to a commercial firm, producers should set up a marketing plan and devise a strategy for getting the program out to desired audiences. Film festival and program markets play a big part in this.

Producers must also make press books, have screeners burned on DVDs, and be ready to schedule screenings and premiers.

## Shaping Your Skills

1. Search for and find a list of film and video festivals with entry dates in the next three months. Look up the winners from the year before and this year's entry fees and assess whether this festival or any of them is worth your time and money.
2. Make a trailer especially for festivals.

# CHAPTER 15

# Distribution

If you are not distributing the documentary yourself, then you must remember that the only business principle that matters to distributors is: Will this film make me enough money to be worth my time and investment . . . or, does it fit my business model.

PRODUCER CJ HUNT

You've got your documentary's online master in a safe place. You've had six months of semisuccess getting the publicity buzz going and securing festival appearances. But you are not off the hook yet.

You have reached your documentary's sweet spot—distribution. This is what you wanted when you began developing the idea. Now, you the producer must shepherd the program rights while choosing either to self-distribute or bring aboard underwriters, distributors, and sales agents. It's a tough slog in another venue—the business world.

## GLOSSARY

**Closed captioning**  The visual display of spoken program text set into the lower third of the screen, usually for television.

**Errors and Omissions (E & O) insurance**  An expensive insurance policy to guard against defamation or rights violations. Broadcasters or distributors will request you secure this.

**Exclusive rights**  When a producer gives a distributor all rights to sales in a particular market.

**Long tail**  When the choice media distribution opportunities are exhausted and the doc is offered to the public through digital platforms like Netflix and Hulu.

**QC**  The quality control assessment done by a production house lab that evaluates whether the video and audio signals are within range for various broadcast or other distribution needs.

**Second Audio Program (SAP)**  A translation of spoken audio that is triggered by equipment in a TV set.

## DISTRIBUTION HAS A LIFE OF ITS OWN

Distribution begins when you hand out your first DVD that isn't a screener; proceeds through complex rights deals with distributors, broadcasters, online sites, DVD sales companies, and educational libraries; and ends years later as sales and interest taper off in a period called the long tail.

Producers must plan for and manage these phases wisely, knowing when to keep rigid control and when to designate the rights to companies that have experience and a track record in their particular area.

## REVISIT YOUR EARLY DISTRIBUTION OBJECTIVES

When you started your doc, whether it is a short student film under 10 minutes long or a feature at an hour and a half, you had envisioned the audiences you wanted to see it. Now, with an expensive color correction finished, audio sweetened, and festivals behind you, it's time to revisit these goals and set up a solid program of staggered releases in different markets to achieve the best possible goals.

Think objectively about the longevity of your program. Is your documentary timeless with a long shelf life (nature, history, profiles, science, experimental) or is there a short window of opportunity (current events, journey, walled city) before its content becomes stale and is replaced by films with newer developments?

Next, identify core audiences who should be approached from the six basic markets: consumer sales, educational sales, national broadcast, international sales, museum and special showings, and theatrical. Then prioritize these markets for release. Some recommend you save the digital streaming distribution platforms for the end, when you enter the so-called long tail.

Finally, answer the most crucial question: Do you have the time and the skills to attempt self-distribution or will you turn it over to professional sales agents and pay them a percentage? You might be eager to start on your next project.

## A VARIETY OF RUNNING TIMES WILL EXPAND DISTRIBUTION POSSIBILITIES

In our era of digital postproduction, it is easy to turn out three or four versions of the same program. And although this process involves wrenching choices of what to cut, making differing length masters from the same material is relatively inexpensive.

Producer Jennifer Maytorena Taylor, for her doc *New Muslim Cool,* wanted to maintain control while still being flexible.

> I had all the stems from the sound mix loaded on my computer. Same with the color corrected master with no titles. So I had all the versions I needed. So if the distributor said we need a 56-minute copy of the film in 10-bit uncompressed with an M & E mix and no titles . . . because the broadcaster would put the titles on. . . . I would make that myself and deliver it on a drive. I just took my time and saved money. Anyone conversant with digital editing can do that.

Her documentary was first cut to an 83-minute feature length for festivals. But shortening it to a 54-minute abridged version for national and international broadcast was a wrenching experience. She also ended up with short segments, leftovers from the feature-length cut, that went on to be released as educational modules, complete with lesson plans. Then, she put other short modules up on the Internet as "conversation starters" to buoy interest for broadcast dates she had secured. One of those short videos, which she called *Pardon Me, Are These Hot Dogs Kosher,* got 100,000 hits on YouTube.

For DVDs, she retained the rights for home sales and sold DVDs on her website, turning over the actual packaging and shipping to a company that specialized in that.

Finally, as interest waned in the 2009 release and she entered the long tail, she agreed to her distributor's suggestion and put *New Muslim Cool* up on Netflix and Hulu, realizing that these digital streaming platforms are the end of the line.

## THE STANDARDS FOR DELIVERABLES

We've mentioned the "deliverables" in many chapters. These are distribution masters in current industry formats, generally HDCAM tapes or files on hard drives, that will ship for use by television or cable networks, distributors, exhibitors, film festivals, or public screenings.

To prepare for this, pay to get a quality control (QC) evaluation of your master. You need to make sure the film meets broadcast standards. These venues will want to know: Where are the signal black levels? Is it in drop or nondrop frame time code? Does the video signal ever exceed the 90 percent broadcast safety zone?

Are there any signal instabilities? Are the CG titles within the screen safe area? This QC check might cost several hundred dollars.

Next, additional lab work might be needed to bring the video specs to those demanded by various distributors or networks. One broadcaster might want a specific program length to be 56:46; others want 58:10. A distributor might want narration audio on certain tracks, whereas another wants a mono program mix on one track, a stereo mix on another, narration on another, and so on. Most want an M & E (music and effects) track separate from spoken dialog. Certain program dubs might need subtitles, second audio program (SAP) language translations, closed captioning of spoken program audio, or CG alerts to websites during certain program portions.

Postproduction houses with the high-end equipment to make these evaluations and changes are usually found in larger cities or regional centers. They may charge $250 per hour of lab time with an operator. Pay it. It could cost $2,000 just to bring older specs up to broadcast standards. Pay that, too.

Anyone planning on PBS distribution should consult the lengthy Producers Red Book (www.pbs.org/producers/redbook/), which lays out the technical parameters and timing checkpoints they employ.

Giving a film to PBS outside their specs means they will charge to bring it up to their standards. For a one-hour doc I edited for PBS, they sent a bill for $600 to fix one internal fade to black that was several frames longer than their tech guidelines. That charge was in addition to the $2,000 we had already spent on postproduction to match their tech requirements and $3,000 for the least expensive E & O insurance we could find.

## RIGHTS

You've produced, shot, and edited a work of art. It might be 5 minutes or 84 minutes, but it is now under your copyright. If you decide to distribute it beyond showing it to your own family, then you must arrange to parcel out the rights to play your program.

Distribution rights are unique to geography and media areas. There are certain rights bundles you can license to a retail distributor, an educational institution, a rental house, a museum, or a broadcast programmer. These can be assigned totally (exclusive) or partially (nonexclusive), a situation where you retain certain distribution capabilities. Finally, you agree to a term and coverage area for the license.

For example, you could distribute to any of these:

Consumer and Internet sales of DVD
    In North America
    In English language markets
    In Spanish language markets
    In other international markets
Consumer streaming digital download
University and trade school educational market, either DVD or electronic

Any U.S. broadcast
Any international broadcast
Theatrical
Public audiences (museums, conventions, etc.)

If you have the skills, you could self-distribute and capture all the revenue to help repay production and editing expenses. Most documentary makers, however, farm out some of the distribution to specialists who know the ropes.

Be very cautious if you plan to give away exclusive rights over a period of time. As with music rights, distribution deals can be short or long term. If you hook up with a distributor, be certain the rights are assigned for only the particular time span that matches the film's distribution goals. When the distributor or agent wants exclusive rights to a number of markets over a specific time period, such as five years, weigh that in relation to your own concept of the shelf life of this documentary. After a five-year term, maybe your doc will seem dated in relation to more recent docs and when the distribution contract ends, you are left with a program without much marketability.

Also, if the film's music or archival licenses expire after a few years, your distributor must know about that.

## HOW TO EVALUATE DISTRIBUTORS

If you are going to bring on reliable experts to help in the distribution, there is no easy way to evaluate them. You have to talk to other filmmakers, look at the company's Web catalog, research their outreach and publicity, and ask about their recent sales totals. See if they specialize in themes in your topic area. While you are checking out the website catalog, make a note of how many films they are offering.

Some distributors have a good reputation and a huge catalog but are not aggressive and do very little outreach. Others might be small, but are proactive and continually promote the film. Make certain that anyone who gets full control over distribution in a particular market for two or three years is aggressive in marketing, keeps good books, and pays royalties on time.

There are distributors who specialize in certain markets. Producer Barbara Grandvoinet, who found herself so busy with new projects that she didn't have time for self-distribution of her doc on street children in Thailand, turned over international rights to the distributor TPI but limited the duration and reserved the Canadian and U.S. markets. Her next effort was to find a distributor for online platforms that made direct sales. After that, she planned to distribute to national North American markets through public television.

I once signed an exclusive two-year international distribution agreement with a reputable foreign company in Montreal. I sent a program master and then waited for the sales and money to pour in. None did. Nor did any communication. My attempts to contact the company only stirred vague messages in return.

Did they sell anything? If they did, they never told me. But for two years, my film was in limbo.

## WHY NOT TRY SELF-DISTRIBUTION?

Self-distribution is an attractive but time-consuming option. It puts the filmmaker adrift in the dog-eat-dog business world. Yes, you don't have to share commissions or royalties and you maintain complete control. However, the hard work and daily chores in distribution are a continuing distraction, making it difficult to focus on the next documentary project.

Producer Ellen Bruno self-distributes her films and says doing this herself is important.

> Because in the process of making the films I'm in touch with a lot of people and organizations and I'm on a mission and I want to get these films out to the world and I know I'm the best person to do that. And so, a lot of the networks I've tapped into already and a lot of those people will use it and use it in very direct ways, lobbying congress and so on. And I also do my own distribution to the educational market and the film has gotten into a lot of universities and that's also a financial incentive.

Producer Emiko Omori began doing self-distribution with co-producer Wendy Slick on their 2008 release *Passion and Power: The Technology of the Orgasm.* "We are hoping that someday we'll get a distributor or rep. We don't want to keep doing this by ourselves . . . because it's time consuming . . . and you know you don't get paid for any the film festivals. And now we've been asked to screen it at universities, like UCLA, where young women want to see it. So, I think that it will eventually return enough to cover what we spent on it."

Producer Ken Kobre began by self-distributing *Deadline Every Second,* his story of 12 international photojournalists working in eight different countries. He mounted an extensive national and international publicity campaign and then identified four areas: international sales, U.S. distribution, the educational market, and consumer DVDs.

After attending the international film market at MIPTV in Cannes, Kobre tried several sales agents over nine months but none clicked. Finally, he found an effective international distributor in Paris. He provided this company with a European format master, European format screeners, and text and photos from the press packet. "It took a while to find a distributor . . . and she took it to MIPDOC in France, where a whole lot of the docs are bought and sold and I've got sales (and prospects) from that."

Kobre was determined to attack the U.S. broadcast market himself. With his goal a national PBS broadcast, he began to approach national satellite distributors such as American Public Television and then individual stations in New York, Boston, and San Francisco. The acquisition editors liked *Deadline Every Second* and suggested that as long as he could find an underwriter, they would run his program and sponsor his outreach to other stations. For this service, they would charge Kobre tens of thousands of dollars.

> My hopes were that I could make enough money back from the broadcast sales of the doc to at least pay the hard money production expenses. I knew there was no

profit in the long run. I quickly learned that it is impossible to get anyone to pay for a single, one-off documentary. If you want to make money, you've got to come up with a series . . . with 10 shows.

I also learned that they want you to have an underwriter . . . someone to finance the documentary in exchange for having their name on the doc at the beginning and end (in the underwrite pod). It's not supposed to be an ad. I found it extremely hard to get an underwriter.

In the end, Kobre approached the stations directly and drew solid audiences in New York and San Francisco, where it did very well. With these successes, he approached other stations, which began evaluating his program.

Although self-distribution can be time-consuming, the producer can appreciate that he or she is setting the agenda. Producer Gary Weimberg says each project is so involving that giving up personal control of any documentary is the indie filmmaker's dilemma. "Do you start making a new film or do you keep working on distributing the last film? And this film (*Soldiers of Conscience*) is really exceptional for me. It may be that I remain active on the distribution of this film for the rest of my life. It's worth it. But, it is certainly not going to be my full-time occupation . . . the DVD sales are not high enough to warrant that."

Paying to have someone else handle various distribution tracks can be expensive. You hire them for a set price or a give up a percentage of revenue from sales. A sales or producer's rep can cost you as much as $15,000 plus a fee against commission or an experienced festival can manage the schmoozing and distribution sales. Finally, if an education distributor agrees to manage the educational and university market, they will take a significant chunk and pay you a royalty.

## SELLING INDIVIDUAL DVDs

If the trailer has been getting exposure but the producer wants to start selling the documentary, then they often turn to a different kind of site. Amazon and iTunes all handle sales of individual DVDs. These sites advertise and offer the programs on a DVD or as a streaming sale. Most protect your rights, discuss the price point and percentage they will take, and send a royalty check. Some offer packaging and others simply link your request to another site. You might have to use their subsidiary to manufacture the DVDs or you will have to personally drop-ship them when someone orders online.

But there are downsides to a successful DVD sales program. You might be ruining your chances for a later distribution deal. Producer CJ Hunt's experience is telling. "If I had known that I would go to a distributor, I would not have sold any DVDs. Because if they (the larger distributor) like it, but you are out there selling it, especially selling it digitally, then you are dead meat." Hunt says his early sales numbers had been so small that the distributor wasn't worried.

Also, individual DVD sales through Internet sites might cut into the sales to the education market, where prices are 10 times as high. As producer Ken Kobre discovered, some instructors wishing to show his *Deadline Every Second*

**Figure 15.1** A campaign to sell individual DVDs should be balanced against its effect on other distribution opportunities.

documentary in their classes bought a personal copy from Amazon and used it in a public setting. So you have to balance one against the other.

If you decide to self-distribute, you might need to get 1,500 units ready for distribution and that can cost $5,000 to $10,000. It is up to you to do sales jobs, pack and ship copies, manage PayPal accounts, muddle through the red tape of Amazon.com, and handle all the tax and license problems that come with retail and wholesale vending. In essence, one filmmaker said, your job is never done. And although your profit is as much as 10 times greater per disc, you will spend hundreds of hours at this job. Sometimes, it's better to leave it to the professionals.

For a distributor in this area, find one who has many contacts, understands the market, takes a master copy, and handles all publicity, catalogs, and distribution. They usually take between 50 and 80 percent of the gross and give you what's left. Some distributors are passive rather than active, seldom doing more than placing your one-sheet in their catalog.

Noel Lawrence of Other Cinema Digital warns that indie filmmakers probably won't get a DVD distribution deal unless they've stirred up some buzz in the festival or theatrical release circuit. Once that has happened, he notes there are two options.

First, you can work with a video label that specializes in certain topics (Women Make Movies, California Newsreel, Criterion, Fantoma, Plexifilm, NoShame, or Other Cinema) and gets it ready for distribution. Second, you can go with a company that handles everything (Facets, Kino, or Zeitgeist). In either case, the filmmaker gives up any control over the cover, the sales, and the distribution, but this contract frees you to move on to other projects.

One important caveat is in order here: The long-term prospects for the home market are dwindling.

## THE EDUCATIONAL MARKET

In the past, libraries, museums, and universities have been good bets for financial return. Their audio/visual buyers, who maintain listings that show the program repeatedly and in many different classrooms or public settings, pay an institutional price for the license that can range from $200 to $500. But a word of caution: Most public A/V libraries are facing financial restrictions, so the market is shrinking.

If you wish to approach this market yourself, you'll need to invest in lists of buyers. These can be had from several commercial services.

For this type of distribution, it is better to turn the process over to a distributor and share the royalties. There are two types of distributors to these markets. General distributors (video supermarkets) PBS Video, Films for the Humanities and Sciences are very big. Among others, you might also investigate Filmmakers Library, Icarus, Cinema Guild, and Ambrose films.

## U.S. BROADCAST MARKETS

The premium cable channels, including HBO and Showtime, IFC, Discovery, Sundance, and the History Channel, commission and acquire documentaries and pay for them. They need to be approached in an organized manner. Documentary producers who have worked with these companies often have the advantage. Forget about the commercial U.S. network broadcast channels because they seldom buy outside their own production structure.

For a first-time producer, the PBS market can be baffling. The model at the bigger stations is standard: They want the documentary producer to come in with an underwriter that pays the bills. For additional thousands of dollars, they will position the doc on a satellite feed and send out advances to the individual stations. They pay a modest honorarium for market exclusive or nonexclusive rights depending on their market size. Call and talk to the program director or whoever does "acquisitions" for the station. Don't be put off by unreturned calls. Get the name of the person and keep calling. Write out a script so that you will say exactly what you need to say when the person finally comes on the line. Have a one-sheet (your synopsis) ready to fax to him or her.

Anyone interested in national PBS should read the book "A Bread Crumb Trail Through the PBS Jungle" (http://www.forests.com), which will help you with public broadcast possibilities. PBS has several umbrella series that might use the shorter form programs, such as *P.O.V.* and *Independent Lens,* and which also use standalone programs. These can be found on the PBS.org website. There is also PBS PLUS, a syndication program that provides programs to local stations but doesn't pay a cent to producers. Although PBS might not pay, it encourages indie producers to find companies who want to be underwriters of the program. The producers then collect money from the underwriters for putting their name at the program's head and tail. This can be a good source of funds for your next project.

In addition, there is American Public Television, which offers a distribution system called Program Exchange. They will put your doc on a satellite distribution and do the advance work for a fee that reaches into the thousands of dollars.

The National Educational Telecommunications Association (NETA) is based in South Carolina and provides a no-fee distribution service for its members and a low-fee service for nonmembers. You can also self-market your program by purchasing satellite time and alerting the stations. In those cases, you must make individual deals with each station, which is a nightmare.

## INTERNATIONAL SALES AT PROGRAM AND FILM MARKETS

There are a number of worldwide program sales markets, such as INPUT every two years; the yearly AFM in November in Santa Monica, California; CINEMART in Rotterdam; Docs for Sale in Amsterdam; IFP in five U.S. cities; and MIPDOC, which is held in April before the MIPTV in Cannes, France. In 2006, AFM reported that more than 8,000 individuals attended. At MIPDOC, 432 companies from 57 countries, and 385 acquisition executives attended.

This isn't Sundance. Documentary producers don't go to AFM or MIPDOC or any film market to schmooze and party (well, some do). These are places to screen the doc, to pitch and negotiate, and hopefully to sell to traditional, usually broadcast outlets. There can be substantial contracts in these sales, where hour docs sell for thousands. For the first-time producer, though, the process can be bewildering.

Two approaches work. The first is to find an international sales agent, someone with a track record, who will rep your doc to the flood of buyers who attend these gatherings. Work on strategies with the agent and agree on which world

**Figure 15.2** At worldwide events, such as MIPTV in Cannes, independent producers on credit card budgets often set up shop at small tables in a bullpen area sponsored by an umbrella arts organization.

markets might be buyers. Broadcast sales to major public broadcasters? DVD home sales? Broadband distribution? English language markets and so on? With luck, the agent might secure placements, co-production money, or even presales. Home DVD and broadband distributors also attend these markets.

If you want to go, set aside the money early. Spend time getting one-sheet glossy handouts, press books, screeners, and other information ready. Register and get access to the booklet directory for the market, find out who will be there, call and e-mail to make appointments ahead of time with acquisition editors. Check *Variety* or *Hollywood Reporter* to find the latest prices for docs in different parts of the world. Then, prepare for an all-out sales effort.

At some of these markets, such as MIPDOC or MIPTV in France, the indie producer might never be able to afford a major sales booth. However, anyone confident in his or her personal sales techniques can hook up with a filmmaker's collective to get a small sales table in a bullpen of independents. The organizers can refer you. Spend some time at the sales table and some time roaming the conference halls, talking to commissioning editors. The international markets primarily are conducted in English.

Another reality check: Your film is up against major distributors with solid track records and buckets of money who are marketing very attractive documentary series in popular genres. You will have to work extra hard to get your film noticed.

## AS INTEREST WANES: THE "LONG TAIL" OF STREAMING AND DIGITAL DOWNLOAD

There are separate markets here: distribution for free with YouTube or Vimeo and general streaming on Netflix or Hulu. Short docs are perfect for the YouTube arena. There is no monetary return, but you can certainly gauge your audience by the numbers you put up. Netflix, of course, is the industry leader in DVD rentals and streaming. Placing your doc with Netflix will allow its 50 million users to access to it. You will be paid a tiny royalty when it is used or streamed. The same goes for Google Video and the iTunes store. Again, placing it there puts it out in the public arena, where it could be ripe for piracy.

### The Mobile Device Market
This is the big unknown right now. Whether documentaries in their entirety can be successfully distributed on personal small screens is very much up the air. Whether this would be financially worth the effort is another question mark.

Perhaps the diminutive screens are better suited for short attention span programs. Everyone is trying to look into a crystal ball on this one and the crucial word is monetize: how to make money by giving something away.

## SUMMARY

After the difficult work of production and publicity, an eternally frustrating job looms in the actual distribution of the documentary. Whether a producer chooses self-distribution or turns the program over to a commercial firm, producers should set up a marketing plan and devise a strategy for getting the program out to desired audiences. Distributors and program markets play a big part in this.

### Shaping Your Skills

1. Assume you have finished a very engaging, exciting, quality 10-minute student film about a local carpenter who has been internationally recognized for repairing pianos for an international nonprofit organization. Discuss the copyright problems and ownership of this film. Investigate any and all distribution possibilities for this film.

2. You have a 2:30 trailer for your hour documentary on organ transplants. Search for websites that accept user-generated material and assess whether or not any of these would carry your trailer. Discuss the pros and cons of putting the trailer up for public viewing or keeping it password protected. Determine the exact format for submission, the optimum length, and the audience you might reach with the trailer. Explain why this audience is important.

# Appendix: Some Docs to See

There are hundreds of documentaries, both historic and current, that will give you ideas on quality, storytelling, and style. Any list like this is controversial, but we are offering some suggestions. We regret we cannot list them all.

## HISTORIC (EARLY YEARS)

*Nanook of the North* (1922) Robert Flaherty First U.S. doc to mix actuality and storytelling.
*Man with a Movie Camera* (1927) Dziga Vertov Art, truth, and modernism mix in USSR.
*The Drifters* (1929) John Grierson Early U.K. reality from noted pioneer.
*Rien Que les Heures* (1926) Alberto Cavalcanti European "city films."
*Plow That Broke the Plains* (1934) Pare Lorenz U.S. advocacy during Great Depression. Voice of god narration.
*Triumph of the Will* (1934) Leni Riefenstahl Artistry and propaganda.
*March of Time* (1930s) Style of early longer form theatrical docs.
*Why We Fight: Divide and Conquer* (1942) Frank Capra U.S. propaganda.
*See It Now* (1950s) Ed Murrow Films on CBS define TV doc style.
*Harvest of Shame* (1960) Ed Murrow End of a big-camera doc style era.

## HISTORIC (LATER YEARS: CINEMA VERITE AND BEYOND)

*Chronique d' une ete* (1962) Jean Rouch Begins French cinema verite.
*Primary* (1960) Drew Associates Start of U.S. verite movement.
*Salesman* (1976) Albert and David Maysles Classic verite explores motives behind a door-to-door bible sales crew.
*Sixteen in Webster Groves* (1965) Arthur Baaron U.S. television (CBS) tries to evolve into more mobile camera era.
*The Day After Trinity: J. Robert Oppenheimer and the Atomic Bomb* (1980) John Else Indie look at dangerous era.
*The War Room* (1993) D. A. Pennebaker Prolific director's backgrounder on U.S. presidential campaign.

*The Thin Blue Line* (1968) Errol Morris A great classic. Uses reconstructed scenes to explore the various stories about a murder.

*Titticut Follies* (1967) Frederick Wiseman The first from a master of U.S. institutional docs and observational camera. See any of his films.

## PROFILES, BIOGRAPHY, AND HISTORY

*American Masters* (series) Susan Lacy High-quality PBS documentary series on artists, musicians, and those with an impact on U.S. culture.

*L'Amour Fou* (2011) Pierre Thoretton Moody portrait of French fashion icon Yves Saint-Laurent.

*No Direction Home* (2005) Martin Scorcese Intimate and often controversial look at singer Bob Dylan for the *American Masters* series.

*Pina* (2011) Wim Wenders Tribute to the German postmodern dancer and choreographer Pina Bausch.

*Rivers and Tides* (2001) Thomas Riedelsheimer Engaging profile of artist Andy Goldsworthy.

*The Farmer's Wife* (1998) David Sutherland Revealing portrait of Nebraska farm couple; example of epic storytelling.

*The Life and Times of Harvey Milk* (1984) Rob Epstein Academy Award-winning biopic on controversial gay political leader.

*Thomas Jefferson* (1996) Ken Burns Great example conveying personality and history. See any of Ken Burns's portraits or series for his iconic style.

*War Photographer* (2001) Christian Frei Study of photojournalist James Nachtwey using inventive techniques for multiple angles.

## WALLED CITY AND JOURNEY

*Buena Vista Social Club* (1999) Wim Wenders Finds soul in Cuba in old musicians' group. Inventive style in many places.

*Cave of Forgotten Dreams* (2010) Werner Herzog 3D look inside the Chauvet caves in Southern France; a stunning film.

*Daughter from Danang* (2002) Gail Dolgin and Vicente Franco An Amerasian woman taken from Vietnam at the close of the war returns to find her mother.

*Detropia* (2013) Heidi Ewing and Rachel Grady A look at desolation in a major American industrial city.

*Maquilapolis* (2006) Vicki Funari and Sergio De La Torre A look at conditions inside a factory along the border, filmed by the workers themselves.

*New Muslim Cool* (2011) Jennifer Maytorena Taylor Follows an ex-con's search to make sense out of major religions.

*Playing With Fire* (2011) Gustavo Vazquez Travels to remote Andean city of fireworks makers.

*20 Feet From Stardom* (2013) Morgan Neville Wonderful, visceral style and fast-cutting make music industry doc exciting.

## EVENT AND PROCESS AND NATURAL HISTORY

*Burden of Dreams* (1982) Les Blank Brilliant study of Werner Herzog's movie making. Blank's films are engaging.

*Deadline Every Second* (2010) Ken Kobre and John Hewitt Reveals inner thoughts of photo-journalists as they cover trouble spots and events internationally.

*Lost in La Mancha* (2003) Keith Fulton and Louis Pepe Tragic-comic look at director Terry Gilliam's attempt to film *Man of La Mancha.*

*March of the Penguins* (2007) Luc Jacquet Beloved characters.

*Spellbound* (2002) Jeffrey Blitz Incredibly popular film that followed contestants in a national spelling bee.

*Wild Parrots of Telegraph Hill* (2006) Judy Irving A delightful bio on birds and their eccentric caretakers.

*Winged Migration* (2001) Jacques Perrin and Jacques Cluzaud Extremely poetic and popular natural history doc.

## PERSONAL AND EXPERIMENTAL

*Baby, It's You* (1998) Anne Makepeace Interesting characters abound in difficult, highly personal topic.

*Super-Size Me* (2004) Morgan Spurlock Host producer eats his way through fast food and wins awards for this reflexive film.

*Rabbit in the Moon* (1999) Emiko Omori Not all Japanese Americans endured their World War II internment with quiet stoicism. With fascinating archival and recently recovered home movies, Omori and her sister Chizuko confronted their own family memories.

*Sacrifice* (1998) Ellen Bruno Personal, cross-cultural work examines the forces at work in the trafficking of Burmese girls into prostitution in Thailand.

*Strange Culture* (2007) Lynn Hershman Leeson Uses multiple formats and actors to explore the U.S government's case against an installation artist.

*The Black Power Mixtape 1967–1975* (2010) Goran Olsson Swedish filmmakers offer newly discovered footage of the Black Power movement in the United States.

*Tongues Untied* (1989) Marlon Riggs Confrontational style in doc on Black and gay culture.

## HOSTED

*Amazing Grace* (1990) Elena Mannes Hosted by Bill Moyers, this Emmy-award-winning film features multiple singers and interpretations of the famous classic.

*Keeping Score: Copland and the American Sound* (2003) David Kennard and Joan Saffa A skillful exploration of an American composer.

*Sicko* (2007) Michael Moore Any of Michael Moore's docs are worthy of viewing.

## CURRENT EVENTS (JOURNALISTIC)

*An Inconvenient Truth* (2006) David Guggenheim (director) Making a powerful, Oscar-winning doc out of Al Gore's PowerPoint presentation.

*Baghdad Hospital: Inside the Red Zone* (2007) Omer Madhi Skillful verite work on journalistic premise.

*Enron: The Smartest Guys in the Room* (2005) Alex Gibney Explores the disastrous collapse of a major U.S. energy corporation.

*Frontline* (any year) PBS Series with highest quality investigative work.

*60 Minutes* (1968–2007) CBS Skillful, aggressive advocacy journalism.

*Harlan County USA* (1976) Barbara Koppel Or any of Koppel's other docs.

*Outfoxed: Rupert Murdoch's War on Journalism* (2004) Robert Greenwald Takes on Fox
   News and its controversial chief executive, Rupert Murdoch.

*Senorita Extraviada* (2005) Lourdes Portillo Investigates overlooked story.

*Shut Up and Sing* (2006) Barbara Koppel A look into controversies when musical artists
   express political ideas.

*9/11: CBS* (2001) *Jules and Gedeon Naudet, James Hanlon* (directors) Powerful story of tragedy.

*When the Levees Broke: A Requiem in Four Acts* (2007) Spike Lee Hurricane Katrina aftermath.

## CULTURAL

*Blossoms of Fire* (2000) Maureen Gosling and co-director Ellen Osborne Features powerful
   women in Zapotec culture and in the region's progressive politics, as manifested in
   their unusual tolerance of homosexuality.

*Nostalgia for the Light* (2010) Patricio Guzman Explores memory, astronomy, and politics in
   a search for the past and present.

# Photo Credits

**Chapter 1**
Chapter Opening Courtesy of Kauthar Umar
Fig. 1.1  Courtesy Lourdes Portillo, photo by Gabriela Cardona
Fig. 1.2  Photo courtesy of Najib Joe Hakim (all rights reserved)
Fig. 1.3  Courtesy Micah X Peled

**Chapter 2**
Fig. 2.1  Courtesy of *Detropia*, photos by Wolfgang Held and Tony Hardmon
Fig. 2.3  Photo by Craig Atkinson
Fig. 2.4  Courtesy Emiko Omori

**Chapter 3**
Chapter Opening Courtesy of Oxana Chumak
Fig. 3.1  Courtesy of Macah X. Peled

**Chapter 5**
Fig. 5.1  Courtesy Charles Hunt
Fig. 5.2  Courtesy Charles Hunt

**Chapter 7**
Chapter Opening Courtesy Maureen Gosling
Fig. 7.1  Courtesy Maureen Gosling
Fig. 7.2  Courtesy Ken Kobre

**Chapter 9**
Fig. 9.1  Courtesy Luna Productions, photo by Ian Slattery
Fig. 9.2  Courtesy of Kauthar Umar

**Chapter 10**
Fig. 10.1  Courtesy of Russell Johnson
Fig. 10.3  Courtesy of Russell Johnson

**Chapter 11**
Fig. 11.1  Courtesy of Luna Productions, photo by Gary Weimberg

**Chapter 12**
Chapter Opening From video frames by Paul Rubicek

**Chapter 14**
Fig. 14.1  *Soldiers of Conscience* poster courtesy of Luna Productions, design by Deutsch
        Design Works, Didem Carissimo. *Deadline Every Second* poster design by
        Ben Barbante
Fig. 14.2  Website design by Ben Barbante

# Index